23.914 Ala
Alan Paton's Cry, the beloved
country /

34028076151761
CC $45.00 ocn401141792
10/06/10

 W9-CNB-433

Bloom's Modern Critical Interpretations

The Adventures of
Huckleberry Finn
The Age of Innocence
Alice's Adventures in
Wonderland
All Quiet on the
Western Front
Animal Farm
The Ballad of the Sad
Café
Beloved
Beowulf
Black Boy
The Bluest Eye
The Canterbury Tales
Cat on a Hot Tin
Roof
Catch-22
The Catcher in the
Rye
The Chronicles of
Narnia
The Color Purple
Crime and
Punishment
The Crucible
Cry, the Beloved
Country
Darkness at Noon
Death of a Salesman
The Death of Artemio
Cruz
The Diary of Anne
Frank
Don Quixote
Emerson's Essays
Emma
Fahrenheit 451
A Farewell to Arms
Frankenstein
The Glass Menagerie
The Grapes of Wrath

Great Expectations
The Great Gatsby
Gulliver's Travels
Hamlet
Heart of Darkness
The House on Mango
Street
I Know Why the
Caged Bird Sings
The Iliad
Invisible Man
Jane Eyre
The Joy Luck Club
Julius Caesar
The Jungle
King Lear
Long Day's Journey
into Night
Lord of the Flies
The Lord of the Rings
Love in the Time of
Cholera
Macbeth
The Man Without
Qualities
The Merchant of
Venice
The Metamorphosis
A Midsummer Night's
Dream
Miss Lonelyhearts
Moby-Dick
My Ántonia
Native Son
Night
1984
The Odyssey
Oedipus Rex
The Old Man and the
Sea
On the Road

One Flew over the
Cuckoo's Nest
One Hundred Years of
Solitude
Othello
Persuasion
Portnoy's Complaint
Pride and Prejudice
Ragtime
The Red Badge of
Courage
Romeo and Juliet
The Rubáiyát of Omar
Khayyám
The Scarlet Letter
A Separate Peace
Silas Marner
Slaughterhouse-Five
Song of Solomon
The Sound and the
Fury
The Stranger
A Streetcar Named
Desire
Sula
The Sun Also Rises
The Tale of Genji
A Tale of Two Cities
"The Tell-Tale Heart"
and Other Stories
Their Eyes Were
Watching God
Things Fall Apart
The Things They
Carried
To Kill a Mockingbird
Ulysses
Waiting for Godot
The Waste Land
Wuthering Heights
Young Goodman
Brown

Alan Paton's
Cry, the Beloved Country
New Edition

Edited and with an introduction by
Harold Bloom
Sterling Professor of the Humanities
Yale University

BLOOM'S
LITERARY CRITICISM
An imprint of Infobase Publishing

Bloom's Modern Critical Interpretations: Cry, the Beloved Country—New Edition
Copyright © 2010 by Infobase Publishing
Introduction © 2010 by Harold Bloom

Bloom's Literary Criticism
An imprint of Infobase Publishing
132 West 31st Street
New York NY 10001

Library of Congress Cataloging-in-Publication Data
Alan Paton's Cry, the beloved country / edited and with an introduction by Harold Bloom.
— New ed.
    p. cm. — (Bloom's modern critical interpretations)
  Includes bibliographical references and index.
  ISBN 978-1-60413-583-1 (hardcover)
  1. Paton, Alan. Cry, the beloved country.   2. South Africa—In literature.   3. Race relations in literature.   4. Apartheid in literature.   I. Bloom, Harold.
  PR9369.3.P37C733 2010
  823'.914—dc22

                                    2010001314

Contributing editor: Pamela Loos
Cover design by Takeshi Takahashi
Composition by IBT Global, Troy NY
Cover printed by IBT Global, Troy NY
Book printed and bound by IBT Global, Troy NY
Date printed: May 2010
Printed in the United States of America

10 9 8 7 6 5 4 3 2 1

Contents

Editor's Note   vii

Introduction   1
     Harold Bloom

Alan Paton's *Cry, the Beloved Country*
     after Twenty-Five Years   3
     Charles R. Larson

The Social Record in Paton's *Cry, the Beloved Country*   9
     J. Alvarez-Pereyre

Fiction and History: Fact and Invention in
     Alan Paton's Novel *Cry, the Beloved Country*   19
     R.W.H. Holland

Cry, the Beloved Country and the Failure of Liberal Vision   33
     Stephen Watson

Alan Paton's Tragic Liberalism   49
     Carol Iannone

"A Corridor Shut at Both Ends":
     Admonition and Impasse in Van der Post's
     In a Province and Paton's *Cry, the Beloved Country*   65
     David Medalie

"Considered as a Social Record":
     A Reassessment of *Cry, the Beloved Country*   83
     Andrew Foley

Alan Paton's Sublime: Race, Landscape
        and the Transcendence of the Liberal Imagination   113
        Hermann Wittenberg

Whose *Beloved Country?*
        Alan Paton and the Hypercanonical   133
        Andrew van der Vlies

Chronology   167

Contributors   169

Bibliography   171

Acknowledgments   175

Index   177

Editor's Note

My introduction considers Paton's artlessly benign vision and humane sentiments as contained in a novel impaired by its minimal characterization and unsurprising narrative development.

Charles R. Larson traces how the literary image of Africa has changed since the novel's initial publication, after which J. Alvarez-Pereyre looks at the contemporaneous social realities the work takes on.

The interplay of fiction and history is explored by R.W.H. Holland, while Stephen Watson contends with the book's failed liberal vision.

Liberalism of a more tragic tenor is a central preoccupation of Carol Iannone, after which David Medalie examines the political and moral impasse in *Cry, the Beloved Country* and another early twentieth-century African novel.

The realm of the sociopolitical returns in Andrew Foley's assessment of the work's enduring significance and impact. Hermann Wittenberg then considers the sublime as it intersects with Paton's liberal imaginings.

In the volume's final essay, Andrew van der Vlies ascribes the novel's enduring appeal to its ability to reflect the evolving racial politics and moral sensibilities of a diverse, worldwide readership.

HAROLD BLOOM

Introduction

Cry, the Beloved Country (1948) is a humane period piece but not at all a permanent narrative fiction. I first (and, until now, last) read it when it was published and I was eighteen. More than sixty years later, I have gotten through it again but only just. Its humane sentiments remain admirable but in themselves do not constitute an aesthetic achievement.

Clearly, I prefer a decently liberal period piece to, say, Ayn Rand's *The Fountainhead*, a period piece that prophesied the emancipation of selfishness by Ronald Reagan and the oligarchic plutocracy that the United States metamorphosed into under George W. Bush, Cheney, Rumsfeld, Ashcroft, and their cohorts. My heart is with Alan Paton but not my long lifetime of sustained reading of the best that has been written. It isn't so much that Paton is not Faulkner but that he evades any authorial identity. The Hasidic rabbi Zusya observed that the Recording Angel would say to him: "Zusya, I do not ask why you were not Moses, but why did you fail to become Zusya?" The black Anglican priest Stephen Kumalo, need not have become Desmond Tutu, but he attains no individuality of his own. Paton *assures* us that Kumalo is a spiritual guide, a Zulu hero of the devotional quest, but we are not *shown* Kumalo. At the novel's close, Kumalo is meant to represent God the Father, a rather difficult role to represent.

Religion becomes religiosity when sentiment goes beyond an author's power of rhetoric and of mimesis. What Paton wanted to write would have been admirable, except that novels are *written through* by Tolstoy and George Eliot, Flaubert and Faulkner, Chinua Achebe and Jose Saramago. *Cry, the Beloved Country* has wonderful intentions but minimal characterization and altogether unsurprising narrative development, as artless as it is benign.

1

CHARLES R. LARSON

Alan Paton's Cry, the Beloved Country *after Twenty-Five Years*

In 1948, when Alan Paton's *Cry, the Beloved Country* was first published, the literary image of Africa was all but controlled by a handful of expatriates who had spent brief periods of time on the continent and later written about their experiences there. Paton's novel was greeted as something new and different, written by someone who had been born and raised in South Africa—an authentic voice, heralding what was certain to be a new group of writers. Charles J. Rolo began his review of the novel in *The Atlantic Monthly* by stating, "There is no large area of the civilized world which we have read less about than South Africa." That was twenty-five years ago, yet with few exceptions Rolo's statement is as applicable today as the day it was written. We still have very little creative literature from South Africa—either by white or black writers—in spite of a number of gifted novelists who began publishing accounts of life in South Africa shortly after the appearance of Paton's first work: Nadine Gordimer, Dan Jacobsen, Alex La Guma, Peter Abrahams, Ezekiel Mphahlele. Perhaps there is no other country outside of Soviet domain where so many promising writers have been given such short shrift by the society that nurtured them.

If it did nothing else, *Cry, the Beloved Country* made us expect that we could look forward to more writing from South Africa—both from Paton's own pen and from the other writers who would surely follow him. In 1953,

From *Africa Today* 20, no. 4 (1973): 53–57. © 1973 by the Indiana University Press.

Paton published his second and only other novel, *Too Late the Phalarope*, and somewhat later, in 1961, a collection of short stories, *Tales from a Troubled Land*, but that is all of the fiction we have had from him to date, though he has written a number of works of non-fiction (mostly political and historical) that appeared in the ensuing years.

Why did Paton's novelistic career come to such an abrupt ending? The answer is all too obvious to anyone familiar with the South Africa political situation since 1948—the year the Nationalists gained control of the country's governmental machinery and apartheid became a reality instead of a slogan. No book that attempts to depict life in South Africa accurately can be published there today. More books are censored in South Africa than in any other non-communist nation in the world. They range from works as innocent as Thomas Hardy's *Return of the Native* and Anna Sewell's *Black Beauty*—banned because of the suggestiveness of their titles—down to the latest novel by white writer, Nadine Gordimer, and all of the works by an increasing number of black writers, most of whom now live in exile. Paton simply chose not to write under these worsening conditions, though ten years ago when a friend of mine visited him, he was considering writing mysteries. (They could, of course, be mindless books which would not have to depict any of South Africa's political or social turmoils.) Under conditions such as these, it is surprising that Paton's three works of fiction have not been banned by the South African government. There is little doubt, however, that if he had continued to write books as timely as *Cry, the Beloved Country*, they would have been outlawed in his own native country.

To a certain extent, the critical reactions toward Paton's first novel have mirrored the dilemma of the South African writer himself. The earliest reviews were almost uniformly laudatory, reviews it should be noted that were written by white literary critics outside of Africa. Paton was riding high on a cloud of critical acclaim. Here was the book liberal whites had been waiting for. American critics especially (the novel was published in the United States before it appeared in English and South African editions) could look at Paton's South Africa and see a disturbing mirror image of the racial tensions of their own country. And now Paton had brought it all out into the open, so things were bound to get better. The book became an immediate best seller; a musical version, *Lost in the Stars*, by Maxwell Anderson and Kurt Weill, played on Broadway the following year; and the movie version which followed in 1951 was bound to open the eyes of millions of people who had never gotten around to reading the book itself. How could anyone be critical of a book like this which brought racial guilt feelings out into the open where they could be talked about?

By the early 1960's, when Paton's novel was just beginning to become popular a second time around with a whole new generation of high school and university students, a group of young black South Africans had emerged who felt that *Cry, the Beloved Country* did not speak for them. They were critical of Paton's novel in a way that no one had ever been before. They spoke harshly of the novel itself and, to a lesser extent, its author, who they felt was guilty of creating stereotypes of the most derogatory kind. Stephen Kumalo, the minister-hero of Paton's novel, they felt, was nothing more than a liberal white's concept of an educated black man, that is, an Uncle Tom. Ezekiel Mphahlele wrote of Kumalo in *The African Image*, "Kumalo ... remains the same suffering, Christlike, childlike character from beginning to end. He is always trembling with humility.... He is always bewildered." And in more critical terms, Lewis Nkosi, in *Home and Exile*, wrote of Paton's hero:

> If we rejected Stephen Kumalo, Paton's hero, it was partly because we, the young, suspected that the priest was a cunning expression of white liberal sentiment. Paton's generosity of spirit, his courageous plea for racial justice, all of those qualities which have earned him the undying respect of many Africans, were not of course, in question. What was in question was Paton's method, his fictional control of African character which produced an ultimate absurdity like Stephen Kumalo; an embodiment of all the pieties, trepidations and humiliations we the young had begun to despise with such a consuming passion.
>
> We thought we discerned in Stephen Kumalo's naiveté and simple-minded goodwill, white South Africa's subconscious desire to survive the blind tragedy which was bound to engulf the country sooner or later; for if the African (anybody else for that matter) was as fundamentally good and forgiving as Stephen Kumalo was conceived by Paton to be, then the white South Africans might yet escape the immense penalty which they would be required to pay.

Mphahlele and Nkosi (writers who live in exile and whose works are banned in South Africa) are a little too hard on Stephen Kumalo. He is more than the flat character Mphahlele sees him to be. True, he does tremble too much, and his humility will not earn him the admiration of today's younger activists. But there are a number of times in Paton's story when we see him acting in ways that can be called anything but timid and meek. Kumalo shows a wide variety of emotions, including rage and desire—not just humility. He quarrels with his younger brother and deliberately lies to him. He tricks his son's pregnant wife into making her believe that he desires her. Toward the end of the story, we are told that he once went up to the mountain alone, so he would not commit adultery with a young school teacher. These and other aspects of his character indicate that Stephen Kumalo is something other than a stereotype. I have to agree, however, with Mphahlele and Nkosi's assessment of Paton's unflagging optimism, which now appears to have contributed regrettably to the novel's datedness.

To a certain degree, Paton's novel was no longer an accurate picture of South African life the year it was published. Once the Nationalists came into power in 1948, they immediately increased the number of pass laws that prohibited almost all forms of contact between blacks and whites in South Africa (The Electoral Laws Amendment Act of 1948; the Prohibition of Mixed Marriage Act of 1949; the Native Laws Amendment Act of 1949; the Population Registration Act of 1950; the Group Areas Act of 1950; the Bantu Authorities Act of 1951, etc.). The list became endless—legalizing separation of the races by marriage, occupation, education, place of residence, etc. Scenes which Paton had included in his novel (black and white priests living together in Johannesburg, the funeral scene in which blacks and whites are both present) were no longer possible in real life. All of this because of the increased legislation during the first few years of Nationalist rule. Today, a South African reading, *Cry, the Beloved Country* must certainly think that he is reading a novel about some other country in some bygone time.

I have taught the novel frequently enough to realize that this is true for the American reader coming across the book for the first time today, too. Paton's story of life in South Africa is almost too tame for today's reader. The situation in the United States has deteriorated so much in the past twenty-five years that much of Paton's novel seems passé. Love, Paton's favorite word, has become a meaningless term:

> there is only one thing that has power completely, and that is love. Because when a man loves, he seeks no power, and therefore he has power. I see only one hope for our country, and that is when white men and black men, desiring neither power nor money, but desiring only the good of their country, come together to work for it.

The war in Vietnam has made us immune to any feelings akin to brotherly love. Even Msimangu's famous statement sounds a little like an empty platitude: "I have one great fear in my heart, that one day when they are turned to loving, they will find that we are turned to hating." Our lives have been attuned to violence in the political and certainly the racial arenas. There can be nothing very shocking about the murder of Arthur Jarvis for the reader who has already seen John Kennedy, Martin Luther King, Bobby Kennedy, and Malcolm X shot down in similar fashion. Harrison's statement to the elder Jarvis—"'I'm not a nigger-hater, Jarvis. I try to give 'em a square deal, decent wages, and a clean room, and reasonable time off. Our servants stay with us for years. But the natives as a whole are getting out of hand'"—sounds as if it were spoken by Richard Nixon, arguing the blessings of busing, law and order. Perhaps the most timely line in Paton's book today is one which once was considered his most pessimistic, "There are times, no doubt, when God seems no more to be about in the world."

No doubt the religious overtones present in much of the story are also irritating to many a contemporary reader. If the world is not as white as it was when Paton wrote his book, the world is not as religious as it was then either. Most of Africa is now independent; many educated Africans have turned their backs on Christianity. Too often it was presented to them with strings attached. One thinks of Mark Twain's invective in an essay about colonialism written in 1901, "To the Person Sitting in Darkness": "shall we go on conferring our Civilization upon these peoples that sit in darkness, or shall we give those poor things a rest?" Paton has always been a deeply religious person, as many of his other writings show us. His didacticism doesn't leave very much for the reader to figure out for himself; instead, his inspirational tone intrudes again and again:

> The tragedy is not that things are broken. The tragedy is that they are not mended again. The white man has broken the tribe. And it is my belief—and again I ask your pardon—that it cannot be mended again. But the house that is broken, and the man that falls apart when the house is broken, these are the tragic things. That is why children break the law, and old white people are robbed and beaten.

Too often the reader feels that he is listening to a sermon, not reading a novel.

Some of Paton's answers to South Africa's social problems seem dated now also, not just his preachy tone, but here I do not think that we can be too hard on him. Once again, the world has moved too rapidly. What might have been answers to some of South Africa's racial problems twenty-five years ago (education and restoration of the land are two possibilities that Paton suggests) simply do not work today. Education is meaningless if there isn't a job available for the person who has completed his schooling. Until the work laws are changed in South Africa, increased literacy is going to lead to nothing but increased disillusionment. Restoring the worn-out land won't help much either as long as twenty percent of the people control eighty-six percent of the land. Ultimately, only one thing will improve all this and that is total elimination of the apartheid laws and governmental control by the majority—the Africans. The chances for that are slim, and that, I suppose, is the most depressing thing about reading *Cry, the Beloved Country* in 1973 instead of 1948. Twenty-five years ago there was still hope for South Africa. Twenty-five years ago there was still hope—period.

I think I've been rather hard on Paton's novel, perhaps intentionally so. The world has not treated Paton's work the way he would have liked it. Reading the novel over again today, it is hard to deny that *Cry, the Beloved Country* is a little too much of a period piece, a thing of the past. Yet it is still a beautifully lyrical novel; it is capable of moving the reader in a way few other novels do these days. As long as fear continues to rule men's lives, Paton's novel will, unfortunately, have something to say to us.

J. ALVAREZ-PEREYRE

The Social Record in Paton's
Cry, the Beloved Country

Dating CTBC

Begun late September 1946, *CTBC* was finished in Feb. 1947: the events related in the book, as well as the general atmosphere of poverty and the description of the inequalities suffered by the non-whites, are clearly contemporary with the last years of the Second World War and the immediate post-war years. There are a few references to the war in the book itself, notably p. 50 ("there has been a great war raging in Europe and North Africa, and no houses are being built") and p. 150 which tells of the Afrikaner's attitudes during the war ("some had joined the army, and some were for the war but didn't join the army, and some were just for neutrality and if they had any feelings they concealed them, and some were for Germany but it wasn't wise for them to say anything about it"). Eric Walker, the historian, says that during this period (of the war and immediately after) "the economic and social structure was rickety, resting as it did on a low-paid, underfed and, on the whole, untrained mass of non-European labour, and depending far too much on gold and diamonds" (*A History of Southern Africa*, p. 745). The situation in the Bantu reserves, that of migratory labour and the erection of Shanty towns, of which we shall hear at length in *CTBC*, are described by Walker in much the same terms as Paton's (p. 752–757). The official statistics point out to the inequalities mentioned in *CTBC* (see Van den Berghe's *South Africa: a Study in Conflict*[1]). Several other books, dealing

From *Études Anglaises* 25, no. 2 (April–June 1972): 207–14. © 1972 by *Études Anglaises*.

9

with the same period, reach the same conclusions: Luthuli's *Let my People go*, especially chapters 9, 10 and 11) and Ezechiel Mphalele's *Down Second Avenue*, both autobiographies (Mphalele worked for a while in Ezenzeleni and lived in Orlando).

We now come to the four events Paton specifically mentions. The bus boycott seems to be that of 1943, for which we have a Government report made public in 1944.

The erection of Shanty Town, or rather of the first of many such 'towns' can be dated 1943, too.

The strike and the discovery of gold at Odendaalsrust both took place in 1946. The strike, as seen from the Africans' point of view, is related in Luthuli's book (pp. 94–95). This relation shows how disillusioned the Africans were at the empty promises of the whites, and Paton wisely deals with the two events in the same breath, as it were (Book II, chapters 6 and 9), to emphasize the gap between the earnings of the white share-holders and the more than moderate demands of the African workers. Another interest of the documents available is that we have (in Baker's book already mentioned) a journalist's account of the discovery of gold at Odendaalsrust (*The Times*, May 13, 1946) which enables us to see in detail the contrast between fiction and document.

The Evidence Itself

Most of the books we have mentioned had not yet been published in 1946. Paton had to rely on contemporary sources, and he must have shown an unusual interest in the affairs of his country since he wrote the book during his few months outside South Africa. Moreover, Paton had been in close contact with Africans from 1935 to 1946 while at Diepkloof Reformatory; we get a glimpse of Diepkloof (in *CTBC* chapter 10, Book I) which lay on the immediate outskirts of Johannesbourg and whose inmates came predominantly from the adjoining slums. Finally, we also know that between 1943 and 1945, Paton wrote a series of documented articles on the general subject of *Society and the Offender*, and that his views are confirmed, particularly by Junod's own conclusions[2]. It is worth remembering too, that the last article of the series to be published before Paton's departure for his tour of other reformatory institutions in Europe and America is entitled "Who is really to blame for the crime wave in South Africa", a title which is strongly reminiscent of one of Arthur Jarvis' papers on the same subject.

The evidence itself is distributed all over the book but introduced 'naturally' through the character of Kumalo who, being at once a 'countryman' and a parson, discovers at the same time the squalid life of Johannesburg and the moral degeneration following the break-down of the tribe and the appalling living conditions in town. When he comes back to Ndotsheni, his eyes are open at last, and only then are we given a picture of the life in the country; in the meantime, thanks to the second book which introduces us into the white neighbourhood, we are in a position to compare the way of living of Africans and whites (English-speaking ones), thus taking stock of the huge differences and inequalities; the conversations of James Jarvis with the Harrisons, and the writings left by Arthur and read by his father, provide a further insight into the mind of white South Africans. Thus the narrative constantly links the individual dramas with the overall national picture, and mixes, or blends, information with narration: the 'thread' of each character is thus part of the warp and woof of the South African texture. We list below, under various headings, the evidence as presented in *CTBC*.

A) LIFE IN THE COUNTRY

On page 7 (the opening page), then on page 22, we hear of the sickness of the land and of its consequences: "the tribe was broken, and the house broken, and the man broken . . . this was true not only in Ndotsheni but also in the Lufafa, and the Inhalavini, and the Unskomaas, and the Umzimkulu".

We hear later of the erosion of the soil, and "how the hills were steep, and indeed some of them were never meant for ploughing" (p. 113). We hear about the ignorance of farming methods, and that there were too many cattle.

But the main fact is that there is too little land, and that is the white man's doing: "Some said there was too little land anyway, and that the natives could not support themselves on it, even with the most progressive methods of agriculture . . . And where was the land to come from, and who would pay for it? And there was still another argument, for if they got more land, what if by some chance they could make a living from it, *who would work on the white man's farms?*" (Book II, 1, p. 114).

The land problem is mentioned again in II, 3, p. 127, by Arthur Jarvis in one of his papers: "We set aside one-tenth of the land for four-fifths of the people. Thus we made it inevitable, and some say we did it knowingly, that labour would come to the towns."

No wonder then that in Book III, the young agricultural demonstrator should exclaim: "What this good white man does is only repayment"; adding: "if this valley were restored, as you are always asking in your prayers, do you think it would hold all the people of this tribe if they returned?".

B) LIFE IN TOWN

Earlier on (p. 1), we have seen the figures showing the differences in the income levels of whites and non-whites. This is exemplified in *CTBC*, especially in chapters 9, 10, 11 and 12 of Book I. For instance, we hear through Kumalo that "to save ten pounds from a stipend of eight pounds a month takes much patience and time, especially for a parson who must dress in good, black clothes" (p. 31). But John Kumalo says of the Bishop that "he lives in a big house, and his white priests get four, five, six times what you get, my brother" (p. 35).

The miners' earnings are first alluded to in John Kumalo's first conversation with his brother and Msimangu: " . . . but it is they who dig the gold for 3 shillings a day . . . When the new gold is found, it is not we who will get more for our labour. It is the white man's shares that will rise, you'll read it in the papers . . ."This prepares the episode of the discovery of gold in II, 6, p. 145, where, in a couple of hours, the shares rise from 20 to 100 shillings. It is difficult not to link John's words: "South Africa is not built on the mines, it is built on our backs, on our sweat, on our labour" (p. 35) with Arthur's first paper: . . ."It is not permissible to add to one's possessions if these things can only be done at the cost of other men. *Such development has only one true name, and that is exploitation*" (p. 126).

So much for the exposure of the inequalities in earnings. When we come to the subject of housing, the picture is not brighter: "ten people in two rooms, and only one door for the entrance, and people to walk over you when you go to sleep" (p. 49). "And of what do we build the houses?—Anything you can find. Sacks and planks and grass from the veld and poles from the plantations" (p. 50). This is taken up again pp. 52, 57, 61: "Pimville, which is a village of half-tanks used as houses, set up many years before in emergency and used ever since. For there have never been houses enough for all the people who came to Johannesburg . . .").

Kumalo notices children in the streets, lots of children: "And these children? Why are they not at school?—some because they do not care, and some because their parents do not care, but many because the schools are full" (Book I, chapter 6, p. 27). Later on, Kumalo's nephew appears: "Into the room, shepherded by an older girl . . . His clothes were dirty and his nose running, and he put his finger in his mouth and gazed at his uncle out of wide saucer-like eyes" (page 30). Arthur Jarvis also alludes to this problem: "Yet we continue to leave the education of our native urban society to those few Europeans who feel strongly about it, *and to deny opportunities and money for its expansion*". So, here, too, the exposure of the white man's responsibility is made by Paton in uncompromising terms. (See, too, p. 79: "Oh for education for this people, for schools up and down the land, where something might be built that would serve them when they went away to the towns, something that would take the place of the tribal law and custom.")

c) CRIME

We now come to the subject of crime itself. Fear and crime are present throughout the book, from the mention, p. 21, that "white Johannesburg was afraid of black crime", to the hanging of Absalom which takes place at the very end of the book. In-between, we hear of several murders and assaults as well as of robberies, either indirectly, in the course of conversations between the various characters, or more directly, by newspapers headlines or by the reports of journalists. This is how we hear of Arthur's murder; there ensue several scenes in prison and in Court.

Before we deal with the subject of justice and Crime, we have to deal with the causes of crime. To poverty, overcrowding, promiscuity, must be added the fact that the lodging of miners (coming from the reserves) in compounds where they must live without their families for long periods breaks whatever custom held them together in more peaceful surroundings. In town, and particularly under the conditions prevailing in Johannesburg, prostitution, liquor brewing, corruption, all concur to the degeneration of people and general spirit. Absalom's wife-to-be 'thinks' she is sixteen, and she has had already three 'husbands'; Gertrude has been one of the shebeen queens, and we are told that many of the rooms in Alexandra are "hide-outs for thieves and robbers". There is nothing but truth in this picture, and Paton will once again deal with the underworld of Johannesburg in some of the short stories in *Debbie Go Home*. Here, too, Paton is quite clear about where the responsibility lies: "I asked Arthur about that" (native crime), Harrison Sr. says, "but he reckoned we were to blame somehow" (p. 122). And in Arthur's often quoted paper, we find this: "the old tribal system was, for all its violence and savagery, for all its superstition and witchcraft, a moral system. Our natives today produce criminals and prostitutes and drunkards, not because it is their nature to do so, but because their simple system of order and tradition and convention has been destroyed. It was destroyed by the impact of our own civilization. *Our civilization has therefore an inescapable duty to set up another system of order and tradition and convention*" (p. 127). Thus, in answer to those white inhabitants of Jo'burg demanding more police, and more prisons, and harsher penalties, one of the anonymous voices, expressing itself very much in Arthur's way, exclaims: "I say we shall always have native crime to fear until the native people of this country have worthy purposes to inspire them and worthy goals to work for" (p. 68).

D) THE INSTITUTIONS

The subject of Justice and Crime hinges on the more general subject of the Institutions in South Africa. If the whites have apportioned the land with the injustice and selfishness we have seen they have also made the laws. As Paton was to write in 1958: "Apartheid, whether partial or total, is essentially something done by someone with power to someone with none" (in *Hope for South Africa*, p. 55). We find the same hint at tyranny and oppression in

Luthuli's *Let my people go*: "The slave system has been nationalised. We are told where we may work, where we may not, where we may live and where we may not; freehold rights are altogether taken from us and we are forbidden by law to strike or to protest against the edicts of an all-white parliament or against exploitation" (p. 80).

So, when it comes to decision-making, we find that it is the white man who decides everything: "If justice be not just, that is not to be laid at the door of the judge but at the door of the People, which means at the door of the White People, for it is the White People that make the Law" (pp. 136–137). It is even the white people that speak for all the non-white population which has absolutely no say in the affairs of the country: "You know these native M.P.'s they have—well, there was talk of getting him to stand at the next elections" (p. 121, II, 2). (Native M.P.'s here means the members of Parliament representing the Natives; but this was abolished in 1959, and the M.P.'s representing the Coloureds in 1968, so that to-day, the white man reigns supreme in a country where he represents one-fifth of the population.)

A Few Questions

If, then, oppression exists in South Africa[3] and there is damning evidence of it, how are protest and resistance to it expressed in *CTBC*?

We hear about Sir Ernest Oppenheimer whose proposals for lodging the miners in villages, not compounds, where they would live with their families, can be only considered as an alleviation, making the system more human.

There are liberal-minded whites who are ready to go farther and sacrifice their own jobs to their ideals of fraternity and restoration (Arthur Jarvis). It would be interesting to list whatever concrete actions they suggest, from Professor Hoernlé to Arthur, not forgetting Father Vincent and James Jarvis. Do the Jarvises represent for Paton individual action at its best or is Paton hinting that only such individual actions are possible in a society which seems to be at the same time 'asleep' (meaning not wanting or not caring to face the facts) and repressive? On the other hand, is collective action possible and fruitful? We do not hear about the issue of the bus boycott, and the strike is crushed ruthlessly. Yet collective action is shown to be possible and fruitful in the episode describing the erection of Shanty Town.

What about the African community itself, then? Between Stephen Kumalo ("the white man's dog") and Napoleon Letsitsi who represents the younger generation, more aware of problems, more restive, too, there is a whole gamut of attitudes and reactions. That of the underworld, for instance, creating its own order based on intimidation and crime; that of Mrs. Lithebe: is she "the native who has come to terms with the white man on his terms, finding a pattern for her life in the ethics of her religion"? (C.P. Harnett).

What about Msimangu? is he socially and politically 'clear'? Why is he retiring in a community? How much of John's portrait is true to life, how much is a caricature? This raises a more general question about all the characters of the book. Are they social types, mere mouthpieces for the author's ideas? What must we think of Mphalele's opinion that "they are nearly all flat" (in *The African Image*, p. 131)[4]?

Finally, what about the role of the Church? On the one hand, we have John Kumalo's assertion: "It is true that the Church speaks with a fine voice, and that the Bishops speak against the laws. But this they have been doing for fifty years, and things get worse, not better" (p. 34). But there are lots of Churches in South Africa, the English-speaking ones and the Afrikaans-speaking churches, and their attitudes are different (see p. 70). More is said about the Church page 163, and about Christianity in South Africa: "The truth is that our civilization is not Christian . . ." (p. 134). Yet, against this last statement must be weighed the actions of such men as Father Vincent, the people at Ezenzelini, some of whom are Afrikaans-speaking, of Arthur and James Jarvis. Must we conclude again that Christian action, in a "Christian" country like South Africa, exercises itself solely on the individual level?

Conclusion

With what picture of South Africa are we left? If the tone used by Paton is never violent, there is no doubt that *CTBC* contains a severe indictment of white South Africa. Yet the way this is done is quite particular to Paton, one might be tempted to write 'unique'. For *CTBC* is no political pamphlet *per se*; but there is direct as well as indirect reference to the political, social and economic life of the country. All the arguments are not listed in a logical, or didactic order, as they would be in a pamphlet: they are dotted here and there, although not in an haphazard way. The question is whether what is lost in pungency and condensation is counterbalanced by the way the individual and national dramas are interrelated, sometimes even interacting? Here again, a study of the structure shows that what is presented theoretically is matched by concrete examples, and that the viewpoint of a given community is confirmed, stressed or even lived out, by another community.

Another question is whether the objectivity used by Paton softens the whole picture, and takes away some of its impact. For instances, who emerges as the villain? The Whites? "But they are not all so" (Msimangu, p. 25). The Afrikaners? " . . . When father says Afrikaners he means Nationalists" (Harrison Jr., p. 132). And we see no Nationalist throughout the book, we never hear the hated address from non-whites to whites: "baas". We only glimpse a 'boy' (meaning the 'native' servant) (pp. 154–5). Yet, too, we are left with terrible complaints: "They give us too little; they give us almost nothing" (Msimangu, p. 26). "God have mercy upon us. Christ have mercy upon us. White man, have mercy upon us" (The anonymous mother in Shanty Town, p. 53).

If the white man is to be in the dock then Paton never puts the onus on any one community: it is never 'they', or 'the Afrikaners', it is 'we'. Thus, in one of the most moving pieces of I, 12, Paton writes: "We do not know, we do not know . . . And our lives will shrink, but they shall be the lives of superior beings; and we shall live with fear . . ." (p. 71). In still another place, he writes: "We are caught in the toils of our own selfishness" (p. 127).

Given such nuances and fairness of spirit and treatment, social protest in *CTBC* is closely related to Paton's Christian outlook on life and philosophy (remember his first title: *God Save Africa*). Yet, such as it is, the book had a strong impact on the non-South African public. For the first time, people the world over realised what it was like to live in South Africa when one did not belong to the white community. "*CTBC* does what no discursive work in political science, sociology, economics, and anthropology could ever do; it makes us understand 'how it feels' to be a South African to-day; it gives the 'form and pressure' of life in South Africa" (Harold Collins: "*CTBC* and the Broken Tribe", in *College English*, XIV, April 1953).

What about the South African public itself? It is difficult to assess the political effect of the book, and to say that it did not prevent the Nationalists from gaining victory in the 1948 elections would be over-simplifying things and attributing to fictional works an importance that most of them, be they best sellers, have not. Its spiritual effects were much greater; but there was certainly a need to carry out one's ideas into the political arena if one wanted to have an influence, and perhaps help to change, the reigning institutions. That is what Paton did by co-founding the Liberal Party in 1954 and leading it for nearly as long as he held the Principalship at Diepkloof. Yet, once again, won over love and faith[5]. Reverting in 1967 to this problem of fear which is central to him, Paton wrote: "Fear of change is, no doubt, in all of us, but it most afflicts the man who fears that any change must lead to loss of his wealth and status. When this fear becomes inordinate, he will, if he has political power, abrogate such things as civil rights and the rule of law, using the argument that he abrogates them only to preserve them . . . I see no hope for the peace of society and the peace of the world so long as this fear of change is so powerful. And this fear will remain powerful so long as the one side has so much to gain and the other so much to lose" (*The Challenge of Fear*, in *Saturday Review*, September 9, 1967).

Notes

1. Van den Berghe reports about the average family incomes in South Africa:

	Whites	Asians and Coloureds	Africans
1938–9	£530	£134	£50,1
1953–4	£1,616	£308	£119,2

All the statistics at the end of this book are interesting and valuable for a comparison of the Kwame Nkrumah.

2. Henri Philippe Junod was for a long time Chaplain of the Prisons. In 1947, he published a pamphlet: *Revenge or Reformation?*, inaugurating a series edited by the *Penal Reform League of South Africa*.

3. Despite the screen of official optimism of which Paton was fully aware: "One can read . . . the brochures about lovely South Africa, the land of sun and beauty sheltered from the storms of the world, and feel pride in it, and love for it, and yet know nothing about it at all" (p. 150).

4. "E.M. Forster says in his *Aspects of the Novel* that when a novelist wants to strike with direct force, it is convenient for him to use 'flat' characters; characters who can easily be labelled and therefore managed. Paton's characters are nearly all flat. We can almost hear them groan under the load of the author's monumental sermon . . ." (*The African Image*, p. 131).

5. Here are the National results in the 1958 elections:

Nationalist Party: 642,069
United Party: 503,639
Liberal Party: 2,934

In 1961, with less then 50% of the electorate going to the polls, the Liberal Party polled 2,461 votes.

R.W.H. HOLLAND

Fiction and History:
Fact and Invention in Alan Paton's
Novel Cry, the Beloved Country

In the author's note at the front of the novel appear the following words:

> Various persons are mentioned, not by name, but as the holders
> of this or that position. In no case is reference intended to any
> actual holder of any of these positions. Nor in any related event
> is reference intended to any actual event; except that the accounts
> of the boycott of the buses, the erection of Shanty Town, the
> finding of gold at Odendaalsrust, and the miners' strike, are a
> compound of truth and fiction. In these respects therefore the
> story is not true, but considered as a social record it is plain and
> simple truth.[1]

These statements are not as direct and guileless as they may seem. Indeed,
they are decidedly artful. The events referred to are documented historically, but the writer tells us that fictional elements are combined with them
in some way. How? As will be seen, the answer is not simple. And how
exactly can a 'story that is not true' be considered as 'a social record' that is
'true'? This may look like a contradiction. But when one realizes that the
term 'true' is being used with two totally different meanings the contradiction is resolved.

From *Zambezia: The Journal of the University of Rhodesia* 5, no. 2 (1977): 129–39. © 1977 by
the University of Rhodesia.

19

Any invented story is untrue in the sense that it has never happened and never likely to; although, if it ever did, the writer persuades us that this is the way it would happen. Paton's first use of 'true' clearly means this. His use of 'truth' for the social record is a little more complex.

Haw can an account compounded of actual and invented elements be true? It cannot clearly be literal truth. Does he mean that the described events are true to the 'spirit' of things, although departing from the facts in some respects? The spirit of anything is open to interpretation and argument. His simple truth is not as simple as it sounds. If *Cry, the Beloved Country* is to be seen as both a social and fictional record, one does not have to read far into the novel to spot that there is an ambiguity somewhere in the chronology of events. It is worth looking closely at Paton's 'plain and simple truth' to find out exactly what it is and to see how he exploits the ambiguity of time-scales for his 'record'.

Events that occur within the time-span established by the invented narrative will be referred to as happening in fictional time; events that have actually occurred, and incorporated into the novel, as happening in historical time. Within the novel, fictional time will be seen to be given preference over historical time.

No author can invent a date in the way that he can invent an incident; unlike a character, it either has occurred or will occur. In a novel, a date acquires an ambiguous status. *Cry, the Beloved Country* is set in the year 1945. What does this claim amount to? Is the date merely a device to give an appearance of historicity to a record that has never happened? Or are real events being dressed up to look like some kind of invention? Is the novel perhaps trying to do both? Do we place the date, then, in fictional or historical time, or in both? The following discussion will try to show that it is best regarded as fictional, 'occurring' within the narrative, rather than at a specific point in history; and, will try to throw light on the questions about truth.

A precise time is first emphasized in Book I, Chapter XI:[2]

At 1.30 p.m. today Mr. Arthur Jarvis, of Plantation Road, Parkwold, was shot dead in his house by an intruder ... [3]

This is offered to the reader as part of a newspaper report; one of the characters, Fr Vincent, brings it to the attention of Stephen Kumalo by reading it aloud to him. There is no ambiguity about the given hour and there is no necessity for it to occur historically—until a day and a date are assigned to it. It is not only fictional, but also essentially timeless, because 1.30 p.m. could, within the book, occur last year, this year, sometime, never. Any one moment is as credible as any other.

However, this particular event of the shooting of Arthur Jarvis is not left timeless. In court, at the trial of Absalom and his friends:

> A white man stands up and says that these three are accused of the murder of Arthur Trevelyan Jarvis, in his house at Plantation Road, Parkwold, Johannesburg, on Tuesday the eighth day of October, 1946, in the early afternoon.[4]

Now the instant of the murder has become actual; a fictional specificness has become an actual specificness. Also it has been linked to a particular place. But when a writer is so precise about the timing of a single incident in a story, he is not necessarily wanting the reader to believe that he is describing a factual event. The happening could be imaginary, but the timing real. He may wish the reader to understand that an action could have occurred at a precise point in history, and that the reader could have experienced it. Such a blending of the invented and the real gives more convincingness to his story. In such instances, reality and fantasy do not conflict.

But if, for example, a character is described as going to the police with information about a murder that has just happened on the day before the murder occurs, we sit up incredulously. A mistake of this kind—an incongruity in fictional time—would destroy the artistic illusion, and writers take care not to make this kind of error. So, giving a real date and time for any fictional event need not throw up any problem of ambiguous chronology, as long as the invented incidents do not conflict with it. We are, thus able to think of Arthur Jarvis's murder as happening in fictional and historical time simultaneously, thereby giving convincingness to an imaginary happening.

But a puzzling ambiguity can occur if a writer does the opposite, that is, introduce into an imaginary account events that are recorded historically. Real calendars and maps are then superimposed on the mock world of the fiction. Alice can live in the day-to-day world, with its formal logic, its measurable space and its regular tick. Or she can walk through the glass and live in the other, with its zany logic, its unpredictable space and its reversible time. Only when one is forced into the order of the other might a breakdown occur.

Yet it is clear from the 'Author's Note' that Paton has fused history and fiction. What consequences does this have for the temporal structure of the novel? In giving his evidence, Absalom (the murderer of Arthur Jarvis and son of Stephen Kumalo) claims that, after the killing, he walked among the Alexandra Bus Boycotters:

> —And on the second day you walked again to Johannesburg?
> —Yes.

—And you again walked amongst the people who were boy-
cotting the buses?
—Yes.
—Were they still talking about the murder?
—They were still talking. Some said they heard it would soon
be discovered.
—And then?
—I was afraid.[5]

This places Absalom, an imaginary character who has committed a murder at 1.30 p.m. in fictional time, firmly into historical time. Because the
Alexandra Bus Boycott is a documented fact, the imaginary crime has been
thrust into the context of history. Flesh and blood boycotters have even
talked about the fictional crime, it is claimed. Obviously, merely to accept
this much, the reader needs Coleridge's 'willing suspension of disbelief for
the moment which constitutes poetic faith'. Of course, readers willingly give
it. However, Paton's claim that his book 'considered as a social record . . . is
the plain and simple truth' prompts the critical reader to compare the novel's
account with the historical record. This is where the trouble begins.

The Alexandra Bus Boycott began on 14 November 1944[6] and lasted
for seven weeks.[7] Absalom's crime is committed on 8 October 1946. The
fictional and historical clocks are striking at different times. Paton has distorted actual chronology for the sake of his story by placing the boycott two
years after its time.

There was, it is true, more than one Alexandra Bus Boycott.[8] Could
Paton be thinking of the other one? Possible, but unlikely, for two reasons.
First, it happened even earlier—in August 1943—and lasted nine days. This
would require a delay of three years to fit the novel's chronology, making
Paton's account of contemporary problems (he wrote the novel in 1947) less
contemporary than need be. Second, the evidence of the novel itself suggests
fairly conclusively that it is the boycott of 1944 he is thinking of.

Alexandra was an African location to the south west of Johannesburg
within the jurisdiction of the Johannesburg City Council; and Paton also
wrote a factual account of it (in addition to the one in the novel) twenty-six
years after the writing of Cry, the Beloved Country. For the historical record,
Paton has had to check his facts; for the fiction, he need not have done so.
Nevertheless, that the novel is based firmly on factual details here is one of
the conclusions that emerges from the comparison:

> African wages were so low that a rise of a penny in any staple
> commodity was a blow to struggling people. The bus fare from

Alexandra Township to the city was raised by just that amount, and the workers of Alexandra, men and women, old men and old women, physical weaklings and cripples, refused to use the buses and walked to and from the city, twenty or twenty-two miles a day. Those who started work at 7 a.m. would have to rise at 3 a.m. and start walking at 4 a.m. If they finished work at 5 p.m. they would get home by 8 p.m. A great part of the distance was the length of Louis Botha Avenue, lined with comfortable white houses, whose occupants had of necessity to watch the daily march. Some white people were deeply moved by the marching protest, and would come daily with their cars to help the old and crippled, often being warned by the police that they were breaking the law. Others were angered by it and thought it should be ended by force. It is a temptation of white authority to this very day to silence black protest by force. Most of the white people of Johannesburg had no conception of the importance of twopence per day to most African people.[9]

The novel's account appears in Book I, Chapter VIII, where Paton makes the old African pastor, Stephen Kumalo (distressed and poor, seeking his lost son Absalom in the squalid locations around Johannesburg) face a walk of eleven miles into Alexandra, and another walk out again of the same distance. In fictional chronology, it happens on 7 October 1946. The similarities of detail in the two accounts will be apparent. The novel reads as follows:

... But here they met an unexpected obstacle, for a man came up to them and said to Msimangu, Are you going to Alexandra, umfundisi?

—Yes, my friend.

—We are here to stop you, umfundisi. Not by force, you see—he pointed—the police are there to prevent that. But by persuasion. If you use this bus you are weakening the cause of the black people. We have determined not to use these buses until the fare is brought back again to fourpence.

—Yes, indeed, I have heard of it. He turned to Kumalo.

—I was very foolish, my friend. I had forgotten that there were no buses, at least I had forgotten the boycott of the buses.

—Our business is very urgent, said Kumalo, humbly.

—This boycott is also urgent, said the man politely. They want us to pay sixpence, that is one shilling a day. Six shillings a week, and some of us get thirty-five or forty shillings.

—Is it far to walk? asked Kumalo.

—It is a long way, umfundisi. Eleven miles.

—That is a long way, for an old man.

—Men as old as you are doing it every day, umfundisi. And women, and some that are sick, and some crippled, and children. They start walking at four in the morning, and they do not get back till eight at night. They have a bite of food, and their eyes hardly close on the pillow before they must stand up again, sometimes to start off with nothing but hot water in their stomachs. I cannot stop you taking a bus, umfundisi, but this is a cause to fight for. If we lose it, then they will have to pay more in Sophiatown and Claremont and Kliptown and Pimville.

—I understand you well. We shall not use the bus. The man thanked them and went to another would-be traveller.

—That man has a silver tongue, said Kumalo.

—That is the famous Dubula, said Msimangu quietly. A friend of your brother John.[10]

The aged, the crippled and the sick are referred to in both; the times given to cover the distance correspond exactly, and the distance itself tallies.[11] Furthermore, references to the lifts offered to Africans by Whites, and references to Louis Botha Avenue, appear in both. Here is the novel again:

So they walked many miles through the European City, up Twist Street to the Clarendon Circle, and down Louis Botha towards Orange Grove. And the cars and lorries never ceased, going one way or the other. After a long time a car stopped and a white man spoke to them,

—Where are you two going? he asked.

—To Alexandra, sir, said Msimangu, talking off his hat.

—I thought you might be. Climb in.[12]

The similarities in the two accounts clearly help to enforce the conclusion that it is the second Alexandra Bus Boycott, of November 1944, that Paton is writing about in the novel.

There is a further piece of evidence to support the view. The first boycott was a totally spontaneous affair and lasted only nine days. The second boycott was quite a different kettle of fish. The first owed almost 'nothing to political leadership',[13] the second owed everything to it. An 'emergency committee' was set up (the main reason the Africans held out for seven weeks) and according to Roux, ' ... The leading figure on the committee was Gaur

Radebe, himself a resident of the township',[14] Gaur Radebe may indeed be a possible prototype for Dubula of the silver tongue.

There was a third Alexandra Bus Boycott; but as that did not take place until March 1957, it can be clearly ruled out. It seems reasonable to conclude that the boycott intended in *Cry, the Beloved Country* is that which began on 14 November 1944.

To return to the matter of fictional and historical time. As there is a discrepancy of two years between the real boycott and the fictional walk of Absalom, the question arises; How shall the incident be regarded? They cannot be simultaneous events. Fictional time has to be regarded as predominant, because it measures the dimension in which the imaginary events of the novel occur and in which the invented characters act out their lives; and it is measured consistently. Thus, the proposal made earlier: it is best to regard the date of the murder, 8 October 1946, as a purely fictional date and not a historical one, as the reader inclines to do at first. The clock of the novel provides the Greenwich Mean Time, and the clocks of history must be made to agree with it.

The foregoing analysis illustrates a technique that is characteristic of the entire novel. Paton uses it first in Book I, Chapter VIII, with the incident discussed above. He uses it almost immediately again in Chapter IX. On occasion its use is even more noteworthy. An examination of the second instance tells a lot about the structuring of the novel, the intention of its author, his beliefs, and the meaning of the work.

Chapter IX is the first of the remarkable choric sections of the book.[15] They are dramatic and lyrical and poetic in a way that helps to give the novel its distinctive flavour and style. Let us consider the temporal function of the section and how it fits into the two chronologies.

The marker of Paton's choric sections is the use he makes of the present tense. He writes in what may be termed the present historic. In English, narrative is normally marked by the use of the past historic in the third person. Indeed, Paton himself uses it orthodoxly for his own purely narrative sections (for example, Book I, Chapter V). The 'tension' that Paton sets up between the narrative sections (in the past tense) and the choric sections (in the present) helps to give urgency, width of reference and social relevance to *Cry, the Beloved Country*. Chapter IX begins thus:

> All roads lead to Johannesburg. If you are white or if you are black they lead to Johannesburg. If the crops fail, there is work in Johannesburg. If there are taxes to be paid, there is work in Johannesburg. If the farm is too small to be divided further, some must go to Johannesburg. If there is a child to be born that must be delivered in secret, it can be delivered in Johannesburg.[16]

The sense that this is happening now implies also that it will continue. Not only do all roads lead at the moment to Johannesburg, they will do so in the future, as they have done in the past. Social problems are thus given a property of timelessness, illustrative of the eternal human situation and eternal dilemmas. This effect is part of what Paton wants, and may be termed the aftermath, or future, function of the present tense.

So, together with this 'aftermath' function, the illusion is kept up that the events are also happening right now. Often, the 'nowness' of the present tense is emphasized by small linguistic changes that suppress or play down the 'aftermath' function. By the use of a simple demonstrative 'this', for example, the 'nowness' of the night is brought vividly out and the 'aftermath' effect diminished:

> This night they are busy in Orlando.

Again, the insertion of 'tonight' has the same effect:

> Let us go tonight and cut a few poles quietly.[17]

Now, we are in the middle of the African slum building itself around us, witnessing the actual process of the erection, subtly made part of it and partly responsible for it.

> This night they are busy in Orlando. At one house after another the lights are burning. I shall carry the iron and you my wife the child, and you my son two poles, and you small one, bring as many sacks as you are able, down to the land by the railway lines. Many people are moving there, you can hear the sound of digging hammering already. It is good that the night is warm, and there is no rain. Thank you, Mr. Dubula, we are satisfied with this piece of ground. Thank you, Mr. Dubula, here is our shilling for the committee.
>
> Shanty Town is up overnight. What a surprise for the people when they wake in the morning. Smoke comes up through the sacks, and one or two have a chimney already. There was a nice chimney-pipe lying there at Kliptown Police Station, but I was not such a fool as to take it.
>
> Shanty Town is up overnight. And the newspapers are full of us. Great big words and pictures. See, that is my husband standing by the house. Alas, I was too late for the picture. Squatters, they call us. We are the squatters. This great village of sack and plank and iron, with no rent to pay, only a shilling to the Committee.

Shanty Town is up overnight. The child coughs badly, and her brow is hot as fire. I was afraid to move her, but it was the night for the moving. The cold wind comes through the sacks. What shall we do in the rain, in the winter? Quietly my child, your mother is by you. Quietly my child, do not cough any more, your mother is by you.[18]

Each separate cameo (enclosed between asterisks in this chapter) is a part of the Africans' general plight, as well as episodes in the account of the building of Shanty Town; we are made to realize that the general points to the particular; all is tending towards the focal point of this particular night. Although earlier the reader was persuaded to accept the situations as timeless, and the comments as those made by the author on an eternal human predicament, he is now made to accept it as an immediately urgent dilemma of one particular night, 7 October 1946, an event of weight and importance in the chronology of the novel. Paton has it both ways: both timeless and timeful. The events happen on his fictional clock, and on no clock at all, for the eternal is timeless.

Roux's account of the historical Shanty Town runs as follows:

The war [i.e. 1939–45] industries had drawn large numbers of African workers into the urban areas. Since Native housing schemes automatically came to an end in 1940, the resulting congestion in the urban locations can be imagined. On the Witwatersrand there were literally thousands of people without homes. Things came to a head at Orlando in April, 1944. The location had become supersaturated with human beings; it could no longer hold all those who were trying to live there. Some thousands of men, women and children left the location and camped on vacant municipal ground nearby. They built themselves shelters of sticks, sacking, old tins, and maize stalks. Thousands of other homeless persons came to join them from other parts of the Reef. Thus was Shanty Town born.[19]

The difference between the two purposes is clear: Roux is out to record the social and historical fact that Shanty Town was built. Paton wants to show Shanty Town in a process of becoming; a variety of aspects emerge, but it is not seen as a sociological phenomenon primarily. Human drama and personal hardship are foregrounded by using the persona of Mrs Seme, an African wife and mother. She seeks lodgings with an Orlando family but is turned away. She hears 'the uncrowned king of Shanty Town' (in real life, Sofazonke Mpanza)[20] propose the building of their shelters:

—And where do we put the houses?

—On the open ground by the railway line, Dubula[21] says.

—And of what do we build the houses?

—Anything you can find. Sacks and planks and grass from the veld and poles from the plantations.

—And when it rains.

—Siyafa. Then we die.[22]

Mrs Seme goes to see an African official of the Johannesburg Housing Committee. He turns out to be corrupt and asks for five pounds.

The whole sequence illustrates the way Paton can bring out the 'aftermath' function of the present, as well as its 'nowness'. In a section that is primarily choric and static, he is nevertheless able to suggest a narrative by exploiting the temporal ambiguity of the tense. From the point of view of fictional and historical time, however, what is important to notice is that Shanty Town is firmly fixed in history in April 1944, whereas, fictionally, it happens on the night of 7–8 October 1946. Paton has again distorted historical time in the interests of fiction by an amount of two years. In fact, the Bus Boycott and Shanty Town were seven months apart. In the novel, this is compressed into about twenty hours. This is the second distortion of time for the sake of the fiction.

Finally, there is another and possibly more revealing discrepancy. The month of the Bus Boycott was November; Shanty Town thus happened first. In the novel, Paton reverses this sequence: Shanty Town follows the boycott.

One of his aims is clear from the extracts given: he wishes the physical upheaval, social suffering and individual misery depicted in the Shanty Town[23] episode to be placed alongside a climatic fictional event—the murdering of Arthur Jarvis by Absalom and all its consequent misery. The two events are thus associated in our minds. This deliberate juxtaposition—the real against the fictional—is fruitful in suggesting that the two are causally related, that the murder of a white man (who, ironically, happens to be active on behalf of Africans) by an unknown Zulu drifting rootlessly about the African locations around Johannesburg has been directly caused by the society that produced Shanty Town. Paton does indeed believe that African crime can be largely attributed to the conditions in which Africans are forced to live.[24] Arthur Jarvis left a paper on Native[25] crime half-written at the time of his murder, directed at the consciences of the white population of South Africa. The irony of his murder is thus sharpened and deepened.

The foregoing analysis illustrates the use Paton makes throughout the novel of actual social events. They are not there simply for their own sakes, as important as they are. They do not simply add background or convincingness to the whole by making sociological 'facts' concrete (although they do this in passing). They are tied to particular fictional events, characters and consequences. They work functionally.

First, Stephen Kumalo leaves the remote Natal village of Ndotsheni and travels hundreds of miles in a train to the thoroughly (for him) alien and bewildering city of Johannesburg. He searches for days amongst the soulless townships for his son, scurrying from Sophiatown to Alexandra, to Claremont, to Pimville, to Orlando, back and forth, unsuccessful, tormented, tired and depressed. It is during this fruitless endless searching that he encounters the Alexandra Bus Boycott, as we have seen. The boycott is a kind of analogue of his own emotional and physical journeying that is getting him nowhere. It is a suitable metaphor of frustration for both Stephen Kumalo, the fictional individual, and the actual African workers. It is a crisis point for Kumalo: he begins to suspect and fear the truth about his son. Later, he confirms this:

> —At first it was a search. I was anxious at first, but as the search went on, step by step, so did the anxiety turn to fear, and this fear grew deeper step by step. It was at Alexandra that I first grew afraid, but it was here in your House, when we heard of the murder, that my fear grew into something too great to be borne.[26]

By causing Kumalo to encounter the Bus Boycott, Paton associates a private and personal trauma with a social one, linking an imagined and a real crisis. Later, ironically, Absalom is able to hide himself among the walkers; it helps Absalom and hinders his father, another significant linking. While Absalom mingles with the boycotters, his father, at the Mission for the Blind, at Ezenzeleni, suddenly has his eyes opened to the truth about his son. Thus, the entire incident is made to work on more than one level.

Second, Shanty Town: its relation to the murder we have already examined. Its function in relation to Stephen Kumalo is twofold: it helps to convince the general reader of the dispiriting extent of Kumalo's search, and to impress the South African reader with the extent of social injustice in his own land. Further it makes another 'step' in the search Kumalo describes in the extract just quoted.

Chapter VIII ends with Msimangu and Stephen Kumalo returning to Sophiatown from Alexandra. The main story-line (of their search) continues at the beginning of Chapter IX:

> While Kumalo was waiting for Msimangu to take him to Shanty Town, he spent the time with Gertrude and her child.[27]

As far as the main narrative of the quest is concerned, the story could have been taken up from this point, without Kumalo having to be shown in Shanty Town. But the need for psychological convincingness means that we must watch Kumalo's fear growing throughout his search in Shanty Town. We are thus persuaded of Shanty Town's fictional reality, besides knowing that it is also a historical reality. Not only that; immediately after his sojourn in there, Kumalo returns to the Mission only to discover that, while he has been searching for his son, Absalom committed murder at 1.30 p.m. on that very day, and his fear 'grew into something too great to be borne'. The social and the personal have become aspects of a single reality: the fictional event has been encapsulated in the social event, the outward becoming the mirror and the metaphor of the inner.

What then, does Paton achieve by altering historical events to occur either later or earlier, and by putting the events themselves out of historical sequence? The answer seems to be that his artistic purpose necessitates the reader in grasping the point that personal tragedy (especially of the Africans) and social evils are inextricably linked. Such an interpretation of social events obviously implies a certain kind of programme to remedy such social evils. In other words, one infers a positive political stance in the writer which, he hopes, will bring about a change in his readers' political and social attitudes. And, as Paton's historical 'distortions' clearly show, political attitudes and social tragedies are human ones first.

Paton's 'plain and simple truth' of the 'social record', then, is neither as simple or plain as he claims. Nor, indeed, is his 'truth' quite as obvious as he implies. The plainness and simplicity of his 'truth' depends very much on the placing of a specific interpretation on the political and social events concerned, and on seeing their relationship to personal dilemmas in a particular way. Many will accept his 'truth' as axiomatic; many will not. It is clear, too, that in the South Africa of 1947, when Paton wrote the book, he himself believed that his plain and simple truth was far from obvious. For who would bother to write a novel to persuade people of the obvious? The 'Author's Note' was just the first shot in his arsenal of persuasive rhetoric, which is the novel itself.

Notes

1. Alan Paton, 'Author's note', to *Cry, the Beloved Country: A Story of Comfort in Desolation* (Harmondsworth, Penguin, 1960), 5.

2. Apart, that is, from the date on the letter to Stephen Kumalo sent by Msimangu (25 September 1946) which starts off the entire action of the novel, *Cry, the Beloved Country*, Bk I, ch. ii, 10.

3. Ibid., Bk I, ch. xi, 65.

4. Ibid., Bk II, ch. v, 137.

5. Ibid., Bk II, ch. v, 143.

6. The dates in E. Callan, *Alan Paton* (New York, Twayne, 1968), 50, 52, appear to be erroneous.

7. See E. Roux, *Time Longer than Rope: A History of the Black Man's Struggle for Freedom in South Africa* (Madison, Univ. of Wisconsin Press, 1966), 318–19.

8. ' . . . twice during the war the workers of Alexandra had defeated the attempts of a bus company to raise fares by walking the twenty miles to and from work each day . . . ', E. A. Walker, *A History of Southern Africa* (London, Longman, 3rd ed., 1957), 756–7.

9. *Alan Paton, Apartheid and the Archbishop: The Life and Times of Geoffrey Clayton, Archbishop of Cape Town* (Cape Town, Philip, 1973), 143.

10. *Cry the Beloved Country*, Bk I, ch. viii, 39–40.

11. I suspect that the reason Paton says 'twenty or twenty-two' in the first and not simply 'twenty-two' as he does in the novel is that he used Walker's History when he came to write the later account; Walker appears frequently in the bibliography to *Apartheid and the Archbishop*.

12. *Cry, the Beloved Country*, Bk I, ch. viii, 41.

13. Roux, *Time Longer than Rope*, 319.

14. Ibid.

15. Other 'choric' examples occur in Bk I, ch. ii, xii; and Bk II, ch. v, vi and ix.

16. Ibid., Bk I, ch. ix, 48.

17. Ibid., 52.

18. Ibid., 52–3.

19. Roux, *Time Longer than Rope*, 322–3.

20. Ibid., 323.

21. It is worth noting that, in the novel, Dubula organizes both the Bus Boycott and the building of Shanty Town. In fact, they were two different men; Gaur Radebe and Sofazonke Mpanza respectively. Another example of artistic distortion.

22. *Cry, the Beloved Country*, Bk I, ch. ix, 50.

23. There were other 'shanty town' incidents that occurred in 1946 at Pimville and Albertynsville, which were recent in Paton's memory when he wrote *Cry, the Beloved Country* in 1947. Roux says that over '25 000 Africans have built themselves shanty towns of some thousands of huts roughly made of hessian stretched over a framework of split poles', *Time Longer than Rope*, 324. These events could account only for some of the details of materials used in the novel's descriptions, such as hessian. But Shanty Town itself was the proper name of one place. The others had different names. Thus, Paton conflates at least two events—a process at work throughout the social-historical events described in the novel. One of the other shanty towns was called Tobruk, which is mentioned specifically by Paton in connexion which Michael Scott in *Apartheid and the Archbishop*, 153.

24. See series of articles by Paton on the relation between society and the offender in *The Forum*, quoted in Callan, *Alan Paton*, 145–6; and Paton's *Tales From a Troubled Land* (New York, Charles Scribner, 1961; published in London in the same year by Jonathan Cape as *Debbie Go Home*), *passim*.

25. 'Native' was the term used in Government papers, in official documents, in newspapers and in ordinary parlance at that time. Post-Verwoerd, it became 'Bantu' [sic]. Recently the South African Broadcasting Company, which is Government controlled, has begun to use the term 'African' and to refer to particular Africans by name in news bulletins. Paton himself never used 'native'. It is employed here for obvious reasons.

26. *Cry, the Beloved Country*, Bk I, ch. xv, 94.

27. Ibid., Bk I, ch. x, 55.

STEPHEN WATSON

Cry, the Beloved Country
and the Failure of Liberal Vision

In any discussion of Alan Paton's *Cry, the Beloved Country* (1948) it is important to note that the writer grew up in an era before South African racial politics had hardened into their present intransigence. As J. F. Cronin has written:

> Paton was born in 1903. He was, thus, already in his mid-forties when the Nationalist Party under Malan ousted Smuts in the General Election of 1948 to establish the first Afrikaner government of South Africa and inaugurated the present régime. It helps towards an understanding of his career to know that he grew up at a time when South Africa's racial issues were not yet as violent and clear-cut as they are today. True, it has often been pointed out that much racially oppressive legislation had found its way onto the statute book in South Africa even before Afrikaner Nationalism came to power, and it may be true that Smuts' United Party was essentially as illiberal in this respect as Verwoerd's National Party came to be, but it was only from 1948 on that *apartheid* began to be applied at all points as a deliberate governmental policy. Paton was by then already in middle life. Growing up as he did in an earlier South Africa than that which saw the youth of Dan Jacobson or

From *English in Africa* 9, no. 1 (May 1982): 29–44. © 1982 by *English in Africa*.

Nadine Gordimer, he would be less likely than they to see the country's problems as susceptible only of extreme solutions.[1]

The important point is that Paton wrote his first and most famous novel at a time when liberalism still seemed to provide an answer to South Africa's problems. In a sense, it represents the culmination of the heyday of white liberal optimism and confidence during the two or three decades preceding the novel's publication, and it is deeply informed by the thinking of South African liberal intellectuals like Hoernlé, Rheinalt-Jones and J. H. Hofmeyer:

> This "Story of Comfort in Desolation" was written when the English United Party was still in power in 1948; and it presents a picture of optimism, together with an assumed confidence in the European's ability to lead and guide Africans to a better condition. Today it is regarded by many who would have praised it then as an old-fashioned paternalist book, which portrays Africans in a sentimental and unrealistic light; and it is probable that Mr. Paton himself, who has since become much more deeply involved in politics (in common with other liberal writers) would agree. Soon after *Cry* was written the Afrikaner Nationalist Party came into power, and liberals have been forced into a more militant and committed position.[2]

This was written in 1957 by an anonymous reviewer in *The Times Literary Supplement*. Yet even when the novel was written, roughly ten years earlier, the liberal vision which finds frequent didactic expression in it was inadequate. The very problems which *Cry, the Beloved Country* first formulates and then endeavours to solve do not admit of a solution in the terms which liberal ideology provides.

If Paton's intentions in *Cry, the Beloved Country* are carefully examined, it will emerge that his primary concern in this novel is to expose a certain state of affairs in South Africa; namely, the social consequences of the destruction of the tribal system by the whites and the general disintegration, both moral and otherwise, which characterizes South African society as a whole. Through the personal sagas of the Reverend Stephen Kumalo, James Jarvis, and their respective sons, he wishes to reveal some of the tragic consequences of this social disintegration and, at the same time, to provide an example of moral and spiritual growth through suffering—a Christian message of comfort and hope despite the prevailing desolation—and to make an appeal to the liberal consciences of his readers.

In order to achieve these purposes, Paton makes use of the literary mode of tragedy. But this is not only because the novel abounds in those fateful contradictions which make tragedy the most appropriate mode for it. As J. M. Coetzee has said:

> A favoured mode among White South African writers has been tragedy (though Afrikaans writers have given much time to a mythographic revision of history). Tragedy is typically the tragedy of inter-racial love: a White man and a Black woman, or vice versa, fall foul of the laws against miscegenation, or simply of White prejudice, and are destroyed or driven into exile. The overt content of the fable here is that love conquers evil through tragic suffering when such suffering is borne witness to in art; its covert content is the apolitical doctrine that defeat can turn itself, by the twist of tragedy, into victory. The tragic hero is a scapegoat who takes our punishment. By his suffering we undergo a ritual of expiation, and as we watch in sympathy our emotions are purged, as Aristotle noted, through the operations of pity and terror.

Tragedy affords a solution, both artistic and otherwise, to that which in reality has not been solved at all. Coetzee goes on to say:

> Religious tragedy reconciles us to the inscrutable dispensation by giving a meaning to suffering and defeat ... The predominant example of religious tragedy in South Africa is Alan Paton's *Cry, the Beloved Country*. A young African comes to the city, falls among bad companions, and in a moment of confusion kills a White. He is hanged. The fathers of the dead men console and learn to respect each other. The hero who bears the blows of fate is here doubled in the persons of the two fathers; we share their suffering as they share each other's suffering, in pity and terror. The gods are secularized as the pitiless justice of the law. Nevertheless, Paton's fable bears the invariant content of religious tragedy: that the dispensation under which man suffers is unshakeable, but that our pity for the hero-victim and our terror at his fate can be purged by the ritual of re-enactment.[3]

It is not, however, only because of its apolitical nature that tragedy becomes a mode which results in mystification rather than revelation. In the final essay of *Language And Silence*, George Steiner, discussing whether revolutionary art will succeed in producing 'high' revolutionary tragedy, remarks:

> no less than a tragedy *with* God, with a compensating mechanism of final justice and retribution, a tragedy *without* God, a tragedy

of pure immanence, is a self-contradiction. Genuine tragedy is inseparable from the mystery of injustice, from the conviction that man is a precarious guest in a world where forces of unreason have dark governance. Lacking this belief, a drama of conflict will hardly be distinguishable from serious comedy, with its pattern of intrigue and mundane resolution (the equations of tragedy cannot be solved, there are in them too many unknowns).[4]

Sophoclean tragedy, for instance, draws much of its mystery and strength, its power to evoke feelings of pity and terror, from its characteristic emphasis on the gap between human and divine judgements. Sophocles writes throughout in the conviction that the laws of the gods are not the same as the laws of men, and what may seem right enough to men may be utterly wrong for the gods. His tragic world is one in which men, acting according to their human nature, are countered and corrected, for evil or for good, by powers outside themselves, and although they may try to work against these, in the end they are at their mercy. The ways of the gods remain a secret and it is not for men to criticize them or even to hope to understand them. What is required is a mood of unquestioning awe and respect. The discrepancy between a divine order and the order of the world is what creates genuine tragedy.

Now it would seem that Paton, in order to make a powerful emotional appeal to the consciences and liberal sentiments of his readers, is concerned to make the causes for the tragic unfolding of events which his novel records ultimately inexplicable, the function of some Fate or divinity whose ways cannot be fathomed by man. For only through this strategy will injustice become mysterious and produce that sense of ultimate mystery which is one of the defining features of tragedy. Consequently, he is continually harping on mystery and the mysteriousness of human existence. The novel abounds in expressions of this sort:

> Who indeed knows the secret of the earthly pilgrimage? Who indeed knows why there can be comfort in a world of desolation?[5]
>
> His son had gone astray in the great city, where so many had gone astray before him, and where many others would go astray after him, until there was found some great secret that as yet no man had discovered. (p. 78)

> I believe, he said, but I have learned that is a secret. Pain and suffering, they are a secret. Kindness and love, they are secret. (p. 193)

> Why was it given to one man to have his pain transmuted into gladness? Why was it given to one man to have such an awareness

of God? ... But his mind would contain it no longer. It was not for
man's knowing. He put it from his mind, for it was a secret. (p. 234)

And just as many aspects of human existence are surrounded by a nimbus
of mystery, so the law is deified, is put into a position where it cannot be
questioned; it is treated as a divine institution which requires unquestioning
awe and respect as an utterly objective arbiter over the subjective follies and
anarchies of men:

> You may not smoke in this Court, you may not whisper or speak or
> laugh. You must dress decently, and if you are a man, you may not
> wear your hat unless such is your religion. This is in honour of the
> Judge and in honour of the King whose officer he is; and in honour
> of the Law behind the Judge, and in honour of the People behind
> the Law. When the Judge enters you will stand, and you will not sit
> till he is seated. When the Judge leaves you will stand, and you will
> not move till he has left you. This is in honour of the Judge, and of
> the things behind the Judge.[6] (p. 136)

Yet in attempting to re-create the mystery of injustice and Fate which
has such potent emotional effects, Paton stumbles into the contradiction
which Steiner has pointed out. For the series of misfortunes which his novel
relates are definitely not the result of the obscure workings of gods (or of
God) whose ways and whims cannot be discovered by man. Like the law
which has been formulated as an expression and defence of the interests of
white South Africa alone, and which therefore has no credibility whatsoever
as an impersonal god, these misfortunes are quite explicable in terms of the
man-made reality and historical conditions of South Africa in the first half
of this century. *Cry, the Beloved Country* is thus a tragedy of "pure immanence"
on top of which a mystifying Christian concern with suffering and joy has
been imposed. In short, it is not genuine tragedy at all.

Part of Paton's technique of mystification is to portray a succession of
unfortunate events and then to dwell on the deep, passive grief which these
cause in various persons. Thus, in the section which dramatizes a housing
shortage in the townships outside Johannesburg and which refers to the death
of a black woman's child and to her subsequent grief, we find generalizations
of the following sort: "Such is the lot of women, to carry, to bear, to watch, and
to lose" (p. 54). Thus we repeatedly find Stephen Kumalo with his "tragic eyes"
and "his face in the mould of its suffering" (p. 105). The description of the mis-
fortune is invariably converted into a drawn out characterization of the almost
insuperable sorrow and mourning which it arouses. And although Paton could

be said to follow this strategy in order to convey the very real helplessness and justifiable bewilderment of the simple-hearted, largely uneducated black in the face of a cruel and alien white world whose domination is ubiquitous and so unfathomable that, like a Kafkaesque one, it takes on all the mysteriousness and arbitrariness of an unknown god, the function of his emphasis on blind, grief-stricken reactions is both to obscure the real reasons (and hence possible solutions) for the tragic incidents and to elicit from the reader a purely emotional identification with the suffering hero so that, again, the real reasons for a predicament are smothered under the flow of sympathy which the reader feels. Brecht's "estrangement" effects, whereby the emotional responses of his dramatic characters are deliberately muted in order that the audience might better perceive that a particular bereavement has specific societal causes and thus can be prevented through specifically social solutions (which perception might make possible a rejection of the fatalities and eternal recurrences of tragedy), might have had a salutary effect on *Cry, the Beloved Country*. For the emotionalism of the novel time and again results in mystification.

There is another type of mystification at work in this novel, one which has equally serious consequences. As a rule, a novel opens by depicting a problematic situation which the rest of the text then seeks to solve. Another way of putting this would be to say that the text (whether it be novel, poem, or drama) is internally dissonant. In the words of Terry Eagleton, it is "never at one with itself, for if it were it would have absolutely nothing to say. It is, rather, a process of *becoming* at one with itself—an attempt to overcome the problem of itself."[7] In its simplest, most conventional expression, this dissonance usually takes the form of a conflict between the dreams and idealism of an individual, and a society whose materialism and determinism prevent the fulfilment of individual ideals. The internal dissonance of the text is produced by a conflict between material-historical conditions and the various forms of necessity which these impose, and an ideology which enshrines values opposed to those determined by these conditions.

Cry, the Beloved Country provides a particularly clear example of this process which is characteristic of almost all literature. The problem that it initially poses and presents is that of the detribalization of blacks by whites and the lawlessness and moral corruption which this enforced social disintegration has caused. The novel describes quite accurately and also explains a certain historical phenomenon which is now a commonplace in the analysis which one finds in South African criminology textbooks.[8] Msimangu formulates the central problem of the novel as follows:

> The tragedy is not that things are broken. The tragedy is that they are not mended again. The white man has broken the tribe. And

it is my belief—and again I ask your pardon—that it cannot be mended again. But the house that is broken, and the man that falls apart when the house is broken, these are the tragic things. That is why children break the law, and old white people are robbed and beaten. (p. 25)

And this is set out more formally in the papers of the murdered Arthur Jarvis:

The old tribal system was, for all its violence and savagery, for all its superstition and witchcraft, a moral system. Our natives today produce criminals and prostitutes and drunkards, not because it is their nature to do so, but because their simple system of order and tradition and convention has been destroyed. It was destroyed by the impact of our own civilization. Our civilization has therefore an inescapable duty to set up another system of order and tradition and convention. (p. 127)

It is this social disintegration which constitutes the central problem to which the novel addresses itself.

At the same time, however, a certain ideology, which is an amalgam of liberalism and Christianity, is brought to bear upon this problem. And it is through this that the internal dissonance of the novel becomes most apparent; it is through this, too, that the major mystification of *Cry, the Beloved Country* is perpetrated. Through the mouthpieces of Stephen Kumalo and Msimangu, Paton attempts to solve what is clearly and statedly a material, sociological problem by means of metaphysics; against the multiple problems caused by detribalization and urbanization he advances the solution of love. Thus Msimangu maintains that "there is only one thing that has power completely, and that is love. Because when a man loves, he seeks no power, and therefore he has power" (p. 37). Of course this is useless; the problem has not been caused by a lack of love in South Africa, and therefore to prescribe an antidote of love for it is simply naïve and beside the point.[9] The actual problem and Paton's solution for it are two completely separate, independent spheres which have no real practical relation to each other. And since there is no possibility of the one really acting upon the other, since crime cannot be solved through love, and also because Paton can see no other solution (his ideology prevents this), throughout *Cry, the Beloved Country* there is a steady displacement of or shift away from the major problem of the book, the sociological one, and an increasing focus on a single consequence of it: the personal sufferings of Stephen Kumalo and, to a lesser extent, James Jarvis. The focus steadily shifts away from the question of what has caused a certain state of affairs and what is to be done about it, and increasingly revolves around the efforts of single individuals to survive and to transcend personal suffering. And since the problem cannot be solved by the Christian love of Msimangu or Kumalo, nor by the liberal change of heart which James Jarvis undergoes and which expresses itself through a paternalistic handout to a "boy's club" and his financial assistance in the restoration of the valley, it is simply subsumed under the religious trials of Kumalo and the symphonic finale to the novel.

When there is an irreconcilable clash between certain historical conditions and an ideology, the invariable result is tragedy. But the mode of tragedy itself is often also a means of transcending this clash. Just as Jarvis and Kumalo are finally united by a mutual sympathy caused by their common loss of a son and, in a microcosmic, symbolic way effect a reconciliation between black and white races in South Africa, tragedy finally collapses the poles of the conflict and finds a solution in the restoration of an ultimate order and meaning which serves to create a calmness of mind. The social failure which is signified by the murder of Arthur Jarvis and the execution of Absalom Kumalo is transformed, by the twist of tragedy, into the moral victory of James Jarvis and the religious exultation of Stephen Kumalo who is restored to an intimation of ultimate order and meaning through his final sense of the nearness of God. Even so, the evidence that this is not a genuine restoration (as in Sophoclean tragedy, for instance) but only an instance of two men who have each, as it were, made a separate peace, is to be found in the fact that Paton quite literally cannot finish his novel. Although, in the final scene, the sun rises in the east and Stephen Kumalo rises in thanksgiving from his mountain vigil, the essential question remains unanswered—the "mystery" of freedom and injustice remains to be solved: "But when that dawn will come, of our emancipation, from the fear of bondage and the bondage of fear, why, that is a secret" (p. 236).

Nevertheless, something of a practical answer to this question is at least suggested in an ideological conflict which the novel promises to elaborate, but which is also collapsed and then abandoned. This conflict is the one feature of *Cry, the Beloved Country* that promises to redeem the novel from its persistent naïveté of tone and its extraordinary lack of political vision. However, that the novel is not redeemed by a development of this conflict is itself a reflection of Paton's commitment to an ideology which cannot allow for certain forms of conflict and which simply cannot countenance them if its credibility is to survive.

As has already been suggested, Paton's ideology is an amalgam of Christianity and liberalism. In a fundamental respect these two ideologies are by no means incompatible. As Leo Marquard has written, "liberals believe in the integrity and worth of every single individual. Religious people would express this by saying that every individual is a child of God; and liberals who are not religious may derive their belief from humanism. But whatever its origin, the belief is fundamental to liberalism and from it flow many of the demands of liberals, such as the rights of the individual and the equality of all in the eyes of the law."[10] In their common concern for and emphasis upon the worth of each and every human individual, liberalism and Christianity go hand in hand. Now a belief in the primacy of the individual is at the very base of liberal ideology; and with this belief it is inevitable that those virtues which will enhance the life of the individual will be emphasized and valued above all others, that there will be a heavy stress on private virtues such as inner strength and integrity, and that there will be a marked suspicion of any political ideas and programmes which make demands of absolute commitment upon men and women since these are perceived to be threatening to the essential autonomy of the individual.

Paton's deep-seated belief in this fundamental liberal tenet is the obvious reason why he would seem to refuse to explore the political implications of the clash of ideologies found in the altercations between John and Stephen Kumalo—a clash which promises much, but is never developed. Perhaps Ezekiel Mphahlele is getting close to this when he expresses the following dissatisfaction: "The priest's brother, John Kumalo, pretends to a roundness and one is tantalized into hoping that the interplay of opposite personalities such as his and the priest's is going to grow into something memorable. John Kumalo is a political speech-maker; he always seems to be addressing a crowd even when he speaks to one person; he does not like Christian convention; he is sensible of the insecurity around him. He will do anything to avoid more pain than is already being inflicted upon him and his people."[11] Yet Mphahlele never fully articulates this failure. In a very real sense these two characters embody the distinction that Arthur Koestler draws in his essay "The Yogi and the Commissar". Stephen is an advocate of "Change from Within", of spiritual purification, and is in favour of passivity, submission, meekness and guidance; John is a proponent of "Change from Without" and of the activism, domination and calculation which this programme for social change demands. John Kumalo believes "that what God has not done for South Africa, man must do" (p. 25). Stephen's faith is "that power corrupts, that a man who fights for justice must himself be cleansed and purified, that love is greater than force" (p. 182).

Now it is all too clear that throughout *Cry, the Beloved Country* Paton is preaching for a revolution of hearts ("Change from Within") rather than for a revolution in social and economic structure ("Change from Without"). Because of his liberal Christian vision and the limits it automatically imposes on the nature and range of political beliefs and practices available to him, he never really questions the power of humility, respect for persons, compassion and the quest for personal salvation to achieve a significant restructuring of society. He himself does not seem to realize (though John Kumalo makes this clear) that although Christianity might offer profound spiritual strength to people at bay (the novel itself is a good illustration of just this), it also imparts a political weakness which dictates, however necessarily and realistically, an acceptance of the hegemony of the oppressor.[12] Nor does Paton ever really question the applicability of the Sermon on the Mount to a political programme. For though it may be possible to establish just relations between individuals purely by moral and rational suasion and accommodation, in inter-group relations this is practically an impossibility. The relations between groups are always predominantly political rather than ethical; they are determined by the proportion of power each group possesses as much as by any rational and moral appraisal of the comparative needs and claims of each group. Paton, with an ideology which commits him to the individual rather than to the group, does not understand this.

Nevertheless, scattered through the novel are a number of passages which either implicitly or explicitly call into question his ultimate faith in a change of heart (an increase in love and the rooting out of fear and hatred) to cure various ills. These passages are usually given to John Kumalo. For example, the following words come from him during a public speech:

> "Is it wrong to ask more money?" John Kumalo asks. "We get little enough. It is only our share that we ask, enough to keep our wives and our families from starvation. For we do not get enough. . . . We know that we do not get enough," Kumalo says. "We ask only for those things that labouring men fight for in every country in the world, the right to sell our labour for what it is worth. . . . They say that higher wages will cause the mines to close down. Then what is it worth, this mining industry? And why should it be kept alive, if it is only our poverty that keeps it alive? They say it makes the country rich, but what do we see of these riches? Is it we that must be kept poor so that others may stay rich? . . . All we ask is justice, says Kumalo. . . . We are asking only for more money from the richest industry in the world. This industry is powerless without our labour. Let us cease to work and this industry will die. And I say, it is better to cease to work than to work for such wages." (pp. 258–59)

In so far as *Cry, the Beloved Country* records an antagonism between a basically materialist view of South Africa's conflicts (which is reflected in John

Kumalo's attitudes and ideas) and an idealist attempt to solve them (reflected in the ideas of Stephen and Msimangu), it can be regarded as a rudimentary novel of ideas. But Paton never develops this antagonism to the point where it would become truly meaningful. Indeed, he cannot; his ideology prevents him from doing so. Through his liberalism and Christianity which demand that people be judged as ends in themselves and not as means, and according to their moral worth and integrity rather than their practical usefulness, he can conveniently dispose of this antagonism. Thus John Kumalo's *moral* corruption is emphasized to the extent that his actual political worth, the substantial accuracy of his many brief analyses, are ultimately ignored and glossed over: "—Perhaps we should thank God he is corrupt, said Msimangu solemnly. For if he were not corrupt, he could plunge this country into bloodshed. He is corrupted by his possessions, and he fears their loss, and the loss of the power he already has" (p. 161). In short, because John Kumalo is not a good man, his politics are not good. Yet, ironically, he is the one person in the novel who displays something of a real political understanding.

The immediate result of this ideological clash being dissolved and disposed of through moral condemnation is that the final political vision which emerges from *Cry, the Beloved Country* is naïve in the extreme. As Ezekiel Mphahlele has written: "Because the message keeps imposing itself on us in *Cry, the Beloved Country*, we cannot but feel how thickly laid on the writer's liberalism is: let the boys be kept busy by means of club activities and they will be less inclined to delinquency; work for a change of heart in the white ruling class (Jarvis's final philanthropic gesture and his son's practical interest in club activities together with his plea to South Africa indicate this)."[13] These practical "solutions" scarcely solve or even begin to suggest a way of solving the problematic historical situation with which the novel deals.

A still further result of this failure to develop the implications of this clash of ideologies is an artistic failure; the novel becomes badly weighted, lop-sided; it becomes a tear-jerker—which is only another way of saying that it is lacking in reality. Its sentimentality is, of course, in accord with one of its express intentions; significantly, *Cry, the Beloved Country* is subtitled "A Story of Comfort in Desolation". Like a good liberal and Christian, Paton is always concerned to console, to lessen any potential conflict, and to appeal to the moral consciences and emotions of his readers. Depictions of pain are always the best means for this latter purpose since they provoke pity and sentimentality. And his liberal desire to reduce conflict perhaps explains his almost obsessive presentations of the *good* white man, of characters like the advocate who takes on Absalom Kumalo's case *pro deo*, Father Vincent, and those helping blacks at a school for the blind: "It was white men who did this work of mercy, and some of them spoke English and some spoke Afrikaans. Yes, those who spoke English and those who spoke Afrikaans came together to open the eyes of black men that were blind" (p. 80). Furthermore, he uses this figure of the *good* white—the liberal hero (Arthur Jarvis), who is destroyed by the harsh South African reality—as a representative figure who atones through his death for the collective guilt of the whites. For the purposes of conciliation he also uses the figure of the *good* black man, the "Uncle Tom" character, who will allay the suspicions and the hostility of whites towards blacks. But the paternalism implicit (and often quite explicit) in his treatment of blacks and all the emotional effects aroused by his attempted reconciliations do not have the final effect of providing comfort in desolation; they merely serve as an incomplete disguise for the limitations in the ideology which informs the novel. In the final analysis, *Cry, the Beloved Country* does not so much display the iniquities of various aspects of South African life; rather, it reveals the poverty of Paton's ideology.

* * *

Given this poverty and also the fact that it has only grown more evident in the more than three decades that have passed between the publication of *Cry, the Beloved Country* and Paton's latest novel, *Ah, but your land is beautiful* (1981), it might have been expected that the latter work, particularly as it is centred around the Liberal Party in South Africa in the fifties, would have shown a greater awareness both of the contradictions within liberalism itself and also in the ways in which it was articulated at that time. And at first sight, this expectation does not seem to have been disappointed. *Ah, but your land is beautiful*, composed as it is of a number of cameos and representative South African voices clearly meant to convey the patterns of conflict in the country during the years 1952–1958, is noticeably more aware of the various alternatives to the liberal programme for social reform than *Cry, the Beloved Country*. Its various liberal protagonists also display an acute awareness of many of the contradictions that are part of their position. For instance, at a Liberal Party celebration one of the whites observes:

> Because of my past I am very conscious that the [Liberal] party is not yet aware of its *tour de force* nature. The question as to why Drummond's diningroom is as big as many a black house has never been raised, nor the question as to why ninety-five per cent of the cars at the conference belonged to white members. The party has committed itself to the fight against all unjust laws, to the elimination of discrimination, and to the destruction of the colour bar ... but there is so far no discussion as to why there are all these laws, nor any discussion as to their economic causes. I have long since ceased

to believe that the causes of all social ills are economic, but so far the party seems almost unaware that many of the causes *are* economic.[14]

Nevertheless, perceptions of this sort are few and far between, and, as with the materialist-idealist clash represented by Msimangu and John Kumalo, they are never developed to the point where they might become truly significant. Although the sources of opposition to liberalism are fully defined in the course of the novel, there is never any attempt to expand upon or reply to the challenge being made to the liberalism of Paton's central characters and to his own liberal vision which dominates the book.

Many of the thematic concerns of *Cry, the Beloved Country* appear once again in his latest novel. There is the same concern with the destructive effects of racial fears, the same belief in the transforming power of personal encounters and the same image of South Africa as a land at once paradisial and purgatorial. Once again, just as in his first novel, there is an episode in *Ah, but your land is beautiful* which testifies to Paton's continuing faith in a personal act of devotion or humility to bring about that change of heart and atonement between races which he so much desires. In this case, a white judge washes and kisses the feet of a black servant at a church service. The episode is then blown up to the point where it might be said to be a symbol of a potential reconciliation between races in South Africa. At the same time, however, Paton also includes the following attack on the incident in the form of an article from *New Guard*:

> The white bourgeoisie is getting itself all worked up because a white judge has kissed the feet of a black woman in a church in Bochabela. Half the bourgeoisie is disgusted, and the other half thinks that a bit of kissing wipes out the scandals of the pass laws and the rape of the blackspots and perhaps indeed lengthens the life of white supremacy.
>
> *New Guard* does not indulge in attacks on the so-called independent judiciary, but will certainly not encourage white people to entertain the delusion that what happened in Bochabela is a solution to something, or that it is an indication of the way 'things are moving'. The episode is totally meaningless and irrelevant, and it shows once more how unrelated to our realities are the bourgeois values of good-will and sporadic benevolence in our South African situation.
>
> The aspirations of the people of South Africa were given unforgettable expression in the clauses of the Freedom Charter. They concerned themselves with government, land, rights,

wealth, industry, education, freedom of movement. They made
no mention of the washing or kissing of people's feet. The Congress of the People would have exploded into incredulous laughter
had any one proposed the inclusion of such fatuities. (p. 248)

Now it is extremely difficult to tell whether Paton has included this
polemic because he considers it to be an incriminating example of left-wing
cant, a serious rejoinder to the episode which he has developed with such
emotional fervour, or a statement which prefigures the less tolerant climate
of the sixties. But whatever his own attitude—and from the weighting that
he gives to the Bochabela incident alone, it would seem to be the first of
these—this attack on the liberal position, like all the others in the novel, is
never answered. The debate, rudimentary as it might be, is left suspended as
Paton switches his focus from one episode to another, from one fragment
in his mosaic to the next. Finally, all such ideological conflicts are dissolved
as the lights go out, the "Golden Age" of the Dr Hendrik (alias Verwoerd)
era begins, and liberal ambitions, like others more radical, enter the political
Dark Ages of the South African sixties. Once again the debate, like the novel
itself, is left hanging.

More importantly, this also means that Paton is dismissing a conflict
which may be more genuinely tragic than any number of those pathetic incidents for which apartheid policies are responsible. Isaiah Berlin, probably the
most renowned liberal theorist of this century, has written time and again
on that particular form of tragedy which results from the clash of ideologies, both practically and theoretically incompatible, and unreconcilable since
there is, in his opinion, no sole, true universal ideal in terms of which all the
warring ideas can be seen as forming a unity. "If, as I believe," he writes, "the
ends of man are many and not all of them in principle compatible with each
other, the possibility of conflict—and of tragedy—can never be wholly elimi-
nated from human life, either personal or social. The necessity of choosing
between absolute claims is then an inescapable characteristic of the human
condition."[15] But the dilemmas which attend this "pluralism"—from choices
at best agonizing to tragedy itself—are never fully articulated. Ironically
enough, a recognition of them may well have provided Paton, as it does Berlin, with the basis for a defence of liberalism, a defence far stronger than the
self-serving arguments which the novel puts forward.[16]

There are other features of this novel which severely weaken it. More
than thirty years after *Cry, the Beloved Country*, Paton's characteristic simplicity of tone and language reads as intolerably *faux-naif*, his "Biblical" style
and its pieties (particularly evident whenever he touches on law and order,
and family life) are simply not equipped to deal with the complex conflicts

of the fifties, scarred as they were by serious ideological and political battles. Clearly one cannot develop much in the way of an historical debate if one is bound to the language of the Sunday school. Nor is his mixture of fiction and historical fact a success: whilst the fictional portions of the book seem to trivialize the historical, the historical merely serves to empty out the imaginative substance of the fictional—with the result that the novel fails both as fiction and as social document. But quite as crippling as these limitations is the fact the *Ah, but your land is beautiful*, a novel which deals with the fifties and a period which saw the founding of the Liberal Party and the consolidation of the policy of apartheid, is controlled and dominated by the ideology of a man who is himself very much the product of the liberalism of that selfsame era. As such, *Cry, the Beloved Country* and *Ah, but your land is beautiful* are not significantly different from each other; the inadequacies of the former are simply repeated in the latter.

Notes

1. J. F. Cronin, "Writer Versus Situation: Three South African Novelists", *Studies* (Dublin), 56 (1967), pp. 74–75.

2. "South African Conflicts", *Times Literary Supplement*, 16 August 1957, p. xxxvi.

3. J. M. Coetzee, "Man's Fate In the Novels of Alex La Guma", *Studies In Black Literature*, 5, 1 (Spring 1974), 17.

4. George Steiner, *Language And Silence* (London: Faber, 1967), pp. 423–24.

5. Alan Paton, *Cry, the Beloved Country* (Harmondsworth: Penguin, 1971), p. 56. All subsequent references are to this edition.

6. It would seem that Paton never fails to fall into contradiction when it comes to a discussion of the Law and of jurisprudence in general. On the one hand, the whole force of *Cry, the Beloved Country* is to prove that there is a species of social *determinism* at work in South Africa; the breaking of the tribal system by the whites has led to a good deal of criminal activity on the part of dispossessed blacks. The one is responsible for the other. On the other hand, Paton continues to attribute *free-will* to his characters and in terms of this they are then totally responsible for their transgressions and particular crimes. Thus, the jurisprudence which is contained in the Court scene in the novel (see p. 171) is completely confused and false. At this point one could easily imagine *Cry, the Beloved Country* turning into a polemic on unjust justice in South Africa. But, in accordance with his desire to create tragedy, Paton has to attempt to legitimize the law. That he fails to do so is quite clear in this section of the novel.

7. Terry Eagleton, *Criticism and Ideology* (London: Verso, 1978), p. 89.

8. See, for example, G. M. Retief, "Social Disorganization, Crime and The Urban Bantu People of South Africa", *Crime and Punishment in South Africa*, eds. J. Midgley, J. H. Steyn, R. Graser (Johannesburg: McGraw-Hill, 1975), pp. 47–55. Paton himself has also written articles on the reasons for crime in South Africa. See, for example, "Who is Really to Blame for the Crime Wave in South Africa", *The Forum*, VIII, No. 37 (December, 1945), 7–8. He is being quite accurate when

he says in his "Author's Note" to *Cry, the Beloved Country* that the book "considered as a social record . . . is the plain and simple truth."

9. Paton creates exactly the same form of mystification in his later novel, *Too Late the Phalarope* (1953). Apart from the fact that it also uses a spurious form of tragedy (the Immorality Act is no substitute for the gods), Paton also sees the problem here as being a tyranny of fear and a lack of love. He does not seem to realize that the rigid Afrikaner Calvinist mentality that he portrays in this novel (and which is exemplified by Pieter Van Vlaanderen's father), its lack of warmth and spontaneity, its many obsessional traits (such as love of Discipline and order, which manifests itself in strict parents and, particularly, in authoritarian fathers) operates as a defence mechanism among the ruling whites, especially the Afrikaners, against a basic national anxiety, arising from a basic national insecurity. In other words, the Calvinist gives evidence of an obsessional and authoritarian national character in an attempt to compensate for an abnormally high level of anxiety originating in a deep sense of national insecurity. His rigid nature, therefore, is due as much to his *political* position in South Africa as to any supposedly inherent traits. But in *Too Late the Phalarope* Paton, through the mouth-piece of Tante Sophie, suggests that the tragedy might have been avoided if sufficient love had been forthcoming. This might, of course, have been true. But in so far as this novel is a study of Afrikaner Calvinism in general, it is to be doubted whether the love, the true love as opposed to the twisted, which he advocates is any solution at all. Once again Paton is attempting to solve what is at root a *political* problem through personal love.

10. Len Marquard, *Liberalism in South Africa* (Johannesburg: Institute of Race Relations, 1965), p. 8.

11. Ezekiel Mphahlele, *The African Image* (London: Faber, 1962), p. 132.

12. Nietzsche's polemic against Christianity: "The Christian faith, from the beginning, is sacrifice: the sacrifice of all freedom, all pride, all self-confidence of spirit; it is at the same time subjection, self-derision, and self-mutilation. This cruel religion of painful subjection softened the slaves by drawing the hatred from their souls, and without hatred there could be no revolt." *Beyond Good and Evil* (London: Foulis, 1909), p. 67.

13. Mphahlele, p. 133.

14. Alan Paton, *Ah, but your land is beautiful* (Cape Town: David Philip, 1981), p. 159.

15. Isaiah Berlin, *Four Essays on Liberty* (Oxford: Oxford Univ. Press, 1969), p. 169.

16. For an example of this, see Robert Mansfield's discussion with Luthuli, pp. 123–5.

CAROL IANNONE

Alan Paton's Tragic Liberalism

In an essay written in 1975, Nadine Gordimer declared that South African literature in English had "made a new beginning with Alan Paton's *Cry, the Beloved Country*, and indeed it could be said that Paton's novel put South Africa on the twentieth-century literary map. Within a few years of its publication in 1948, it had become a worldwide best-seller and was eventually translated into twenty languages. At the time of Paton's death in 1988, it had sold over fifteen million copies and was still selling at the rate of one hundred thousand copies a year. It is not solely in literary terms that a South African novel of the twentieth century must make its mark, however, and Gordimer went on to say that Paton's "was a book of lyrical beauty and power that moved the conscience of the outside world over racialism and, what's more, that of white South Africa as no book had done before."

A 1980 essay was still able to claim that "no single work of South African literature either before or since has attained such fame." Despite Gordimer's own rise to Nobel stature, and the coming to prominence of a number of South African authors, that assessment can be repeated today—no single work has achieved such fame. At the end of the century, it remains South Africa's most significant novel and a rare example of the successful wedding of literature and social conscience. As such it is a reflection of the life of its author.

From *American Scholar* 66, no. 3 (Summer 1997): 442–51. © 1997 by *American Scholar*.

At the time of the novel's publication, Alan Paton (pronounced with a long a) was a forty-five-year-old principal of a black reformatory school. He was born in 1903 in Pietermaritzburg, Natal, a colony of Great Britain until the South African union was formed in 1910, joining Natal and the other British colony, the Cape of Good Hope, with the two Afrikaner republics, the Transvaal and the Orange Free State. His parents were associated with the fundamentalist Christadelphian sect, but in general Paton matured in the kind of Victorian-Edwardian-Anglican ambiance that seemed to define a lot of English South Africa at that time, a world of now old-fashioned virtues like "manliness, decency, honor," as Paton's biographer, Peter F. Alexander, names them.

Having skipped a few grades, Paton entered Natal University College at age sixteen and graduated with a Bachelor of Science degree. There he met Railton Dent, an older student and the son of a missionary; Dent became the greatest individual influence on Paton's life by imparting to him "one thing," as Paton explains it, "that life must be used in the service of a cause greater than oneself." Paton goes on to elaborate: "This can be done by a Christian for two reasons: one is obedience to his Lord, the other is purely pragmatic, namely that one is going to miss the meaning of life if one doesn't." It proved for Paton to be the prescription for a long and industrious life, full of service, courage, and accomplishment.

If reading the life of the average twentieth-century literary figure can make us glad we are not like its subject, reading about Paton's can make us wish we were. Christianity was central to Paton's life from first to last. He left the Christadelphians to become a Methodist, and then in 1930 he became an Anglican, joining the church of his wife, Dorrie, whom he married in 1928 and with whom he had two sons. He was eventually to become a lay leader and to participate in the church's repudiation of racialism and separatism.

After graduation from college, Paton taught white children for some years and became increasingly active in Christian benevolent organizations. In 1934 he fell deathly ill with enteric fever, lost over a third of his body weight, and was confined to a hospital and convalescent home for six months. When he recovered, a friend told him that after such an experience he would not be able to resume his old work, and this proved to be true. Under the direction of Jan Hofmeyr, one of South Africa's liberal Afrikaner statesmen, the Department of Education was undertaking the transformation of both black and white reformatories from virtual prisons to something closer to schools.

Paton was put in charge of Diepkloof, near Johannesburg in the Transvaal, where he was responsible, at different times, for from 360 to more than 600 black pupils, officially aged nine to twenty-one and called "boys" at both the white and black institutions. They had been committed for offenses ranging from pilfering fruit from street stalls to rape and murder. Here he worked veritable miracles of humanization, with the help of an enlightened supervisor at the ministry, several sympathetic outside government overseers, and an excellent staff whom he largely trained himself.

Paton had always shown a literary bent and had been writing poetry and attempting novels since his college days, but the pressures of work and family prevented him from bringing any mature work to fruition. After twelve years at Diepkloof, this was to change. In 1946, he embarked on an extended journey to review correctional institutions in Europe, the United States, and Canada. One September at twilight, he found himself sitting in Norway's Trondheim cathedral, admiring its beautiful rose window and longing for home. He went back to his hotel and began writing, completing in three months as he continued his trip the novel that was to become *Cry, the Beloved Country*. He gave the manuscript to the friends whom he was visiting in the United States; they were much and tearfully taken with it, suggested changes, and found a publisher, Scribner's, where Maxwell Perkins, the editor for Ernest Hemingway, F. Scott Fitzgerald, and Thomas Wolfe, advised acceptance. In appreciation for their efforts Paton granted his friends a generous percentage of what were to be the novel's considerable profits thereafter, and Scribner's went on to be the American publisher of the rest of Paton's twenty or so books, including two more novels, *Too Late the Phalarope* and *Ah, But Your Land Is Beautiful*, a book of short stories, a play, two volumes of autobiography, two biographies, some devotional literature, and several collections of essays, poems, stories, and political writings, much of it interesting and even important, but none quite the equal of his exquisite first novel.

In later years, Paton often observed that South Africa had very little to unite it—what with myriad African tribes, a population of Indians and "coloreds," and two different white "races," all with separate languages, cultures, histories, values, and symbols. South Africa's union had been brought about by war and politics more than by shared ideals. Only the physical land itself might inspire common loyalty. As Maxwell Perkins observed, the land is one of the chief characters in *Cry, the Beloved Country*. The novel opens with a lyrical description of the spectacular landscape of the Ixopo district in Natal:

> There is a lovely road that runs from Ixopo into the hills. These hills are grass-covered and rolling, and they are lovely beyond any singing of it. The road climbs seven miles into them, to Carisbrooke; and from there, if there is no mist, you look down on one of the fairest valleys of Africa. About you there is grass and bracken and you may

hear the forlorn crying of the titihoya, one of the birds of the veld. Below you is the valley of the Umzimkulu, on its journey from the Drakensberg to the sea; and beyond and behind the river, great hill after great hill; and beyond and behind them, the mountains of Ingeli and East Griqualand.

The grass is rich and matted, you cannot see the soil. It holds the rain and the mist, and they seep into the ground, feeding the streams in every kloof. It is well-tended, and not too many cattle feed upon it; not too many fires burn it, laying bare the soil. Stand unshod upon it, for the ground is holy, being even as it came from the Creator.

The narrative then shifts to a very different terrain, one that reflects the division in the society itself:

Where you stand the grass is rich and matted, you cannot see the soil. But the rich green hills break down. They fall to the valley below, and falling, change their nature. For they grow red and bare; they cannot hold the rain and mist, and the streams are dry in the kloofs. Too many cattle feed upon the grass, and too many fires have burned it. Stand shod upon it, for it is coarse and sharp, and the stones cut under the feet. It is not kept, or guarded, or cared for, it no longer keeps men, guards men, cares for men. The titihoya does not cry here any more.

The great red hills stand desolate, and the earth has torn away like flesh. The lightning flashes over them, the clouds pour down upon them, the dead streams come to life, full of the red blood of the earth. Down in the valleys women scratch the soil that is left, and the maize hardly reaches the height of a man. They are valleys of old men and old women, of mothers and children. The men are away, the young men and the girls are away. The soil cannot keep them any more.

This poorer district is named Ndotsheni by the author. The action begins when the main character, Stephen Kumalo, a devout Zulu parson of an impoverished rural Anglican parish, receives a letter from a stranger summoning him to Johannesburg. According to the letter, Kumalo's much younger sister Gertrude is in need. Gertrude went to the big city with her small son some time before to find her husband who had gone to work in the gold mines. Kumalo's son Absalom is also in the city; he went to look for Gertrude and has lost touch with his old parents. Once Kumalo arrives in Johannesburg, he is helped by a group of Anglican priests, both black and white, who minister in a black slum called Sophiatown.

Kumalo finds his family drastically changed. His brother John, who moved to the city some years before, is living with a woman not his wife and has become a racial militant, full of the germinating anger of the de-tribalized, de-Christianized, urbanized South Africa that Paton saw waiting in the wings. Moreover, Kumalo learns with sorrow that his sister Gertrude has sunk into prostitution and that, during the very course of Kumalo's desperate search for him, Absalom has committed murder while breaking into a house with two companions.

Meanwhile, James Jarvis, a wealthy English-speaking farmer from the fertile area described in the opening passages, has learned that his grown son Arthur has been shot to death in his home in Johannesburg. The elder Jarvis and his wife must also journey to the city for the funeral and trial. There he learns from the police what has since brought Stephen Kumalo almost to the breaking point, that Absalom Kumalo is the killer of his son. Thus the two worlds collide.

A later critic faulted Paton for not giving Absalom's point of view, but the novel works from the standpoint of the older generation. As the two fathers struggle to understand what has become of their sons, the anguish of the beloved country unfolds. "When people go to Johannesburg they don't come back," murmurs Kumalo's wife, Grace. Absalom fell in with "bad companions," one of them his own cousin Matthew, John's son, but Kumalo remains aghast at how his well brought up boy could have committed so terrible a deed. For his part, Jarvis too will learn more about a side of his son that he barely knew. Arthur had been president of the African Boys Club and a proponent of racial reform, so his death at the hands of a young native seems ironic. Among Arthur's effects Jarvis finds manuscripts and articles through which he learns, painfully and in detail, about his son's strongly held racial views. At the funeral, which is attended by all shades and colors of people, Jarvis finds himself shaking black hands for the first time in his life.

The novel's success may have been due, in part, to the moment of South African history that it captured, 1946, before the imposition of "grand apartheid" was to consume the country completely in politics. The depression and war had passed. Industrialization and urbanization were breaking down tribal customs, even as the increasing population of blacks and whites in the cities was worsening the tensions under separatism. The novel strips away the surface assurances of white supremacy to reveal what has in some respects become a wasteland—a literal wasteland in the case of the sordid slums and the dying tribal lands, but also a spiritual wasteland, characterized by alienation and mistrust among races and peoples and families and generations.

"It is fear that rules this land," says Msimangu, one of the black priests who helps Kumalo.

So painful is the reality depicted in *Cry, the Beloved Country* that when the playwright Maxwell Anderson adapted the novel for the stage (with music by Kurt Weill), he called it *Lost in the Stars*, and made it a cry against a God who had abandoned his creatures. This was done much to Paton's consternation. His perspective is thoroughly Christian, though in the sense of a struggle for the light, not in the application of received truths. The novel manifests both Christian and tragic qualities. The final answers are "secrets" and "mysteries" that reside only with God, and at any given moment the divine may not be evident or clear. The characters must bear up in the face of desolation, injustice, pain, and loss, but there is also hope, comfort, and consolation.

Thus despite the good liberal intentions behind the novel to move white South Africans over conditions in their society, *Cry, the Beloved Country* does not evidence the kind of superficiality that Lionel Trilling felt was typical of what he called "the liberal imagination." Avoiding easy answers, Paton enters into the perspective of both "victims" and "oppressors," and demonstrates a humility and acceptance before the unknown and unresolvable.

Both the 1995 film version (starring James Earl Jones) and the Anderson play evince the thinner imaginative capacity of much contemporary liberalism and thus provide an instructive contrast to Paton's greater subtlety. In the film, worthy on many other counts, the delicacy that Paton achieved in portraying Jarvis's racialism is partly destroyed by the drive toward ideological simplification. In the film, James Jarvis refers to blacks as kaffirs, an insulting word that is out of character for the Jarvis of the novel. Even more untrue to Paton's vision, the Jarvis in the film refuses to shake the black hand that is proffered to him at his son's funeral. In an even greater departure from Paton, the Jarvis figure in the Maxwell Anderson adaptation is an out-and-out white supremacist spouting forth on the necessity for the white man to dominate the black. But Paton knew that South Africa's problem lay as much in the softer, unarticulated sort of racialism as in the ideological kind.

The 1951 film, directed by Zoltan Korda and written by Paton, with Sidney Poitier as Msimangu, is faithful to Paton's nuanced tragic vision. Although it might be too low-key for some tastes and was not commercially successful ("When does your film start?" asked Alexander Korda, Zoltan's brother, at an early screening), it is deeply moving, especially for those who know the novel.

Paton's rejection of easy racial moralism does not mean that he exonerates the South African system. Far from it. But he doesn't go in for the blanket indictment of South Africa that became typical in later years. Msimangu castigates the white man for giving "too little . . . almost nothing" to the blacks, but he also acknowledges the gift of Christianity and appreciates the good white people who do what they can. On the other side, the fiery speech of John Kumalo demanding higher wages makes a lot of sense, notwithstanding the menacing anger that informs it.

In one of Arthur's writings, a work in progress discovered by his father after his death, Paton provides a lengthy version of his own thought, though skillfully tailored to reflect Arthur's younger, more naive understanding. Arthur carefully distinguishes what was "permissible" from what was "not permissible" in South Africa's history. Reflecting an earlier understanding of colonialism, he does not feel it necessary to delegitimize all of white South Africa:

> What we did when we came to South Africa was permissible. It was permissible to develop the great resources with the aid of what labour we could find. It was permissible to use unskilled men for unskilled work. But it is not permissible to keep men unskilled for the sake of unskilled work.
>
> It was permissible when we discovered gold to bring labour to the mines. It was permissible to build compounds and to keep women and children away from the towns. It was permissible as an experiment, in the light of what we knew. But in the light of what we know now, with certain exceptions, it is no longer permissible. It is not permissible for us to go on destroying family life when we know that we are destroying it.

This aspect of the novel has perhaps not been fully appreciated. Paton had a tragic grasp of the way good and evil are interwoven in human history. In Arthur Jarvis he created a character who understood the inevitability of civilizational progress and expansion and the conflict and loss that they bring. At the same time, Arthur insists that the colonizers take responsibility for the damage they have done in the process:

> The old tribal system was, for all its violence and savagery, for all its superstition and witchcraft, a moral system. Our natives today produce criminals and prostitutes and drunkards, not because it is their nature to do so, but because their simple system of order and tradition and convention has been destroyed. It was destroyed by the impact of our own civilization. Our civilization has therefore an inescapable duty to set up another system of order and tradition and convention.

Knowing that South Africa prides itself on being a Christian nation, Arthur reproaches it for its hypocrisy, and, by the by, renders a shrewd analysis of the psychology of racism:

> The truth is that our Christian civilization is riddled through and through with dilemma. We believe in the brotherhood of man, but we do not want it in South Africa. We believe that God endows men with diverse gifts, and that human life depends for its fullness on their employment and enjoyment, but we are afraid to explore this belief too deeply.... We say we withhold education because the black child has not the intelligence to profit by it; we withhold opportunity because black people have no gifts.... We shift our ground again when a black man does achieve something remarkable, and feel deep pity for a man who is condemned to the loneliness of being remarkable, and decide that it is a Christian kindness not to let black men become remarkable. Thus even our God becomes a confused and inconsistent creature, giving gifts and denying them employment.... The truth is that our civilization is not Christian; it is a tragic compound of great ideal and fearful practice, of high assurance and desperate anxiety, of loving charity and fearful clutching of possessions.

These are nearly the last words that Arthur wrote before his murder.

As bad as social conditions are for blacks, however, they do not entirely explain the senseless murder of a son, husband, and father, and a man "devoted to our people." There were those who had tried to help Absalom. He had spent time in a Diepkloof-like reformatory, where a young official obtained a job for him and arranged for his release so that he might assume responsibility for the girl he had made pregnant. But such aid could not overcome the temptations and confusions Absalom faced in the big city.

At the trial, the judge acknowledges and perhaps even partly concedes the arguments by Absalom's lawyer regarding the "disastrous effect" of tribal breakdown that the victim Arthur Jarvis himself wrote about. But, the judge asserts, "even if it be true that we have, out of fear and selfishness and thoughtlessness, wrought a destruction that we have done little to repair ... a Judge may not trifle with the Law because the society is defective.... Under the law a man is held responsible for his deeds."

Under South African law, a conviction of murder requires that "an intention to kill" be established. Absalom's lawyer argues that the young man did not mean to kill but only fired his gun out of fear. The judge finds an intention by "inference" in Absalom's carrying a loaded gun while breaking into a home.

In ruling so, the judge is applying a standard of legal responsibility and conscious deliberation where conditions of social disorder and disadvantage have eroded the moral sense of many young people. "It is as my father says," Absalom dutifully responds to Kumalo's prodding, but he cannot himself explain his own actions. And exactly why Absalom did what he did remains one of the "mysteries" to which there will be no answer.

Nevertheless, Absalom confesses, marries his girl to give the baby a name, and bears up under his fate. His two accomplices, egged on by the militant John, simply deny their involvement. They are completely exonerated owing to what the judge and his assessors deem insufficient proof, while Absalom is condemned to death. Some have taken Paton to be criticizing South African justice, so particular within the courtroom and so negligent without, but the author's accomplishment is that the reader can both understand the reasoning behind the guilty verdict and yet wince at the pronouncement of the sentence.

Ultimately, the humility, honesty, and persevering hope of Kumalo and his friends prove more fruitful than the corrosive anger and cynicism of John and the two thieves (who are involved in other criminal exploits). Good emerges from the wreck of the tragedy. Jarvis and Kumalo meet in a deeply moving but understated scene of shared and interlocking grief. Where Jarvis once saw only "a dirty old parson" from a "dirty old wood-and-iron church," he now sees a human being in anguish as great as his own. Jarvis's eyes open to his son's concerns for the blacks and he begins to help them where he can. He contributes to the boys' club, arranges for an agricultural consultant to help restore the ravaged earth of Ndotsheni, and determines to build a new church for Kumalo. For his part, Kumalo returns home with an expanded family, consisting of Gertrude's little son (Gertrude has mysteriously disappeared back into the big city) and his pregnant daughter-in-law. He also becomes more active, working with the agricultural consultant and encouraging the local chief to serve his people rather than indulge his arbitrary and trivial power over them.

The beauty of the language is part of the magic of *Cry, the Beloved Country*: the poetic Zulu speech, the cadences of the King James Bible, the mythic quality of much of the prose. Paton threads through sounds and images that make the story come alive: the gold of the mines that cause the devastation of the slums and the golden words of Msimangu's sermon that restore Kumalo's heart; the raucous, irresponsible laughter in the black townships; the cacophony of white voices addressing the "native problem" (vaguely reminiscent of the empty discourse in the pub in *The Waste Land*); the rush of the river when torrential rain stops. And the description of Kumalo's vigil the night before his son's execution is sublime.

After initial widespread adulation, critics began to find fault with *Cry, the Beloved Country*, seeing it as sentimental and propagandistic, more a treatise than a work of art. The novel tends to survive these objections, however, because the whole is greater than the sum of the parts. Wherever one probes a weak spot, the novel resists at some other point; as Lewis Gannett put it, it is "both unabashedly innocent and subtly sophisticated." The mythic narrative involving the search for the lost son blends with a realistic picture of a modern society. The novel's earnest idealism is offset by the amorphous sense of fear that pervades the country and by the suppressed fury the characters carry within them. Kumalo and Msimangu can erupt in anger and yield to subtle cruelty, and the brows of the young official at Diepkloof are constantly knitted against the difficulty of his work. (Paton's own increasingly tight-lipped expression was his response to the frustrations he faced.)

Where *Cry, the Beloved Country* grows too fable-like it suddenly turns analytical; where too discursive, it waxes poetical. Edward Callan, Paton's chief critic, has done a thorough job of delineating Paton's techniques, but, at the same time, it is not necessary to overstate the novel's purely literary pretensions in order to appreciate its achievement. Dan Jacobson, the self-exiled South African novelist, put *Cry, the Beloved Country* above strictly literary, political, or moral considerations into a category of works he called "proverbial."

Behind much of the criticism of Paton's novel one can make out a political edge. Early objectors to the novel tended to be white South Africans who bridled at its grim portrayal of black life. When the first film version was shown, the wife of the nationalist Afrikaner politician D. F. Malan remarked, "Surely, Mr. Paton, you don't really think things are like that?" The novel was not permitted in the schools until a few years before Paton's death. Later objections came from black militants and their sympathizers, who saw the novel as an expression of white liberalism and mocked Paton's belief in boys' clubs, for example. But the author was not so shallow as to imagine that boys' clubs *per se* were the ultimate solution to South Africa's dilemma. Paton makes clear in the novel that the renewed ameliorative efforts in the aftermath of the tragedy are a good beginning: but "when that dawn will come, of our emancipation, from the fear of bondage and the bondage of fear, why, that is a secret."

Nevertheless, Paton was modest enough to appreciate the good such measures could do. Paton personally paid for the education of countless black youngsters, gave financial help to many others who were in need, and contributed enormous amounts of time and money to his church, to charitable organizations, and to institutes working for social improvement. These commitments expressed his larger conviction that, as he said elsewhere, "the only power which can resist the power of fear is the power of love"—that the only way to achieve justice in South Africa was through a change in the hearts of enough people to make a difference. The militants who faulted Paton for proposing "love" as a solution to social and political injustice did not seem to realize how much of the groundwork for their political activism had been prepared through voluntary organizations of the kind Paton labored in and supported.

So, too, with the novel itself. Noting the blows it took from later militants, the black South African novelist Richard Rive defended *Cry, the Beloved Country*, calling it a "watershed" in South African fiction in that it brought the racial question into literary purview and widely influenced later writers. The Angolan writer Sousa Jamba read the novel at age fifteen in a second-hand copy that smelled of kerosene because, he surmised, its previous owners had stayed up nights to read it. Jamba carried it with him everywhere, and "forgot that what I was reading was written by a white man."

Even disdainful black writers such as the South African poet Dennis Brutus had to admit the novel's power and influence. And while deploring much in the characterizations, Ezekiel Mphahlele, another South African writer, concedes that *Cry, the Beloved Country* is "the first work in the history of South African fiction in which the black man looms so large." Although he did not like the portrait of the humble Zulu priest (preferring the angry John Kumalo instead), Mphahlele implicitly admits that it was true to life.

In Stephen Kumalo, Paton has painted a full picture of an African man, a good but flawed human being, complete with an inner life and a moral compass. The judge's sophisticated legal reasoning in no way surpasses the rural parson's own horrified grasp of his son's murderous act. Furthermore, Paton portrays his black characters in the dignity of individual responsibility even as he shows the restricted circumstances in which they must maneuver.

Paton's preoccupation with individual responsibility must partly have been derived from his experience at the Diepkloof Reformatory, where he stressed education, introduced extensive vocational training, and made many improvements in diet, clothing, sanitation, and living conditions. He became famous for successfully putting into practice the theories of experts in juvenile delinquency who believed that freedom could be used as an instrument of reform and rehabilitation. Paton canceled many of the harsh and restrictive rules that had been in operation before his tenure, and the results were gratifying. The rate of escapes plunged sharply. After a rocky start, his furlough and home-leave program was an astonishing success. Thousands and thousands of boys took their respective leaves and returned with no trouble; very few absconded. Alas, one furloughed boy did commit a serious crime, breaking into a white woman's home and murdering her. He became the basis for the character Absalom Kumalo.

In some ways what Paton achieved at Diepkloof was the fulfillment of a liberal dream, epitomized when he had the high barbed wire gates of the compound torn down and replaced with ... flower beds! The freer the boys were, the less subject to punitive rules, the better they behaved, and the less likely they were to escape. But this behavior was not achieved through the simpleminded "compassion" in currency today. It developed within a framework of authority through which Paton labored to develop his charges' capacity for internal control. He employed military-style discipline in the work details and had the boys march and drill in parades conducted by his capable Afrikaner assistants, who were themselves in a civilian wing of the military service during the depression and war. Surprisingly or unsurprisingly, depending on one's point of view, these parades were relished by the boys, who took great pride in them.

Paton instituted daily Bible lessons and encouraged evening hymn singing, often conducted by his one black assistant or by Paton himself. He gradually built up his pupils' self-discipline by exposing them to the temptations they would face on the outside, and he granted them more and more freedom as they showed themselves more and more capable of handling it. He kept careful files on all of them and exercised great care in choosing them for furloughs. Furthermore, he sealed their behavior through pledges of responsibility. In solemn ceremonies, the boys made promises of trust and Paton issued badges of honor. Two boys who absconded while on separate furloughs eventually turned themselves in to the local police; when asked by the police why they had turned themselves in, both replied that it was because of their "promise."

The point is that while Paton did believe that the "root causes" of black crime lay in conditions in South Africa, for which whites were largely responsible, he also knew what painstaking care, what investment of self, and what demands on the individual black person were involved in undoing the effects of these causes. He knew that even his best efforts did not always succeed; with all the good he was able to accomplish at Diepkloof, he was never able to eliminate corporal punishment entirely. All this gave him a kind of clear-eyed wisdom that served him well in his activities after 1948.

To the surprise and consternation of many, the 1948 elections saw the defeat of the relatively liberal United Party under the great Boer War general and statesman Jan Smuts and with him his liberal ministers, in favor of the Afrikaner Nationalist Party under D. F. Malan. The Nationalist victory, combined with the success of his novel, convinced Paton to leave Diepkloof, where the new regime would eventually undo all his work. He tried for a while the life of a man of letters. But the worsening political situation in the country and his commitment to service, as well as his relative lack of literary inspiration following his first success, led him to politics.

Like Arthur Jarvis, Paton never condemned the Afrikaner people as such, only the extremes of Afrikaner nationalism. Although he had been painfully disappointed by the arrogance and exclusivity he saw at the time of the Centenary of the Great Trek in 1938 (for which he grew a commemorative beard), he admired what was good in Afrikanerdom and, unlike most English-speaking South Africans, he knew Afrikaans. He appreciated the Afrikaners' position, their humiliation under the British, and their peculiar vulnerability as an isolated minority culture, even with their numerical superiority over the English. And Paton was always able to see the individual behind the ideology; he recalls in his autobiography that the only person ever to return the salute of the head boy who kept the gate at Diepkloof was an Afrikaner nationalist.

Such Afrikaner statesmen as Smuts and Hofmeyr, Anglophiles with a larger perspective on South Africa's future, gave some hope that racial conditions in the country might improve. But now a new phase of Afrikanerdom was beginning under Malan and his minister of native affairs, Hendrik Verwoerd, who was to become prime minister in 1958: apartheid, grand apartheid, total apartheid, "separate development," constituted a social engineering project of dreadful hubristic proportions, aiming to separate all of the races and tribes in every area of life, ostensibly in order to preserve their God-given identities, languages, and cultures, but really to retain white supremacy and Afrikaner security. These were the years when, as Paton wrote, "one draconian law after another was passed," backed up by terror and force.

Paton was dismayed not only at the fresh and monstrous injustice that the new policy inflicted on blacks, but at its demented unrealizability. Much mixing had already taken place, industrialization had produced a great deal of interdependence among groups in the labor force, and great numbers of blacks had no real tribal affiliation and spoke only Afrikaans. Paton thought that Verwoerd, in his obsession to create security for the Afrikaners, had constructed something contrary to nature—not to mention nature's God.

In 1953 Paton helped found the Liberal Party to uphold the hope of a non-racial South Africa, and he wrote and spoke extensively on behalf of its principles, both at home and abroad, even after the Party itself was proscribed in 1968. (All reports portray him as an electrifyingly gifted orator.) The Liberal Party was against violence and staunchly anti-Communist, and its classical rights-based premises differed from the socialist Freedom Charter of the African National Congress. During these years Paton lost his wife to emphysema, endured a miserable period of widowerhood, and, fortunately, married his second wife, Anne, in 1969.

Paton's politics can make us wonder how "wishy washy liberal" ever became a common epithet. His liberalism was a matter of strength and courage all the way through. He discarded his early and rather casually accepted racialism as he came to see, in the face of the majority white view, that white supremacy was at odds with Christian theology (and was driving South Africa toward disaster). Later, he maintained his moderation against the growing radicalism around him—again, at least partly because of his religious understanding.

As Paton's biographer Peter F. Alexander points out, the whole metaphor of Paton's two-part autobiography, *Towards the Mountain* and *Journey Continued*, suggests that Christian perfection is not something to be had in this world, but only to be worked toward. Paton was an idealist, but not a political utopian. He was aware of the built-in limitations in South African society and was patient with incremental change. For this reason he was to fall into disfavor as the racial activism in his country became more fierce, but he stood fast against enormous pressure, mockery, and contempt. The attacks were not only on him but on liberalism itself and came from blacks and whites, including many former allies. On speaking tours in the United States, he encountered the vociferous anti-apartheid opposition on American campuses that branded him a paternalistic relic.

Paton angered the radicals in three areas, writes Alexander. One, he opposed trade sanctions in the 1980s because he felt that they would hurt the black poor most of all. To this we can add another reason: his experience at Diepkloof, which had taught him that punishment did not lead to true reform; he continued to believe in the need for moral suasion to lead people to free and enlightened choice. He also continued to hold out against violence, although he testified for mercy in the sentencing of Nelson Mandela. Two, he gradually came to favor federalism instead of a unitary state, at least as a transition to one man one vote for South Africa. And, three, he admired Chief Buthelezi, a fellow Christian but, for the militants, a thorn in the side.

Paton took plenty of heat from the government during these years. Although, as the author of *Cry, the Beloved Country*, he was spared arrest and banning, his passport was temporarily revoked, his mail opened, his phones tapped, his house searched, and his property damaged. At certain times he was watched and followed; he received ugly threats and letters from white racists. But his quarrels with the militant left are perhaps of greater interest today.

Paton demanded to know where the "young white Radicals who sneer at liberals and liberalism" would have been without previous liberal efforts. They "would have been in darkness until now," he asserted. "One cannot measure past labour in terms of present demands." He went on to caution that "if black power meets white power in headlong confrontation, and there are no black liberals around, then God help South Africa. Liberalism is more than politics. It is humanity, tolerance, and love of justice. South Africa has no future without them." Paton's fictional character, Msimangu, says something similar, though more lyrically, in one of the novel's most memorable lines: "I have one great fear in my heart, that one day when they turn to loving they will find we are turned to hating."

Paton often compared the South African situation with the American. He admired the United States as an example of democracy to the world and wrote that American citizens "should go down on their knees and thank God for their Constitution, their Bill of Rights, and their Supreme Court," since, he felt, these had prevented the United States's racial problem from exploding like South Africa's and resulting in cycles of all-out oppression and violence. He was also canny enough to recognize the difference in demographics. To righteous white outsiders who demanded "moral solutions to political problems" he dryly remarked that it was easier to be good when you are secure—that is, when you are the majority.

Paton's tendency to compare the United States and South Africa invites several observations today. In some ways, the two countries are the positive and negative of each other. Aside from an almost exact reversal in racial demographics, South Africa, according to Diana Wylie, an American academic writing in the *Yale Review* of her recent visit to South Africa, is without common narratives or unifying myths or founding principles to unite its disparate peoples and is struggling to reach for them now. We have such common narratives and principles and are doing our best to delegitimize them. The idea of preserving different groups in separate enclaves was one of the delusions of Afrikaner nationalism, and tribalism and ethnicity persist as problems in the new South African state, while here we disfavor the old assimilative American model and energetically promote ethnicity and separatism under the rubric of "multiculturalism." If South Africa watched tribal breakdown and did nothing to remedy its effects, we watch family breakdown and do nothing. Finally, Wylie notes that Christianity has and continues to be a unifying force in South Africa. In contrast, our rights enthusiasts labor to strip religion from the public square.

Although Paton's political labors and political writing pretty much overshadowed his literary work after *Cry, the Beloved Country*, and his two later novels show the strain of politics, he did manage to produce a few fine stories and an important biography of Hofmeyr. But it was his supreme and lasting achievement to uphold a model of humanity in the face of suffering and injustice and to have limned it in an extraordinary and enduring novel.

Paton harkens us back to the moral discipline of the early civil rights struggle in our own country, and he stands for something lost in our post–civil rights era of radicalized demands, grievances, and entitlements: the tragic sense, the mature recognition that "suffering is an inescapable part of life" and that human character is formed in response to it. He held to the belief that love is greater than hate, and that persuasion and reason are better than force and intimidation. He never lost the to us now perhaps distant conviction that "a man who fights for justice must himself be cleansed and purified." He resisted the simplified ideologies of both Left and Right. His liberalism was not the narcissism of good intentions, but the lifelong commitment of a man who saw reality whole.

Cry, the Beloved Country claims our attention through its unembarrassed simplicity, its nuanced complexity, and its textured beauty, as well as through the qualities of mind of an earlier age that it manifests, a turn-of-the-century belief in the dignity of the individual, a modest acceptance of the limits of the human condition, and an affirmation in the power of reason, faith, and goodness. As such it commends itself to the turn-of-another-century's end.

DAVID MEDALIE

"A Corridor Shut at Both Ends": Admonition and Impasse in Van der Post's In a Province and Paton's Cry, the Beloved Country

Laurens van der Post's *In a Province* (1934) and Alan Paton's *Cry, the Beloved Country* (1948) are both Jim-Goes-to-Jo'burg stories: the many differences between the two novels notwithstanding, the basic pattern of the unsophisticated young rural man who is corrupted by the city and becomes estranged from his cultural heritage is the same. In each case, this results in the young man's becoming a criminal. In both novels, well-meaning individuals who understand this lamentable trajectory prove unable to avert its tragic course. The unconsummated sympathy is transferred, instead, to the reader: both novels admonish the beloved country, urging it to understand more fully, to feel more keenly, to behave more justly.

Towards the end of *In a Province*, Johan van Bredepoel is forced to admit that his liberal good intentions have not yielded any positive results. Despite his sincere desire to befriend and assist Kenon Badiakgotla, the young black man whom he met in the city of Port Benjamin, the latter, nonetheless, slipped into crime and has met with tragedy:

> "Ah," he thought, "we were brothers in misfortune and inadaptability, but I could have helped him, and I didn't. Remote from one another we passed through life like two shadows over a hill, darkening it,

From *English in Africa* 25, no. 2 (October 1998): 93–110. © 1998 by *English in Africa*.

but not altering it at all. Our lives were set in a corridor shut at both ends." (Van der Post 1953, 337)

Although Van Bredepoel seems to be accepting responsibility and berating himself for not coming to the aid of his "brother," his remarks imply that there was, from the start, an element of tragic inevitability. There is the suggestion that, unbeknown to him and Kenon, their efforts were overlaid by something which divided them inexorably. They sought to find their way out of a labyrinth, but it turned out to be "a corridor shut at both ends."

The metaphor Van der Post uses is a particularly resonant one: although it refers explicitly to the relationship between Van Bredepoel and Kenon, it may also be seen as an expression of a more general political and moral impasse, one which both Van der Post's and Paton's first novels present. For all their explicit didacticism, in particular the insistence upon liberal solutions to the political and social problems confronting South Africa in the 1930s and 1940s respectively, there is nevertheless a sense of a moribund present which cannot be invigorated either by the traditions of the past (located in the country) or the possibilities of the future (associated with the city). Just as Van Bredepoel believes he ought to have done more to help Kenon, yet feels vaguely that something was deterministically preventing him from doing so all along, so the novels themselves, within their vigorous polemic, have already foreclosed upon both the past and the future, as the succeeding discussion will suggest, so that the corridor of history itself seems to be shut at both ends. Thus two works which follow closely the classic liberal scheme of urging a change of heart in the individual, leading in turn to effective change within the wider society, are nonetheless marked by a curious inertia; by the "paralysis of will of the liberal," linked to a "failure of vision of a common society with a common destiny," which David Hemson has identified in *Cry, the Beloved Country* (Hemson 1994, 35).

As far as the future is concerned, it is significant that both novels firmly rule out the possibility of a viable urban black culture. The city and the various phenomena of modernity are represented in each case as vitiating indigenous culture and identity: " . . . it did not take [Kenon] long to realise that, in the strange and complex life in which he found himself, the traditions of his people were no longer certain guides" (Van der Post 1953, 97). Absalom Kumalo and Kenon Badiakgotla are swallowed by the city—Johannesburg and Cape Town (Port Benjamin) respectively—and, although Kenon returns briefly to his rural origins after he is released, it is clear that his spirit has been irredeemably stained by his experiences in Port Benjamin: we are told, after he comes out of the prison, that there "seemed to be no vitality left in him, his old vividness was dulled. This Kenon was a strange person" (132). He is alienated from himself; his sense of inner continuity is gone: "'I am not I,' he said to himself, shaking his head" (141).

Paton presents urbanisation for the most part as a tragic inevitability, although Stephen Kumalo manages, in Book Three, to rescue some of the lost inhabitants of the city (Gertrude's child and Absalom's young wife) and take them back with him to Ndotsheni, thus reversing partially the apparently remorseless pattern which is indicated towards the beginning of the novel:

> All roads lead to Johannesburg. Through the long nights the trains
> pass to Johannesburg. The lights of the swaying coach fall on the
> cutting-sides, on the grass and the stones of a country that sleeps.
> Happy the eyes that can close. (Paton 1958, 12)

The city is thus presented as a place of near-hypnotic compulsion, a centripetal force which sucks in people from the countryside.

Paton's descriptions of rural Natal in the first chapter of the novel are marked by rhetorical devices which equate pastoral plenitude with syntactical lushness, as seen in the following sentence, where the almost limitless vistas are captured in the proliferation of clauses and the leisurely meandering between commas and semi-colons:

> Below you is the valley of the Umzimkulu, on its journey from the
> Drakensberg to the sea; and beyond and behind the river, great hill
> after great hill; and beyond and behind them, the mountains of
> Ingeli and East Griqualand. (7)

In contrast, the city is presented as the place of jagged rhythms—the incomplete sentences in the description below suggest that modernity itself is a kind of frenzy:

> A great iron structure rearing into the air, and a great wheel above
> it, going so fast that the spokes play tricks with the sight. Great
> buildings, and steam blowing out of pipes, and men hurrying about.
> A great white hill, and an endless procession of trucks climbing
> upon it, high up in the air. On the ground, motor-cars, lorries,
> buses, one great confusion. (17)

Part of the appeal of the countryside lies in the fact that it delights the senses—"you look down on one of the fairest valleys of Africa . . . you may hear the forlorn crying of the titihoya. . . . Stand unshod upon (the grass), for the ground is holy ..." (7). In contrast, however, the bemusement of the onlooker in response to the urban commotion implies that the city is fundamentally *inhuman*; what is more, it deceives its luckless inhabitants, sending confusing sensory messages, as suggested by the comment that "the spokes ... play tricks with the sight."

In Van der Post's novel, the seductive cunning of the city makes Kenon dissatisfied with the rural environment in which, prior to his going to Port Benjamin, he lived contentedly. As in *Cry, the Beloved Country*, the countryside is associated with ennobling simplicity, the city with degrading complexity:

> He remembered the cheerful crowds, weaving and interweaving in the complicated mesh of their intentions, and there came back to him the excitement he had felt walking amongst so many strange people, seeing them at their best, not knowing the sordidness they came from and would go back to before midnight, but projecting both forwards and backwards in his mind a picture of them in the same attractive clothes, the same carefree mood. (143)

The narrator indicates clearly that nothing positive will come of Kenon's new enthusiasms: the "weaving and interweaving" of the inhabitants of the city in "the complicated mesh of their intentions" is another version of "the corridor shut at both ends," the dilemma from which there is no escape. The city is deceptive because its glitter conceals a "sordidness," which is presented in such generalised terms that it amounts to another kind of determinism—an endemic moral corruption. In Port Benjamin, according to Van Bredepoel, "the form of our lives is order, but their content is chaos" (160). Kenon is not irretrievably lost when he goes to prison, but when he finds himself wishing that he were back in the city—described later by Van Bredepoel as "that world of hate and blood" (345)—his tragic fate is sealed.

The city is also presented in both novels as the site of militant (or potentially militant) political activity. It is significant that the low-cost housing on the outskirts of Port Benjamin is described as "row[s] of uniform houses, the shoddy products of democratic precipitation" (14): democracy itself is thus associated with inconsiderate haste, one of the characteristics of the urban milieu as depicted by Van der Post.

Collectivist politics, whether in the form of trade unions, strikes, boycotts (or, in the case of Van der Post, communism), is invariably shown in both novels as emanating from the city. Although the countryside has escaped this kind of political activity thus far, it is under threat—particularly in *In a Province*, where the communist "agitator," Burgess, has extended his activities and influence beyond the metropolitan centre to the town of Paulstad.

Collectivist behaviour at its most nightmarish and repugnant always takes the form of a maddened mob, intent upon acts of violence. In Van der Post's novel the threat becomes a catastrophic reality (the riot at Shepherd's Place, the massacre at Paulstad), while in Paton's it remains a hovering and ominous possibility.

David Maughan Brown's analysis of the treatment of the crowd in three South African novels of the 1950s and 1960s—Harry Bloom's *Transvaal Episode* (1956), Jack Cope's *The Golden Oriole* (1958) and Laurens Van der Post's *The Hunter and the Whale* (1967)—may be applied usefully to these two earlier works as well. He argues that the novels of Bloom, Cope and Van der Post reveal "an identical, almost paranoid, fear of the crowd which would appear to derive from a profound, and quintessentially liberal, faith in individualism and concomitant distrust of collective political action" (Maughan Brown 1987, 4). Indeed, both *In a Province* and *Cry, the Beloved Country* repeatedly suggest that human beings are ontologically at their best when they act as individuals, and at their worst when their individuality is ceded and they act as members of a group or crowd. This is clearly seen in the behaviour of the crowd at Shepherd's Place, where the loss of individual identity is the precursor to the outbreak of violence: "all the odds between one individual and another had gone; here there were neither rich nor poor, but only cells of a single organism" (209). This suggests devolution, a regression to a lower, non-individuated life form. Collectivist behaviour and violence are thus presented as part of the same atavistic impulse.

The "pervasive drive towards animalizing the crowd" (Maughan Brown 1987, 5) which forms part of this anti-collectivist rhetoric is readily seen in both novels. Msimangu describes John Kumalo's oratorical skills and his capacity to incite the crowd in precisely those terms: "They say he speaks like a bull, and growls in his throat like a lion, and could make men mad if he would" (Paton 1958, 37). Oratory—even when practised by John Kumalo, whose skills in that area cannot be denied—becomes, therefore, a potentially base form of behaviour: a strange inversion of the Edenic situation, where language, meant to distinguish humankind from the animals, is associated instead with a tendency to regress and become animalistic, a betrayal of the higher faculties and aspirations of humankind. Yet, when Msimangu preaches in the chapel at Ezenzeleni, the situation could not be more different, even though he, too, is addressing a crowd:

> For it was not only a voice of gold, but it was the voice of a man whose heart was golden, reading from a book of golden words. And the people were silent, and Kumalo was silent, for when are three such things found in one place together? (81)

Part of the redemption that Msimangu offers is the redemption of *language*, purging it of demagogy—which is equated in the novel with "political" forms of persuasion only, and no other tendentious use of language—and, instead of inflaming the crowd, as John Kumalo does, his words induce calmness and reflection in them. Whereas John Kumalo is shown to be hypocritical (self-seeking and cowardly, in contrast to what he urges others to do), here the perfect internal consistency of the golden voice, the golden heart and the golden word—"found in one place together"—establishes Msimangu as the pinnacle of human (and humanistic) evolution, almost recreating a prelapsarian world where language has not yet been corrupted, and there is no discrepancy between intention, conduct and utterance.

The ultimate endorsement of Msimangu and his message lies in the fact that, although he addresses a number of people, each person in the audience feels as if the words are being addressed to him or her *individually*: "Yes, he speaks to me, in such quiet and simple words. . . . I hear you, my brother. There is no word I do not hear" (82). His address to the crowd is therefore transformed into a series of intimate interpersonal communications, rescuing the individual from the collectivist danger. Msimangu speaks as a Christian and as a liberal; not, it would seem, as a demagogue. The highest compliment paid to black people in both novels is the implicit assertion that they are capable of being liberals (intuitively, perhaps, rather than consciously) and that their traditional beliefs do not preclude their becoming so:

> [Van Bredepoel] knew how sensitive black people were to individual qualities, he knew that, unlike many Europeans, they saw and judged men purely and directly as men, that there were few social associations to interfere with the clarity of their judgement. (Van der Post 1953, 324)

Hence, despite the fact that Van der Post places a great deal of emphasis upon tribalism as an essential constituent of black identity, there is nonetheless the suggestion that the commendable propensity of some black people to behave like liberals supersedes any tribal affiliations, leading, where necessary, to the suppression of "social associations" in favour of the dispassionate appraisal of individuals: "they saw and judged men purely and directly as men." Having done so much to attest to the richness of the tribal heritage which, tragically, Kenon loses, the endorsement here of a capacity in black people to consider individuals in deracinated terms strikes one as a curious paradox. What it shows is that the tribal context is admired only when it is compatible with the liberal (and, in Paton's case, also the Christian) perspective. Thus, in *Cry, the Beloved Country*, Msimangu's criticism of the role played

by colonialism in the destruction of tribal life—"The white man has broken the tribe" (25)—deliberately excludes indigenous or traditional religious
practices from the tribal legacy which is being mourned: "It was a white man
who brought my father out of darkness" (25).

The Paulstad massacre is presented by Van der Post as a contest between
progressive individuality and regressive collectivism in which, tragically, the
latter holds sway. In the sentences that follow, the "crowd" becomes a "mob";
the loss of its humanity is the consequence of this dehumanization:

> It seemed to van Bredepoel that all the faces in the crowd had lost
> their individual expression. Every black man looked alike. The mob
> no longer saw outside themselves . . . (321)

The crowd "seemed to Van Bredepoel a many-footed monster with a single
voice" (325): the loss of individual identity has made it grotesque. In contrast, Van der Post offers the heroic behaviour of the Colonel of police,
hitherto a minor character in the novel, who tries single-handedly to pacify
the three drug-crazed black men (Kenon being one of them) whom Atkins,
the nefarious detective, has armed and persuaded to incite the crowd:

> Slowly the Colonel walked out towards the three Natives. It
> seemed to van Bredepoel that there was something infinitely heroic
> about his action, that this obscure Colonel of police in an obscure
> country village had suddenly become great, not because of anything
> attaching to his own life, but because he placed himself like a bridge
> between the conception and execution of a duty that was greater
> than himself. Bearing himself like someone inspecting a troop on a
> fashionable parade-ground, he continued to move forward until he
> reached the old Native, who had danced into position ahead of his
> companions. The black man raised his rifle to strike the Colonel,
> but before it could fall the Colonel caught his arm and said coolly:
> "Jan Makatese, you're a fool. I always thought you were a fool, but
> now I think you are a bigger one. Give me that rifle and go over to
> Major Atkins there." (323–324)

Amidst the incipient chaos and the irrationality of both the black crowd
and the reactionary farmers, this brief episode brings together many of the
defining virtues of the liberal creed, especially the status and responsibility of
the individual. In appealing to the old black man as an individual, using his
name and reminding him of their past association, the policeman is attempting to restore his humanity by distinguishing him from the amorphous crowd,

the "many-footed monster." The courageous behaviour of the Colonel and his transformation from "obscurity" to "greatness" suggest that the potential of the individual is never circumscribed: "there was something infinitely heroic about his action." In contrast to the references to devolution which characterise the descriptions of the crowd, here there is a suggestion of ontological ascent and amplitude.

The comment that "he placed himself like a bridge between the conception and execution of a duty that was greater than himself" points to the way in which Van der Post envisages liberal-humanist interventions as a "bridge," a response to the racial and political polarization which has reached its most extreme form in Paulstad. More telling is the notion that the bridge lies between "the conception and execution" of the duty the Colonel assumes, for it is precisely the gap between "conception" and "execution" which is the great quandary of both *In a Province* and *Cry, the Beloved Country*. Here again the moment in which the Colonel is cast into prominence is revealing: although the old man gives up his rifle and submits to the authority of the police, "ashamed and crestfallen" (324), Kenon assaults the Colonel, an act which prompts the irruption of violence and leads to the massacre. The Colonel has not succeeded in staving off the tragedy, his admirable heroism notwithstanding; he himself becomes one of the victims of the bloodshed. Although we are told that Van Bredepoel "admired his determination to be just to both white and black. It seemed to him that there was some compensation for the Colonel in the way he had died" (337), this elegiac tribute does little more than establish the Colonel as a model of individual rectitude. His plan has failed, just as Van Bredepoel's attempts to help Kenon have come to nothing.

In both novels, the most important representatives of the liberal creed, Johan van Bredepoel and Arthur Jarvis, are murdered. In Van der Post's in particular, tragedy seems greater than proscription. This cannot but be disabling to the liberal agenda, particularly if one sees the need to be adaptable and efficacious as a crucial component of liberalism, as Eric Voegelin suggests:

> [Liberalism] is not a body of timelessly valid scientific propositions about political reality, but rather a series of political opinions and attitudes which have their optimal truth in the situation which motivates them, and are then overtaken by history and required to do justice to new situations. (Voegelin, quoted in Rich 1984, 123)

The fact that both *In a Province* and *Cry, the Beloved Country* are so implacably opposed to modernity in its various manifestations suggests, in itself, an inability or unwillingness "to do justice to new situations"—as we have seen, Van Bredepoel identifies "inadaptability" (Van der Post 1953, 337) as something which he and Kenon have in common. Instead of moving with the grain of history, there is indeed a sense that the various initiatives are being "overtaken by history" and that programmes for reform are turning in upon themselves.

In one of his arguments with Burgess, Van Bredepoel confesses to feeling like an "anachronism" (216). Burgess's reply, even granted the fact that it is spoken by a character for whom there is little or no authorial approval, cannot, nevertheless, merely be dismissed:

> "You would have felt an anachronism in whatever age you had lived," Burgess broke in warmly, and then, as if frightened of going too far, held his peace. (216)

In general, Burgess has no qualms about criticising Van Bredepoel and his liberal beliefs. Here he hesitates, for, presumably, this is the most devastating criticism of all: the implication is that the liberal ideology is inevitably, irretrievably, out of step; that, in Voegelin's terms, it will always be "overtaken by history," never equal to the situation, never opportune. The novel does not lend support to such a view, but it does not convincingly negate it either. Van Bredepoel gives his life to save Burgess, but the effect of this is merely to entrench the latter in his views and to make him even more of an ideologue: he turns Van Bredepoel, whose antipathy towards communism has grown steadily through the course of the novel, into a hero of the communist struggle, saying "They shall pay for this, when the revolution comes" (349). The implication is clear: he has learned nothing.

Both Van der Post and Paton present the educated, articulate, urban black person as one of the most dangerous and meretricious manifestations of modernity. The presentation of "the Doctor" is strikingly similar to that of John Kumalo: in both cases, their education has given them nothing but demagogic glibness and hollow rhetoric. Even before "the Doctor" speaks, the quasi-Dickensian absurdity of his appearance indicates that he is unlikely to have anything cogent to say:

> He was bareheaded, but his chin was so tightly supported by a high, stiff collar that he could not turn his head without turning his body as well. Round the collar was tied a black silk kerchief in the fashion of the 'nineties. His chest was puffed out, his stomach drawn in, and his posterior projected so much that the lines of his figure resembled those of a stuffed and corseted pouter pigeon. (152)

"The Doctor" is doubly damned: as an African he is too modern, and as a white man he is a parody, his dress style out of date and in no way deflecting attention from his protruding "posterior," that physical attribute which the colonial eye has dwelt upon so often, and with such pathological fascination. After such a description, it is less than surprising to find "the Doctor" described as "a pompous windbag ... circling in his vague bombastic way round the mysterious source of (the crowd's) frustrations" (159).

Yet, if one looks past the tendentious descriptions of the two orators, one finds that what they say is not particularly radical. "The Doctor" speaks of the alliance between colonialism and Christianity—"The white man had the Bible and we had the land; to-day he's got the land, and we the Bible" (154)—and advances the idea of the unchristian Christian society (the same paradox, incidentally, which Arthur Jarvis identifies in his writings in *Cry, the Beloved Country*). The claim that "Christ himself ... was black!" (154) may outrage the white racists present, but should scarcely cause offence to liberally-minded people. The only aspect of the speech made by "the Doctor" which could possibly be construed as discrepant with the liberal agenda of the novel as a whole is his appeal to the crowd to join (and contribute money to) the African Workers' Union in the spirit of the slogan "Christ, Combination and Co-operation" (156).

The text of John Kumalo's speech (as opposed to what is said *about* it) is equally innocuous. He asks that black people be given a share in what their labour has produced; he asks for a decent wage, particularly for those employed in the mining industry. His polemic is aimed at a discrete, rather than a general injustice:

> All we ask is justice, says Kumalo. We are not asking here for equality and the franchise and the removal of the colour-bar. We are asking only for more money from the richest industry in the world. (Paton 1958, 159)

He urges the crowd to consider the option of a strike, and equates economic justice with freedom:

> ... it is a man's freedom to sell his labour for what it is worth. ... It is for that freedom that many of our own African soldiers have been fighting. ... Not only here ... but in all Africa, in all the great continent where we Africans live. (160)

The seditiousness of what he says lies, apparently, in this last comment, as suggested by the response of the crowd: "The people growl also. The one meaning of this is safe, but the other meaning is dangerous" (160). It is far from clear what the "safe" and "dangerous" meanings are, especially since, as the subsequent discussion will indicate, Paton's novel is itself so ambiguous in its attitude towards Africa, the "great continent." Presumably Kumalo is referring to something that goes beyond industrial action, perhaps to revolution itself. But it is not enunciated explicitly and his speech, if one sets aside the interpolations of the omniscient narrator, consists essentially of reasonable and modest demands.

What, then, is so reprehensible about "the Doctor" or John Kumalo? Since the hostility towards them does not seem to be sufficiently rooted in what they say, presumably it lies in what they *do not say*: firstly, their perspective is urban, not rural; secondly, they do not ask the members of the crowd to respond as individuals—hence, they are not black liberals; and, thirdly, although they both make reference to pre-colonial African society, they do not do so in an attempt to restore lost or atrophied cultural practices, but rather to increase dissatisfaction with the contemporary political situation. Their words are full of Africa, but it is not, apparently, the right kind of Africa.

In focusing upon the attitudes towards modernity expressed in the two novels, one should note that there is one aspect of modern life which the two novels present very differently, namely justice and the Rule of Law. In *Cry, the Beloved Country*, strenuous efforts are made to insist upon the exemption of the Rule of Law—a cornerstone of a liberal society—from the general corruption of a fundamentally illiberal society. A strange paradox results: Absalom's crime is clearly not equal to his punishment, and there is sympathy for him as a result; yet, at the same time, we are asked to accept the punishment as *judicially* correct, as the judge indicates in his summation:

> . . . it is one of the most monumental achievements of this defective society that it has made a Law, and has set judges to administer it, and has freed those judges from any obligation whatsoever but to administer the Law. But a Judge may not trifle with the Law because the society is defective. If the Law is the law of a society that some feel to be unjust, it is the Law and the society that must be changed. In the meantime there is an existing Law that must be administered, and it is the sacred duty of a Judge to administer it. (171)

The judge's role is almost hieratic, suggested by his comment that his duty is a "sacred" one. In administering the Rule of Law in such absolute terms, dismissing both the effect of the "defective society" and the responsibility of the judiciary in relation to it, the judge admonishes the corrupt society and the criminals it produces, yet is somehow removed from it. The Rule of Law protects him, even as it fails to protect Absalom. What is more, the narrator of the novel lends further support to this view, so that the pressure upon the reader to accept the sacerdotal status of the judiciary is very great indeed:

> In South Africa men are proud of their Judges, because they believe they are incorruptible. Even the black men have faith in them, though they do not always have faith in the Law. In a land of fear this incorruptibility is like a lamp set upon a stand, giving light to all that are in the house. (137)

When an omniscient narrator has to make use of generalisations so sweeping that they are as likely to bring into question what is being declared as to bolster it, it is a sign not only of ideological desperation, but also of *narrative* desperation. The narrator, presented implicitly from the start as one who may be trusted to guide the reader through the moral quandaries of the novel, just as he guided him or her authoritatively through the hills and valleys of rural Natal, has now to fall back upon his own authority and offer it as a justification in itself. His role has thus changed from one of guidance to one of admonition. It is the narrative equivalent of the inflexibility of the judge, who also uses the authority invested in him as its own justification. In confronting this stern moral purity, the reader is unable to ascertain what he or she should do with the compassion for the young man which the novel has taken pains to inculcate. The "lamp" or beacon of the Rule of Law notwithstanding, the trial is an impasse for the reader, as, in a different way, it is for Absalom and his father.

In Van der Post's novel, in contrast, the Rule of Law is shown to be thoroughly complicit in the workings of an unjust society. During Kenon's trial after the violent incident outside Tommie's place, his ignorance of the procedures of the court result in his being unjustly convicted of a "murderous assault on three white men" (122). In the magistrate's comment, during his summation, that "unprovoked assaults by men of your race on white people are becoming far too common in this district" (122–123), Van der Post points to the racial paranoia that sways the ostensibly objective operation of the Rule of Law. When Van Bredepoel learns what has happened to Kenon, he thinks to himself that "The law . . . is, after all, concerned only with the law. It sees the human being only at the point where he comes into conflict with the law" (124). This is essentially the same argument put forward by the judge at Absalom's trial, but, where Paton uses this insight to separate and protect the Rule of Law from the pervasive social corruption, Van der Post shows how it limits the capacity of the law to protect people like Kenon. In this regard, Van der Post's liberalism may be regarded as more thorough and true to itself than Paton's, for Paton is prepared to plead the case of a set of abstract principles in conjunction (or even in competition) with the invidious situation of an individual human being, while Van der Post does nothing to dilute the impact of Kenon's plight.

Even more damning than the unjust treatment of Kenon, which becomes the first stage in his apparently irrevocable decline, is the depiction of the magistrate in Paulstad, a man of integrity in whose eyes Van Bredepoel sees "the shadow of a profound and intelligent disillusionment" (252). This unnamed man, branded by the other whites in Paulstad as "too much of a negrophobolist" (256), presents a view of the operation of justice in an unjust political situation which is directly at odds with that enunciated by the judge in *Cry, the Beloved Country*. For a start, he rejects the notion of "an abstract conception of justice" (258), arguing instead that, in a colonial situation, there can be no arbitrary separation between the colonial rule and the Rule of Law:

> " . . . we won't allow the black people to enter into the system of living for which our justice was obviously devised. By refusing to do so, we imply that they are psychologically and racially in a different class. Yet we proceed very illogically to inflict our system of justice on them as if they were like ourselves. . . . We forbid them the sort of life their law demands, and give them our law without the sort of life that our law demands." (259)

The law cannot, therefore, be exempted from the general social malaise. Where power relations are fundamentally unequal, there is no possibility of a disinterested or untainted justice. In fact, true justice would entail nothing less than the dismantling of those power relations *per se*, as Van Bredepoel recognises, with great honesty, towards the end of the novel: "I don't know if I want justice, lest in justice being done to others justice should be done to me" (339).

Like Van Bredepoel, however, the magistrate is an impotent figure whose superior insight has no effective consequences whatsoever. Whereas Paton seeks to grant correct understanding some measure of practical usefulness, as seen in particular in the attempts to renew the community of Ndotsheni in the last part of the novel, Van der Post presents those who think incisively as enmeshed in a kind of torpor, doing little more than remonstrating and then sinking into further disillusionment. Van Bredepoel thinks of the magistrate as "another who has lost faith" (261):

> "He has come to mistrust so much the system of which his administration of justice is part, that he can no longer see a case

by itself, but only as something in which, no matter how just he himself is, his justice will be coloured by the general injustice of the system." (261)

The magistrate's awareness of his own complicity as an agent of "the system" becomes, in other words, not a redemptive insight, but the ultimate expression of his moral paralysis. The finest, fairest and most sympathetic minds—Van Bredepoel's and the magistrate's—are overcome by a sense of helplessness and futility. In tandem with this, the novel's polemic itself peters out and we are left with a dead Kenon, a dead Van Bredepoel, a moribund magistrate and an unrepentant ideologue, Burgess, who has learned nothing from the tragic events that have resulted, in part, from his own actions.

One of the major differences between *In a Province* and *Cry, the Beloved Country* is that the former makes tragedy an ending and a climax, whereas the latter ends with an attempt to ameliorate the tragedy that has occurred and to achieve a recuperation of sorts. In that regard, the shape of Paton's novel is far better suited to a polemical and reformist agenda than Van der Post's, for to urge change and then show change taking place is a much more persuasive trajectory in a didactic work than to urge change and present despair. Book Three of *Cry, the Beloved Country* clearly corresponds to the last stage of a traditional, formal elegy, where the nadir of sorrow is partially left behind and forms of consolation are sought. Significantly, this is also the part of the novel which brings the return to Ndotsheni and the countryside and the final abandonment of the city. In Book Three, the process of recovery is marked by a grudging acceptance that traditional, conservative black society needs to adapt if it is to be retained as a pragmatic political solution. For instance, unwise farming methods need to be abandoned, and an agricultural demonstrator, Napoleon Letsitsi, is brought to Ndotsheni to teach the people that some of their traditional practices are harmful. This educated young man is endorsed by the narrator and clearly represents a palatable and non-threatening form of modernity; yet the recommendations he makes are extremely problematic if considered in terms of the novel as a whole:

> So the young man told them . . . how the people must stop burning the dung and must put it back into the land, how they must gather the weeds together and treat them and not leave them to wither away in the sun, how they must stop ploughing up and down the hills, how they must plant trees for fuel, trees that grow quickly like wattles, in some place where they could not plough at all, on the steep sides of streams so that the water did not rush away in the storms. But these were hard things to do, because the people must

learn that it is harmful for each man to wrest a living from his own little piece of ground. Some must give up their ground for trees, and some for pastures. And hardest of all would be the custom of lobola, by which a man pays for his wife in cattle, for people kept too many cattle for this purpose, and counted all their wealth in cattle, so that the grass had no chance to recover. (215)

After all the novel has purportedly done to validate traditional African practices, the advice given by the demonstrator seems curiously antipathetic within its ostensible sympathy. The sub-text of what he recommends is that the continued survival of rural communities is the overriding priority, and if that means the loss of tribal practices such as *lobola*, then so be it. Not only are non-indigenous plants (such as the wattle) recommended as a way of preserving the indigenous way of life, but so, too, are modes of behaviour which are radically discrepant with existing traditions. Interestingly, even a kind of collectivism is put forward as a solution, whereby the right to private property (one of the tenets of traditional liberalism) is to be ceded in favour of the common good, for "it is harmful for each man to wrest a living from his own little piece of ground."

The espousal of traditional, rural black society in *Cry, the Beloved Country* and in *In a Province* is entirely consistent with contemporary liberal thinking. According to Paul B. Rich, "by the mid-1930s the main body of South African liberals looked ... to the rural reserves as the main repositories for African political and economic rejuvenation" (Rich 1984, 125). This political orientation was bolstered by "a growing ideological and intellectual influence from research in anthropology" (54). The liberal interest in indigenous cultures, as reflected in Van der Post's and Paton's novels, is highly selective: as we have seen, the advice given by the demonstrator in *Cry, the Beloved Country* makes one question seriously whether indigenous culture is truly being valued for itself and on its own terms. Traditional religion has already been disparaged by Msimangu; if the idiosyncratic mix of old and new advanced as a solution by Letsitsi is to be implemented, the result will, presumably, be a further attenuation of tribal practices under the guise of their preservation. What Rich calls the "'adaptionist' ideal" (59), whereby tribal life is promoted only if it can be satisfactorily channelled in certain directions, is evident in a 1932 *Report of the Native Economic Commission*, which advocates a "wise, courageous, forward policy of development in the Reserves" (quoted in Rich 1984, 58):

To develop the Natives and the Reserves: to make the dead hand of tribalism relax its grip; to convert tribalism into a progressive force; to set the Native mass in motion on the upward path of civilisation, and to enable them to shoulder the burden of their own advancement—such must be ... the main approach to the solution of the Native problem in its economic aspect. (quoted in Rich 1984, 59)

There is no unambiguous appreciation of "old Africa" in either *Cry, the Beloved Country* or *In a Province*. The loss of an indigenous identity is identified as a problem with wide-ranging social and political ramifications, yet the destruction or attenuation of old Africa turns out to be a false or merely ostensible etiology; what is more, the possibility of its resurgence is the subject of apocalyptic anxieties rather than elegiac laments. Van der Post does far less than Paton to establish cultural authenticity: Kenon belongs to a fictitious tribe, the Bambuxosa, who live in Bambuland; he admires a heroic ancestor, a chief called Masakama. Like Paton, Van der Post presents the countryside as simultaneously bucolic and increasingly untenable: the people lead "unchanging lives," enshrouded by "an atmosphere of timelessness" (70); the walls of the valley are "like the frame round a picture in which life is sealed and transfigured in one calm, unperplexed and unchanging moment" (70). Yet we are also told that "there are far too many people even for so seemingly rich a soil, that often it does not rain, that the taxes are heavy" (73). The rural life is thus both preserved from change and beset by it.

The comparison of the community to a picture "in which life is sealed and transfigured" is revealing, for it suggests that pre-colonial life, despite all the nostalgia with which it is imbued, is only approved of when it is hermetic and static. In both *In a Province* and *Cry, the Beloved Country*, the threat of militancy and irrational mob behaviour is associated with the resurgence of old Africa: before "the Doctor" addresses the crowd at Shepherd's Place, a song—described alternately as a "hymn" and a "battle song" (Van der Post 1953, 152)—is sung, part of which Van Bredepoel is able to translate: "Long have you waited, long have you slept, O Africa! But now you shall awake!" (152). What is more, the prediction that "one day Masakama will come back to his people on the clouds with many warriors and much cattle" (88) is partially fulfilled in Paulstad as the "dark mass of Natives ... listen in to another world, to a succession of worlds, through which the Bambuxosa had slowly come, the great Masakama at their head" (321). But the greatness of the past becomes nothing more than bloody mass hysteria; the mythological wealth, Van der Post implies, should never have been unsealed.

Similarly, when John Kumalo's stirring oratory is described, the greatest danger, according to the narrator, is that he should inflame the mob by suggesting to them that the past may hold future possibilities within itself:

What if this voice should say words that it speaks already in private, should rise and not fall again, should rise and rise and rise, and the people rise with it, should madden them with thoughts of rebellion and dominion, with thoughts of power and possession? Should paint for them pictures of Africa awakening from sleep, of Africa resurgent, of Africa dark and savage? (Paton 1953, 158)

The old Africa is thus only valued when it is quiescent; when it inspires people to strain towards "rebellion and dominion . . . power and possession," its resurgence is presented as a sinister kind of atavism: "Africa dark and savage." One of the great ironies of *Cry, the Beloved Country* is that it is John Kumalo, a man thoroughly sullied by modernity, who has the potency of old Africa available to him (even if he chooses not to exploit it in full), rather than Stephen Kumalo or Msimangu. The past and the future, in other words, coincide in John Msimangu and they become the same thing: a cul-de-sac masquerading as a way out.

A further indication that the allegiances expressed in these novels should be regarded with a measure of scepticism is to be found in the language used. In Van der Post's novel, despite the ostensible embracing of an authentic African identity, the narrator's non-African affiliations are almost perversely insisted upon—so much so, that the positioning of local experiences in relation to European, Asian or North American reference points becomes a habitual method of conferring meaning. Examples of this include the following: "the bagpipe music of mosquitoes" (21); "a storm coming over the veld . . . like a brigade of Tartar cavalry" (22); "the yellow light within takes on a glowing Rubenesque fullness" (50); "the clouds . . . rebounded and scattered from the rocks below like the spray of some vast, unimagined Niagara" (158); "the light of a tortured afternoon flowing like a Pacific surf around them" (267); "[the native] had a large black and white blanket wrapped around him like the toga of a Roman senator" (299); "there seemed to hang over [the two men] the mystery of an El Greco picture" (301); "a current of feeling . . . swept the observation away like a cork before a Yangtze tide" (312). Such comparisons show that the posture of embracing Africa is undermined by the language in which it is couched; as Maughan Brown has argued, there is in Van der Post a "blindness to . . . the ideological origins and implications of much of his own terminology and discourse" (Maughan Brown 1992, 139).

Having said this, however, it is important to acknowledge that what *In a Province* does *not* do is to suggest, as *Cry, the Beloved Country* does, that what the reader has before him or her is a work of simple language and simple truths. Van der Post's novel contains a number of modernist elements, many of which have to do with what the schoolmaster, Meneer Broecksma, ascribes to Rembrandt: a mind "which was always sombre with shadows" (164). For the complacent communist, Burgess, even the tragic events in Paulstad leave "no shadow on his mind" (340), but Van Bredepoel's mind is, as he puts it, "on a slant" (167), and this equips him better to understand a country which is itself, as it were, "on a slant" and "sombre with shadows."

In *Cry, the Beloved Country*, however, there is an air of narrative ingenuousness which is often misleading. J. M. Coetzee has pointed to the way in which the language given to and associated with characters such as Stephen Kumalo relies on inauthentic archaisms and an "artificial literalism" (Coetzee 1988, 127): this, rather than being simple and innocent, is elaborately contrived. Nonetheless, the reader is warned against convoluted formulations: "Wise men write many books, in words too hard to understand" (Paton 1958, 57); and, as we have seen, Msimangu's speech contains "quiet and . . . simple words" (82). Yet there are many "hard" words in the novel (the writings of Arthur Jarvis, one of Paton's "wise men," for instance, or the judge's summation), not to mention forms of narration which require the response of a reader attuned to sophisticated literary devices—the "collage" of black voices in Chapter 9 of Book One, for example, counterbalanced by the "collage" of white voices three chapters later. Despite the suggestions that a simple language will lead to simple (therefore consensual and practicable) truths, and that the novel makes both available, what we find is that its language is not simple at all, its truths are quirky, and its admonitions (as in Van der Post's novel) are easier to hear than to heed.

Works Cited

Coetzee, J. M. 1988. *White Writing: On the Culture of Letters in South Africa*. Sandton: Radix; New Haven, London: Yale UP.

Hemson, David. 1994. "*Cry, the Beloved Country*: Land, Segregation and the City." *Alternation* 1.2: 27–42.

Maughan Brown, David. 1987. "The Image of the Crowd in South African Fiction." *English in Africa* 14.1: 41–64.

———. 1992. "Laurens van der Post." *Perspectives on South African Literature*. Ed. Michael Chapman, Colin Gardner and Es'kia Mphahlele. Johannesburg: Ad. Donker.

Paton, Alan. 1958 (1948). *Cry, the Beloved Country*. Harmondsworth: Penguin.

Rich, Paul B. 1984. *White Power and the Liberal Conscience: Racial Segregation and South African Liberalism, 1921–1960*. Johannesburg: Ravan.

Van der Post, Laurens. 1953 (1934). *In a Province*. London: Hogarth Press.

ANDREW FOLEY

"Considered as a Social Record":
A Reassessment of Cry, the Beloved Country

I

As 1998 marks the fiftieth anniversary of the publication of Alan Paton's *Cry, the Beloved Country*, it seems appropriate to offer a reassessment of the value and significance of the novel. In particular, it is worth considering how a book which has been the subject of so much adverse criticism over the years continues to exert such a powerful hold over its readership half a century after its first appearance. The novel has, after all, been condemned by a diversity of critics as paternalistic, naïve, simplistic and irrelevant, and its author labelled misguided, conservative and anachronistic. Indeed, Paton's work has been ill served even by sympathetic commentators who have tended to highlight and laud the novel's simplicity, spirituality and universality, and so have downplayed or ignored what constitutes a vital part of its meaning, its depiction and analysis of South African social and political conditions on the eve of the advent of apartheid. This article, therefore, intends to argue that *Cry, the Beloved Country*, far from being inaccurate or reductive in its social analysis, in fact provides a keen insight into the problems facing South African society at the time, an informed and subtle understanding of contemporaneous socio-political debates, and a sensitive appraisal of the possibilities for the country's restoration on a number of different levels.

This is not to suggest, of course, that *Cry, the Beloved Country* is little more than a sociological tract, or to undervalue the fictional story at the

From *English in Africa* 25, no. 2 (October 1998): 63–92. © 1998 by *English in Africa*.

centre of the book. A key element in the novel's achievement lies in its moving and evocative presentation of the struggle of the two main protagonists, Stephen Kumalo and James Jarvis, towards mutual understanding and reconciliation in the twilight of their years. But it appears that very often this aspect of the work has been emphasised to the virtually total neglect of its socio-political dimension. Significantly, one of the novel's earliest commentators, Max Perkins, editor for Charles Scribner's Sons (the first publishers of the work), felt that the final segment of the book, dealing with the amelioration of socio-economic conditions in the tribal reserves, was anti-climactic and should be revised (see Callan 1991, 16). And almost fifty years later, Darryl Roodt's film version (1995) of the book concentrated almost entirely on the basic story line, and quite ignored the question of social restoration which the novel explores. In order to redress the critical balance, as it were, and to meet some of the charges levelled against the novel, this article will focus in some detail upon the social and political aspects of the work. At the same time, however, as will become clear, the sociological features of the novel are not really separable from those dealing with individual characters, for in Paton's view it is the human individual who constitutes the primary unit of social or political value. This view represents the core principle of liberalism as a political philosophy, which may be seen to underpin the fundamental meaning of the novel as a whole. As such, this article will attempt to read *Cry, the Beloved Country* on its own ideological terms of reference as a novel offering a consciously liberal perspective on South African social problems and seeking liberal solutions to those problems.

Following the structure of *Cry, the Beloved Country* itself, the article will divide into two main sections. The first will deal with Paton's depiction of the difficulties confronting South African society at the time, and will examine Paton's credentials as a social commentator. The second section will turn to Paton's exploration of the possibilities for restoration, and will evaluate the plausibility of his social diagnosis. Finally, the article will consider the continuing relevance of *Cry, the Beloved Country* in the South Africa of the 1990s.

II

In evaluating the quality of Paton's thought as a social commentator, it is important to note that he was not always a proponent of liberal values. He was not born into a liberal-minded family, nor did he display particularly liberal attitudes in the early part of his life. Although he was clearly a decent, moral young man, concerned about his neighbour, and eager to serve his community, he could not be termed a liberal because he had not yet comprehended the importance of what he later identified as the defining characteristic of liberalism in South Africa, "its particular concern with racial justice" (Paton 1958, 6). Indeed, in his autobiographical essay, "Case History of a Pinky" (1971; in Paton 1975, 235–236), Paton relates his experience directly to that of Arthur Jarvis in *Cry, the Beloved Country* (reported in Arthur's "Private Essay on the Evolution of a South African"), in claiming that he was brought up by "honourable parents" and taught all he should know about "honour and charity and generosity," and yet of other ethnic groups in South Africa, he "learnt nothing at all" (Paton 1988a, 150).

The seminal event which served to precipitate the start of Paton's "learning" about South Africa was his decision at the age of thirty-two—following a life-threatening bout of enteric fever—to take up the post of Principal at Diepkloof Reformatory for African Boys. Speaking of himself in the third person in "Case History of a Pinky" (Paton 1971; in Paton 1975, 238–239), he comments:

> It opened his eyes. For the first time in his life . . . he saw South Africa as it was. . . . During those years at Diepkloof Reformatory he began to understand the kind of world in which Black people had to live and struggle and die. I won't say that he overcame all racial fear, but I will say that he overcame all racial hatred and prejudice.

Two further crucial events in Paton's life brought him to full liberal consciousness. Firstly, he served on the Anglican Diocesan Commission of 1941 under the chairmanship of Geoffrey Clayton, then Bishop of Johannesburg, which had the task of attempting to define "what it believed to be the mind of Christ for South Africa" (1973a, 116). Paton (1973a, 117) has recounted that his involvement in the Commission was for him like coming from the darkness into the light as he began to understand at last that one could not be a Christian in South Africa and claim to love justice and truth without becoming actively concerned about the socio-political problems of the country. As he trenchantly remarks in *Towards the Mountain* (1980, 248), "the bishop's commission . . . didn't change the heart of the nation but it changed me." Secondly, there was Paton's virtually epiphanic encounter at the funeral of Edith Rheinallt-Jones, recalled in his essay, "A Deep Experience" (1961). While Paton had been impressed with Edith's work at the South African Institute of Race Relations and the Wayfarers, as well as with her relationships with blacks, whom she treated as absolute equals, his real revelation came at her funeral in 1944 at St George's Presbyterian Church in Johannesburg (1961, 24): scores of people of every colour and creed "had come to honour her memory—their hates and their fears, their prides and their prejudices, all for the moment forgotten." For Paton the experience was profoundly significant:

> In that church one was able to see, beyond any possibility of doubt, that what this woman had striven for was the highest and best kind of thing to strive for in a country like South Africa. I knew then I would never again be able to think in terms of race and nationality. I was no longer a white person but a member of the human race. I came to this, as a result of many experiences, but this one ... was the deepest of them all.

By the mid-1940s, then, Paton had come to understand and accept the basic precepts of liberalism. Far from merely representing the adoption of conventional or convenient views, Paton's social and political understanding had developed through hard personal sacrifice and experience, and through a gradual, uneven intellectual evolution. Thus, in writing *Cry, the Beloved Country* in 1946, Paton came to the task not as an uninformed neophyte but as a middle-aged professional man with a mature apprehension of racial and political issues in South Africa.

As has been well documented (Paton 1980; Alexander 1994), Paton began writing *Cry, the Beloved Country* in an unpremeditated manner under the inspiration of homesickness during a lengthy tour of overseas penal institutions. Nevertheless, the novel is fundamentally the product of Paton's urgent need to utter, as he put it (1980, 272), "a cry of protest against the injustices of my own country." It was, indeed, part of Paton's express intention, in writing the novel, to "stab South Africa in the conscience" (in Callan 1982, 29), and to effect this he set out to portray the country's social ills with uncompromising candour. Thus, in the "Author's Note" that precedes the novel (and from which this article derives its title), Paton observes that his book is a work of fiction rather than fact in its primary aspects, but he goes on to stress that in terms of its social analysis of South Africa it is both valid and accurate: "In these aspects therefore the story is not true, but considered as a social record it is the plain and simple truth."

Such a claim is of course rhetorically exaggerated, but Paton's basic point is that the novel's depiction of South Africa's social problems derives neither from sensationalistic embellishment nor from mere conjecture, but is based upon the actual conditions obtaining in the country at the time. It is a point which is directed specifically at those South Africans who would simply not accept the authenticity of the scenes of black deprivation and suffering presented in the novel: one recalls, for instance, Prime Minister D. F. Malan's wife, at the premiere of the 1949 film version of the book, refusing to believe that such township ghettos existed in Johannesburg (Paton 1988b, 53–54). Paton's point could also be turned against those critics who accuse him of socio-political ignorance or ingenuousness, for it must be remembered that Paton's situation and background had put him in a very advantageous position to write a novel of this kind. Most evidently, Paton's experiences, over ten years, as Principal of Diepkloof Reformatory had placed him personally and directly in touch with the effects of racial discrimination in South Africa, at the level both of the individual and of the society at large. Furthermore, as a social analyst and commentator, he had over a long period of time wrestled with the question of the underlying causes of these effects, and had frequently presented statistical and other evidence before various public and private bodies (see Callan 1968, 52).

By way of example, shortly before the composition of *Cry, the Beloved Country*, Paton had published a series of articles in the journal, *The Forum*, and elsewhere during 1943–1945, which deal critically and objectively with many of the issues raised in the novel, especially that of the causes of crime and its elimination (see Paton 1943a–c; 1944a–c; 1945a–c). These pieces propounded the basic message, as one of their titles suggests, that the "real way to cure crime" was for society to "reform itself"; in particular, a society should provide its members with a sense that they were "socially significant" because "to mean something in the world is the deepest hunger of the human soul" (1944a, 24). Another article, entitled "Who is Really to Blame for the Crime Wave in South Africa?" (1945c, 7–8), is in fact obliquely referred to in *Cry, the Beloved Country* through the title of one of Arthur Jarvis's speeches (Paton 1988a, 72). In this article, Paton sets out to offer an explicitly liberal alternative to the prevailing official view, embodied, for instance, in the 1943 committee under S. H. Elliott, chief magistrate of Johannesburg, which with gross insensitivity recommended simplistically that the way to combat the increase in crime was merely through stricter enforcement of the pass laws (see Davenport 1987, 340). Paton, in contrast, warns that the causes of the crime wave are to be found not simply in the fact of the rapid urbanisation of the post-war period—though this is certainly relevant. Rather, he asserts that the more important underlying cause is the alarming disintegration of traditional African society under pressure of the impact of Western social and economic forces. This decay in the moral and spiritual support structure of African society, both in the tribal reserves and in the cities, which had for some time been gradually worsening, had now reached crisis proportions and required urgent attention. Typically, though, Paton is not content to suggest a solution merely along abstract economic lines. Instead, he maintains (1945c, 8) that ultimately "moral and spiritual decay can be stopped only by moral and spiritual means," and that social regeneration can only occur if the conditions are created where morality and social responsibility can flourish: "men obey the laws when they are pursuing worthy goals, working for some good purpose, making the most of their seventy years, using their gifts." He makes the further telling point that the real reason why white society denies blacks opportunities to develop these gifts is out of blind, irrational "fear," a fear which obscures the causal connection between African social frustration and its criminal consequences (see also especially Paton 1943b, 1944a, 1945a).

Clearly, then, the details of the "social record" which emerge in *Cry, the Beloved Country* derive not from unsubstantiated imaginative fancy but from direct personal experience and authentic knowledge of social conditions. It is these details with which Paton confronts the reader in the first movement of the novel, through his presentation of the parallel experiences of Stephen Kumalo and James Jarvis as they are forced to recognise and to understand the nature and the full extent of their society's problems for the first time in their lives.

To begin with Stephen Kumalo, the initial circumstances which set off the dramatic conflict correspond closely to the situation described in Paton's *Forum* article discussed above (1945c). Kumalo, a humble village parson in Ndotsheni in rural Natal, is compelled into a journey to Johannesburg to try to find three missing members of his family and re-unite the family structure. The attempt ends in failure, however. His sister, Gertrude, has become a loose and dissolute woman, who, after briefly repenting, finally disappears. His brother, John, is a corrupt, self-serving politician, who wants nothing to do with Ndotsheni. And, worst of all, his son, Absalom, has become caught up in criminal activities and is, by the time Stephen finds him, the confessed murderer of Arthur Jarvis. Stephen's quest does, nevertheless, serve an important purpose in that it forces him into a greater understanding of himself and his society. He has simply never been fully confronted by the fundamental problems of his society at large and has no experience of how to deal with them. He now embarks not merely on a physical journey but also on a spiritual journey of discovery and learning. In an important sense, Paton positions his readers so that they share the journey and experience, with Kumalo, the often brutal nature of their own society, something of which they too may well have been ignorant.

In Johannesburg, then, Kumalo is brought face to face with the poverty and squalor of the townships; he is appalled by the descent into crime, wrongdoing and corruption of so many people, including his own relatives; he is confronted everywhere in the city by the fact of white oppression, racial inequality and injustice; and he is horrified by the infrastructural inadequacies of African life in the city as a whole. These realities are given immediate expression in the first of three choral chapters in the novel, where the voices of the townships clash and mingle to speak directly of the crushing misery and frustration suffered by thousands of black South Africans daily. This chapter (chapter 9) serves the purpose both of widening the perspective of the novel beyond that of Kumalo alone to include the society in general, as well as of providing a form of external confirmation of Kumalo's alarmed personal response to what he sees.

What Kumalo comes fundamentally to understand is that the root cause of this degradation and corruption lies in the disintegration of traditional African society. Furthermore, Kumalo's failure to re-unite his family and restore the traditional kinship structure suggests, metonymically, the impossibility of restoring the former tribal system generally. It is Msimangu, Kumalo's physical and intellectual guide in Johannesburg, who makes the point explicitly and draws the relevant conclusion:

> The tragedy is not that things are broken. The tragedy is that they are not mended again. The white man has broken the tribe. And it is my belief—and again I ask your pardon—that it cannot be mended again. But the house that is broken, and the man that falls apart when the house is broken, these are the tragic things. That is why the children break the law, and old white people are robbed and beaten. (25)

Kumalo does eventually accept the validity of Msimangu's assertion and he begins to recognise that this reality is as relevant to Africans living in the rural areas as it is to those in the cities, his words echoing the narratorial description of the rural waste scene of the opening pages of the novel:

> The tribe was broken and would be mended no more. The tribe that had nurtured him, and his father and his father's father, was broken. For the men were away, and the young men and the girls were away, and the maize hardly reached to the height of a man. (79)

However, even in this moment of dark despair, there is already forming in his mind an incipient thought about the possibility of a way forward in restoration:

> He turned with relief to the thought of rebuilding.... After seeing Johannesburg he would return with a deeper understanding to Ndotsheni.... One could go back knowing better the kind of thing that one must build. He would go back with a new and quickened interest in the school, not as a place where children learned to read

and write and count only, but as a place where they must be prepared
for life in any place to which they might go. Oh for education for his
people, for schools up and down the land, where something might
be built that would serve them when they went away to the towns,
something that would take the place of the tribal law and custom.
For a moment he was caught up in a vision.... (79)

Thus, already present at this point in the novel—barely a third of the
way through—is the implicit faith in the potential for the regeneration of
society. Indeed, it is part of the general ethos of the book that even though the
world might seem to be pervaded by evil and destruction there still remain
many sources of goodness and generosity, and so it is possible for there to be,
at least potentially, in the words of the novel's sub-title, "comfort in desolation." Even in his bleakest moments, Kumalo is comforted and sustained by
Msimangu and others, and finds succour in sources unimagined:

Who indeed knows the secret of the earthly pilgrimage? Who
indeed knows why there can be comfort in a world of desolation?
(56; see also 187 and 224)

The implication is that this principle applies with equal validity at the level
of the social and political. So, in one sense, the novel records the extent of
the problem:

Cry for the broken tribe, for the law and the custom that is gone.
Aye, and cry aloud for the man who is dead, for the woman and
children bereaved. Cry, the beloved country, these things are not
yet at an end. (66)

but it also suggests that there is enough humaneness and practical good-will
in the world for the beloved country to be regenerated as a just and racially
harmonious society. For example, although Kumalo is confronted continually by the injustice of a political system of white oppression, so too does
he meet several instances of white men who have dedicated themselves to
fighting that system and aiding the oppressed: the Afrikaner official at the
Reformatory; Father Vincent at the mission; Mr Carmichael, the lawyer
who takes Absalom's case pro deo; the white motorists who help the bus
boycotters; and, of course, Arthur Jarvis himself.

It is, in fact, clearly part of the novel's main purpose to make plain that
the large proportion of blame for the current disintegration of black society
in South Africa is to be laid squarely at the door of the whites, and so it is

in large measure their responsibility to make amends and help to construct a new, integrated and equitable social order. Msimangu, in affirming that the old tribal structure cannot be mended, makes this clear:

> It suited the white man to break the tribe, he continued gravely. But it has not suited him to build something in the place of what is broken. I have pondered this for many hours and must speak it, for it is the truth for me. They are not all so. There are some white men who give their lives to build up what is broken. But they are not enough, he said. They are afraid, that is the truth. It is fear that rules this land. . . . They give us too little, said Msimangu sombrely. They give us almost nothing. (25–26)

Msimangu's speech raises two vital issues in the novel: the responsibility of whites to participate actively in the restoration of society; and the pervasive fear which militates against their doing so. If the chorus of African voices in chapter 9 serves to confirm the extensiveness of the frustration and hardship suffered by black South Africans, then the corresponding chorus of white voices in chapter 12 emphasises the ubiquitous fear and confusion in white society generally:

> Have no doubt it is fear in the land. For what can men do when so many have grown lawless? Who can enjoy the lovely land, who can enjoy the seventy years, and the sun that pours down on the earth, when there is fear in the heart? . . . There are voices crying what must be done, a hundred, a thousand voices. But what do they help if one seeks for counsel, for one cries this, and one cries that, and another cries something that is neither this nor that. (67–68)

Paton's response is to provide a portrait of one white man who does manage to move beyond his own prejudices and fears towards a greater understanding not only of the fundamental problems of his country, but also of the urgent necessity of attempting to solve them.

Like Stephen Kumalo, James Jarvis is a basically decent man living a sedentary farmer's life in the Natal hills. His quiet, comfortable world is shattered, however, by the news of his son's murder in his home in Parkwold, Johannesburg. As a result, he is led, again like Kumalo, on a quest to Johannesburg for his son, which becomes a voyage of discovery and learning about himself and his society. Although his son is already dead when he begins his journey, his search is to understand his son, through his writings and achievements, as he had never done when he was alive.

Jarvis readily admits that "my son and I didn't see eye to eye on the native question" (119), but he is led into a re-appraisal of his son's views and devotion to the cause of racial justice partly as a result of his son's writings which he encounters in Johannesburg and partly because of his realisation of the extent of his son's reputation and accomplishments. His son's brother-in-law and friend, John Harrison, pays tribute to his standing in the community, and this is confirmed by the extensive media coverage and the many and diverse sympathy notes which follow his death, but most especially by the numerous guests of all creeds and colours who attend his funeral. As a result, in a way reminiscent of Paton's "deep experience" at Edith Rheinallt-Jones's funeral, Jarvis undergoes his own spiritual and political enlightenment and comes to question and eventually reject his previously held conventional and conservative views.

Jarvis finds his own attitudes challenged and changed to a large extent by reading his son's articles and essays. His son's study itself, where he does the reading, with its pictures of Christ and Abraham Lincoln and its great variety of books, gives an initial impression of the quality of his son's character—broad-minded, tolerant, enlightened, compassionate and deeply concerned about his fellow man—an impression which is substantiated by his son's writing. Jarvis reads three pieces, in particular, which affect him profoundly. The first, a fragment which he finds on the desk, deals with the very same issue of the broken tribe that Msimangu had broached earlier. In essence, Arthur's piece focuses on the way in which the whites who came to South Africa conquered the black peoples, and then proceeded to exploit them both politically and economically. It distinguishes carefully between what is "permissible" and what is not, or between what was once considered permissible but which is no longer "in the light of what we know":

> It was permissible to allow the destruction of a tribal system that impeded the growth of the country. It was permissible to believe that its destruction was inevitable. But it was not permissible to watch its destruction, and to replace it by nothing, or by so little, that a whole people deteriorates, physically and morally. (126–127)

Like Msimangu, Arthur concludes that whites have "an inescapable duty" (127) to make appropriate reparation for the harm they have wrought on African society. Indeed, this commonality of concern between Arthur Jarvis and Msimangu is not an insignificant point. For if the ineluctable interconnectedness of the white and black communities in the novel is affirmed in a negative way by the fact that Kumalo's son kills Jarvis's son, then the similarity of Arthur's and Msimangu's views suggests in a positive manner the actual common ground that exists between the two communities as well as the potential for eventually establishing a fully integrated, common society in South Africa.

The second article, entitled, "The Truth About Native Crime" (119), embodies once more many of the arguments which Paton himself advanced in his *Forum* articles of 1943–1945 discussed earlier. In it, Arthur Jarvis highlights the fact that crime is frequently a result of African social frustration which in turn arises out of the hypocrisies and prejudices of a white community which refuses to allow blacks the opportunities to better themselves and achieve advancement. He goes on, in some of the last words he wrote, for he was busy with this manuscript when he was killed, to expose the mendacity of so-called white South African Christian society in so far as it condones, even by its silence on the matter, the practice of racial discrimination:

> The truth is that our civilisation is not Christian; it is a tragic compound of great ideal and fearful practice, of high assurance and desperate anxiety, of loving charity and fearful clutching of possessions. (134)

"Deeply moved," James Jarvis begins to comprehend the validity of his son's argument, and to move towards the adoption of his son's views and attitudes.

The final turning point occurs when he reads the third piece, "Private Essay on the Evolution of a South African," which it was noted earlier Paton felt was directly applicable to himself. James Jarvis is at first "shocked and hurt" (150) to read his son's comment that although he had learned from his parents the values of "honour and charity and generosity," he had learned "nothing at all" about South Africa (150). But, having recovered, he reads on and recognises the truth of what his son has written, and that it is he, indeed, who must "learn" about South Africa from his son. In particular, he is "moved" by the closing paragraphs, which include Arthur's dedication to the cause of justice and truth in his country:

> Therefore I shall devote myself, my time, my energy, my talents, to the service of South Africa. I shall no longer ask myself if this or that is expedient, but only if it is right. (151)

Jarvis walks out of the house into what he now realises has been "a strange country" to him, determined that "he was not going that way any more" (152). The implication is that his conversion is complete and that he has decided to take up and pursue, in his own limited way, his son's goals. As such, he finds guidance through reading one of his son's heroes, Abraham Lincoln; in particular, Lincoln's famous Gettysburg Address, a speech mentioned though not actually quoted in the novel (127):

> It is rather for us to be here dedicated to the great task remaining before us—that from these honored dead we take increased devotion to that cause for which they gave the last full measure of devotion; that we here highly resolve that these dead shall not have died in vain . . .

Significantly, before Jarvis leaves to return to Natal, two incidents occur which reveal how his attitudes have changed. In the first, he coincidentally encounters Stephen Kumalo himself at Springs, where he had gone with his wife to visit her niece, Barbara Smith. Kumalo in turn is there to look for Sibeko's daughter as he has promised to do. Kumalo, in great distress, reveals to Jarvis that it was his own son who murdered Jarvis's son. Despite his shock, Jarvis treats the old man with kindness, unlike Smith's daughter, and the mutual respect shown by the two bereaved men foreshadows their closer contact later on. In the second incident, Jarvis gives John Harrison an envelope containing one thousand pounds for the Claremont African Boys' Club, whose letter to Arthur, their president, Jarvis had come across in his son's study. He expresses the hope that the club might be renamed the "Arthur Jarvis Club," though he does not make this a condition of his donation.

These incidents immediately and directly raise the issue of what sorts of solutions the novel proposes to the problems which it has identified. In particular, it is necessary to consider to what extent these solutions, which are presented from a specifically liberal perspective, constitute a valid, practical and adequate response to the socio-political circumstances described by the novel in South Africa at the time.

III

In addressing the question of the nature and form of the solutions which are advanced in *Cry, the Beloved Country*, it is useful to begin by considering some of the various criticisms levelled against this aspect of the novel. Most of the criticism directed against *Cry, the Beloved Country* is of two kinds: in the first place, the novel is accused of embodying a paternalistic attitude towards Africans; in the second, it is condemned for its political naïveté and the ideological inadequacy of its vision for the practical transformation of South African society.

The tone for the first form of criticism—that of paternalism—is set by an anonymous writer for the *Times Literary Supplement* in an article called "South African Conflicts" which formed part of a "Special Insert" on "Modern Literature" (1957, xxxvi). After disparaging liberal politics in South Africa in general, the writer goes on to assert that, because the political situation has changed so much since *Cry, the Beloved Country* was published in 1948, the novel has come to be "regarded by many who would have praised it then as an old-fashioned, paternalistic book, which portrays Africans in a sentimental and unrealistic light." This line of attack is picked up by Ezekiel Mphahlele in *The African Image* (1962) and developed in some detail by Paul Rich (1985), who argues that the novel is in essence a nostalgic pastoral romance with little sense of historical reality, and he claims that

> the novel completely bypasses the emerging black culture of the townships and slums of the Witwatersrand, which are seen only through the deadening lens of Paton's paternalistic moralism that had been fortified by his experiences as Warden of the Diepkloof Reformatory for "delinquent" African boys outside Johannesburg. (1985, 56)

The give-away phrase in this quotation is "delinquent," placed in emphatic inverted commas in an attempt to imply that Paton himself patronisingly regarded his charges as "delinquents." Such an attempt reveals that Rich is either alarmingly unfamiliar with Paton's attitudes and work at Diepkloof (Paton deliberately replaced the title "Warden" with "Principal," and strove to transform the institution from a corrective to an educative one) or he is deliberately distorting the facts to bolster his critique. Similar strictures could be levelled against the *Times Literary Supplement* writer, who seems quite mistaken in stating that Paton knew little of the "African struggle" before writing *Cry, the Beloved Country* and only become familiar with South African politics much later (1957, xxxvi); as well as against Mphahlele (1962, 157), who makes several disturbingly inaccurate assertions such as that Stephen Kumalo in the novel "remains the same suffering, child-like character from beginning to end" when the novel is clearly concerned with his maturation and development. Nevertheless, despite the evident limitations of many of these critiques of *Cry, the Beloved Country*, the charge of paternalism against the novel continues to be made, and so it will be addressed shortly.

The second line of criticism has centred around the view that Paton's liberal outlook is jejune and inefficacious in dealing practically with South Africa's real social problems. Once more, a good deal of such criticism often seems unjust and inaccurate. Mphahlele (1962, 159–160), again, for example, seems very far from the mark when he claims that

> because the message keeps imposing itself on us in *Cry, the Beloved Country*, we cannot but feel how thickly laid on the writer's liberalism is: let the boys be kept busy by means of club activities and they will be less inclined to delinquency; work for a change of heart in the white ruling class (Jarvis's final philanthropic gesture and his son's practical interest in club activities together with his plea to South Africa indicate this).

Nevertheless, Mphahlele is quoted approvingly by Stephen Watson (1982)—before he resiled from a Marxist orientation—who goes on to maintain (1982, 35) that Paton in *Cry, the Beloved Country*

> advances the solution of love. . . . Of course, this is useless; the problem has not been caused by a lack of love in South Africa and therefore to prescribe an antidote of love for it is simply naïve and beside the point.

Watson alleges, moreover, that Paton appears unaware that the social problems in the novel "are quite explicable in terms of the man-made reality and historical conditions in South Africa in the first half of the century" (1982, 33), and therefore he is quite wrong to be "preaching for a revolution of hearts . . . rather than for a revolution in social and economic structure" (1982, 37). This argument represents one of the classic Marxist critiques of liberal texts, namely that their understanding of political and economic realities is deficient and that their proposed solutions in terms of "personal love" (Watson 1982, 44) are inadequate. It should be clear from our foregoing discussion of Paton's background as a social analyst and reformer that Watson's aspersions on his experience and understanding are unfounded. Similarly, Watson's assertion that Paton's proposals for social transformation may be reduced to a plea for increased personal love reveals that Watson has failed to comprehend what the term, "love," means in the context of the novel. Nonetheless, the charge of political naïveté against a liberal writer like Paton is a grave one, however clumsily it is presented, and it will be treated seriously in the following discussion.

Edward Callan (1982, 38) has pithily labelled Book Three of *Cry, the Beloved Country* "the Book of Restoration," and there does indeed seem to be in it a shift in tone and mood, as well as in content, beyond an unsettling portrayal of social distress towards a vision of restorative possibilities for the beloved country. Far from being paternalistic and/or naïve, however, this section of the novel offers a variety of valuable, feasible and acceptable short- and long-term solutions to many of the problems which have been identified earlier, as well as providing informed theoretical debate about some of the most difficult dilemmas of the time. These proposed solutions may, in fact, be sub-divided into at least four different levels at which they operate: the level of basic material resources; the physical restoration of the land; the spiritual; and the political. Each of these will be discussed in turn, though naturally, as will be seen, a certain degree of overlap exists between them.

Firstly, in what has often been misrepresented by antagonistic critics as a series of empty paternalistic gestures, Jarvis provides help in the form of resources at a basic material level. As has already been noted, he donates one thousand pounds to the Claremont Boys Club, a huge sum of money in those days, and by no means an exiguous portion of his reserves. Back in Natal, he provides milk to the black schoolchildren of Ndotsheni when he learns of their shortage from his grandson. And he supplies the materials to repair Kumalo's leaky church, whose dilapidation he notices during his visit there. It is important to see that these actions are not designed as terminal solutions, but as short-term measures to meet urgent needs. Jarvis does not perform them in a patronising manner, or out of a desire to establish himself in a position of control over the people, or out of some misplaced sense of guilt. On the contrary, he acts from a wish to lend real practical assistance where it is manifestly necessary; in the spirit, one might say, of Archbishop Clayton, who was wont to suggest that, in times of difficulty about what to do, one should "do the next right thing" (in Paton 1973a, 140). As such, Jarvis's actions, coming from a man who had hitherto not even noticed the needs of the people around him, let alone addressed them, represents real moral progress.

This is not, in any event, the only kind of assistance which Jarvis provides. At a second level, he seeks to facilitate a more permanent and extensive upliftment of the people of Ndotsheni through the restoration of the land, which has become waste through poor farming methods as well as the drought. To help achieve this, he hires a young black agricultural demonstrator, Napoleon Letsisi, whose task it is to teach the people more modern and successful farming techniques, and thus to help them to help themselves. Jarvis's intention, therefore, is to empower the people to become agriculturally and financially autonomous and self-supporting rather than in any way dependent upon either his skills or his largesse. Once more, it is difficult to see in this case how charges of paternalism may be made against this aspect of the novel. Indeed, at the end of the book, Jarvis announces to Kumalo that he will be leaving his home in Natal to live in Johannesburg with his daughter and her children, thus symbolically giving up his "High Place" (the name of his farm), though he assures Kumalo of his continued support for the "work" in Ndotsheni. This complex issue of land ownership will be examined a little later, though it is worth noting at this point that it is one with which Paton is clearly concerned.

For Kumalo's part, he too has not been content to do nothing after his return from Johannesburg. Aware of at least the partial validity of his brother's dictum that "what God has not done for South Africa, man must do" (25), Kumalo seeks actively to effect some positive changes:

> Kumalo began to pray regularly in his church for the restoration of Ndotsheni. But he knew that was not enough. Somewhere down here upon the earth men must come together, think something, do something. (195)

However, his initiative proves at first a failure: his visits to the chief and the headmaster bear no fruit, because the chief is a mere figurehead with no insight and no real power, and the headmaster, though well-intentioned, is hopelessly out of touch with the everyday needs of the people, caught up as he is in education department bureaucracy and barren theorisations:

> The headmaster explained that the school was trying to relate the life of the child to the life of the community, and showed him circulars from the Department in Pietermaritzburg, all about these matters. He took Kumalo out into the blazing sun, and showed him the school gardens, but this was an academic lecture, for there was no water, and everything was dead. (198)

Nevertheless, despite Kumalo's failure to mobilise the leaders of the community into effective action, the novel suggests that through his and Jarvis's combined actions—a white man and a black man coming together and thinking and acting in concert—the land may at least partly be restored, an idea symbolically emphasised by the fact that the drought breaks when they commune together in Kumalo's church (208–209). It is efforts such as these, it is implied, that will help the present "waste land" (188) to be revitalised as "Africa, the beloved country" (189) once more.

The clear allusion to T. S. Eliot's poem, *The Waste Land*, in which the moral and spiritual decay of early twentieth-century Europe is laid bare, suggests that Paton is not concerned only with the physical and material regeneration of South Africa. And, indeed, the third level at which the possibility of restoration is explored is the spiritual. Paton remained a deeply committed Christian all his life, and his vision in this novel of the restoration of the land and its people is suffused by his Christian belief in a God who is not merely transcendent but coterminously immanent in the world and involved in human life. It is not only individual souls, but also the fate of society as a whole, of Africa, which rests in a fundamental sense in the hands of God, as expressed in the anthemic prayer, "Nkosi Sikelel' iAfrika: God save Africa" (191). As such, the Christian message which Paton propounds in the novel is one which resonates at both the individual and the social level.

The novel ends, for instance, with the profoundly religious experience of Stephen Kumalo, his faith restored after his bleak moments of near total despair in Johannesburg, going up the mountain to endure a vigil in which he shares the agony of his son's last night before execution. Like the biblical King David, who also lost his beloved but aberrant son, Absalom, and like the first Christian martyr, Stephen, after whom he is named, Kumalo must confront real pain and suffering. But he has by this stage learned the great Christian lesson that "kindness and love can pay for pain and suffering" (193) and that Christ's divine suffering and love can provide the ultimate "comfort in such desolation" (187). Finally, just before the awful moment, he breaks bread and drinks tea in a private mass recalling Christ's sacrificial redemption of mankind. Significantly, as he stands facing the dawn, he sees that "the sun rose in the east" (236), suggesting not merely the beginning of a new day, but also, through the profound pun, the promise of resurrection and new life.

Episodes such as this suggest that God is truly present in human affairs and that the Christianity preached and practised in the novel is neither otherworldly nor uninvolved in history. At the very heart of the novel, in fact, is Msimangu's sermon at Ezenzeleni, a sermon concerned with both personal and social liberation. His text is taken from chapters 40 and 42 of the book of Isaiah, the beginning of what is known as Deutero-Isaiah or Second Isaiah, which prophesies the emancipation of the Israelites from Babylonian captivity, sustained by the power and love of God (see Bright 1980, 354f). As such, while the sermon certainly is meant to provide succour for personal suffering—such as physical blindness—it also affirms the efficacy of God's intervention in political history. In addition, much of the novel's implicit political value system seems to derive essentially from the fundamental principles of Christ's teaching. The Beatitudes (Matthew 5, 1–10), in particular, for example, are concerned not only with individual comforting and heavenly reward, but also, vitally, with such socio-political issues as peace-making, righteousness and justice on earth.

The Christian theme of *Cry, the Beloved Country* seems, therefore, to impinge directly upon the political, appropriately enough since, from Paton's perspective, the two were intimately connected. Throughout his career, in fact, Paton insisted on the crucial affinity between his liberal political ideals and his Christian beliefs. He has stated (1958b, 278), for instance, that: "Because I am a Christian I am a passionate believer in human freedom, and therefore, in human rights." He has also expanded (1958c, 11) on what he viewed as the Christian underpinnings of much liberal thought, with specific reference to the South African Liberal Party of which he was a founding member:

> Now although the Liberal Party is not a Christian organisation, its policies have a great deal in common with Christian ethics, and its philosophy has been influenced by Christian theology. I shall not apologise for writing something about these things. If one is a Christian, one believes that there is a spiritual order as well as a temporal, but one also believes that the values of the spiritual order—justice, love, mercy, truth—should be the supreme values of the temporal society, and that the good state will uphold and cherish them. Further one believes that the Church, while without temporal power, has the duty of championing these values in the temporal world.

This is not to suggest, of course, that Christianity and liberalism are inter-changeable or identical, but simply that for Paton certain cardinal values are shared by both. It may, therefore, be observed that much of the religious dimension *Cry, the Beloved Country* functions also as an extension or confirmation of the liberal ideas which are advanced in the novel as a whole.

While acknowledging the pervasiveness of the religious perspective in the novel, it is still viable to isolate a fourth level at which the text offers a sense of the possibility of restoration, namely, the political. This specifically political aspect is conveyed through both the words and the deeds of the various characters in the book. Most obviously, something very close to the liberal political views of Paton himself and other leading liberals of the day is expressed through the writings of Arthur Jarvis, which have already been discussed in some detail. These pieces provide a lucid and coherent outline of liberal political philosophy, based upon both moral grounds and intellectual conviction, and supply a clear course for positive practical action. If there is some objection to them, it may be that they are presented in somewhat too pat a fashion in the novel, rather than growing organically out of the plot structure. Nevertheless, the views expressed in these pieces are lent an urgent immediacy of context through the character, Msimangu, who acts as Kuma-lo's intellectual as well as physical guide in Johannesburg. It is he, as has been noted, who asserts that the tribe is broken beyond mending and who insists on the moral responsibility of whites to aid in the development of a new society. It is he also who speaks of the practicalities involved in a transition to a new society where political power will be shared between black and white. Just as Msimangu is scrupulously honest in holding whites largely culpable for the present social and political problems in the country, so he is candid in warning of the dangers inherent in a sudden acquisition of power by the oppressed. Such power, he feels, may very likely become "corrupted" through pride or greed or desire for revenge, and so it is crucial that this power be informed by love:

> But there is only one thing that has power completely, and that is love. Because when a man loves he seeks no power, and therefore he has power. I see only one hope for this country, and that is when white men and black men, desiring neither power nor money, but desiring only the good of their country, come together to work for it. (37)

And he goes on to observe, sombrely and gravely:

> I have one great fear in my heart, that one day when they are turned to loving, they will find we are turned to hating. (38)

It is this speech of Msimangu's, which is repeated at the end of the novel, that has particularly led to the novel's condemnation by critics like Stephen Watson (1982) for offering a solution based on love rather than hard political theory. Yet it is, in fact, a speech precisely about politics. What it is vital to understand is that by "love" as it is used here, Paton—via Msimangu—does not mean simply some vague notion of interpersonal goodwill. More properly, the term, "love," may be glossed here as the desire to create and live in a just society, and so the act of loving may be thought of as right political conduct which will help bring about a more equitable socio-political order where all persons can live as freely and fully as possible. It ought, in any event, to be clear from the political context of Msimangu's remarks that he visualises such love in terms of black and white South Africans actively and selflessly working together for "the good of their country" as a whole. This understanding of the political meaning of love lies at the centre of the liberal enterprise, which upholds the principle of social and political corrigibility and amelioration, and believes in the general will and desire of the majority of persons to live under a just system of government. The alternative to liberalism, especially in the politically volatile South African context, is one which Paton, like Msimangu, dreaded. In an article entitled, "On Turning 70," Paton (1973b; in Paton 1975, 258) offered a trenchant response to those who continued to sneer at proponents of a liberal solution to South Africa's problems:

But if Black power meets White power in headlong confrontation, and there are no Black liberals and White liberals around, then God help South Africa. Liberalism ... is humanity, tolerance, and love of justice. South Africa has no future without them.

In *Cry, the Beloved Country* itself, Paton is at pains to make clear that the mere verbalisation of liberal sentiments is not enough, and that these sentiments need to be accompanied by meaningful action at the level of the economic and political structures and conditions of society. Hence, it is important to see that characters like Arthur Jarvis and Msimangu do take active steps to change their society. Msimangu, as Tony Morphet (1983, 7) points out, "is exemplary in showing what to do," tirelessly striving to improve the welfare of his fellow South Africans and inspiring others, like Stephen Kumalo, to emulate his efforts. Similarly, Arthur Jarvis does not simply write articles and correspond with an African boys club, as Mphahlele (1962, 159–160) suggests, but is actively involved in numerous charitable and social organisations, from Toc H and the YMCA to the Society of Christians and Jews and various African social groups. Moreover, he has, as Mr Harrison rather disapprovingly observes, intervened directly in the socio-economic sphere, calling for "more Native schools," protesting "about the conditions at the non-European hospital," and insisting on "settled labour" on the mines (121). In so doing, he shows not only courage and compassion, but also a sound grasp of the social and economic roots of many of his country's problems, as well as an understanding of the basic need for racial equality in the fields of education and health care, and the elimination of unjust labour practices like the migrant worker system. Far from seeming naïve and uninformed, as Stephen Watson (1982, 35) avers, Paton, in *Cry, the Beloved Country*, reveals an ability to comprehend and address the fundamental problems of his country in a way which even from this vantage point in time appears remarkably perspicacious and illuminating.

What Paton refuses to condone in this novel, or anywhere else for that matter, is what Watson (1982, 37) calls social and political "revolution," to be brought about through the use of violence, if necessary. Throughout his life, Paton resisted any notion of violent revolution, not because he felt personally threatened by it, but because he believed that it would do more harm than good. In *South Africa and Her People* (1957, 151), for example, he asserts that revolution would not "solve any problems. It would in my opinion bring chaos, from which we would take generations to emerge." It is a tenet which he espoused constantly during the dark days of the sabotage trials of the young members of the Liberal Party who had secretly formed the African Resistance Movement in frustration at the intransigence of the Nationalist

Party government; writing of John Harris, the A.R.M. member who was convicted of murder for the Johannesburg Station bomb, Paton (1965, 2) states categorically:

> By temperament and principle I am opposed to the use of violence. By intellectual conviction I am opposed to its use in South Africa, believing that it will not achieve its declared purpose of making this country happier and better.

And in his assessment of Hendrik Verwoerd following the Prime Minister's assassination, Paton (1967; in Paton 1968, 269–270) again broaches this most difficult of all liberal dilemmas:

> Of course there are some South Africans who feel so deeply and disturbedly about the injustice of the status quo that they declare that violence is the only solution left, and they declare that a person like myself secretly wishes to preserve his own state of privilege, or is simply a coward. I can well understand these views, but I have no intellectual trust in them. If a situation seems unchangeable, there is no reason to believe that violence will change it. One draws back from the prospect of an unending history of murders and assassinations.

This is not to say that Paton, like many other liberal opponents of political injustice in South Africa, was never tempted by the idea of a radical solution to this country's ills. Even in *Cry, the Beloved Country*, there is a telling scene where Stephen Kumalo, playing with Gertrude's son, acts out a symbolic violent overthrow of the city and, by extension, the political system:

> So they brought out the blocks, and built tall buildings like the buildings in Johannesburg, and sent them toppling over to destruction with noise and laughter. (105–106)

But this anarchic impulse passes, for Paton's more considered view is that such violence is ultimately counter-productive and futile, and that there can be no viable alternative to a society founded on the rule of law and transformed, where necessary, only through non-violent means.

It is, perhaps, for this reason that Paton chooses to depict the potentially revolutionary John Kumalo in such a negative light. It is, of course, quite mistaken to think that Paton in this novel was critical or distrustful of black politicians in general. He clearly approves of Dubula and his wife, for example, especially since they strive, like Msimangu and Arthur Jarvis, to translate their beliefs into positive action. Indeed, Paton fully condones the bus boycott and the creation of Shanty Town as legitimate political action consonant with liberal principles of peaceful protest and passive resistance. John Kumalo, on the other hand, does nothing in the service of others and can offer the people little more than his "golden voice," which is disparagingly contrasted with Msimangu's "golden words."

Nevertheless, there remains a problem with Paton's portrayal of John Kumalo. As a number of critics have remarked, his depiction as a selfish coward and corrupt hypocrite detracts from the several valid points which he makes in conversation and in speeches. For instance, when Stephen Kumalo and Msimangu first visit him, he observes quite rightly that the "tribal society" is "breaking apart" and that a "new society is being built" (34), and he goes on to claim with some justification that the church, like the old chiefs, is doing little to facilitate this social renewal, while the people suffer (35). Even Msimangu is compelled to admit that "many of the things he said are true" (37). Furthermore, his speech to the mine workers seems eminently reasonable, merely calling for decent wages and proposing legitimate strike action, but by no means demanding "equality and the franchise and the removal of the colour-bar" (158–160), as, for example, the A.N.C. had in actuality recently done (see Robertson 1971, 31). As such, it is difficult to know what to make of the narrator's remark that Dubula and Tomlinson listen to his voice "with contempt, and with envy" (158), or of Msimangu's comment:

> Perhaps we should thank God he is corrupt. . . . For if he were not corrupt, he could plunge this country into bloodshed. (161)

because such statements inevitably serve to undermine the political validity of the speech itself. The difficulty is exacerbated by the fact that the gold mining industry in particular, and materialistic white society in general, have just been excoriated in the third of the choral chapters in the novel, that dealing with the gold rush at Odendaalsrust (145–149).

In fact, the problem is further compounded by Msimangu's strange decision to retire into a religious community where he "would forswear the world and all its possessions" (183), since this seems precisely to remove him from the sphere of practical action and influence which Paton has been highlighting in the novel. It would appear, moreover, to substantiate the views of Msimangu's unnamed critics in the novel who, following Marx's axiom that religion is the opium of the people, despise Msimangu for preaching "of a world not made by hands. . . . making the hungry patient, the suffering content, the dying at peace," and for sending the people "marching to heaven instead of to Pretoria" (82–83).

These elements in the novel are genuinely problematic, and nothing is to be gained from trying to ignore them or wish them away. Perhaps they ought to be viewed as indicative of a real tension in Paton's thinking at that time between his desire for urgent, fundamental change in his society and his apprehension that too rapid or extreme a process of change could prove destructive rather than regenerative, and bring with it widespread social suffering and misery. It must be recognised, for example, as Robertson (1971, 28–39) points out, that many black nationalistic demands of the 1940s, which seem quite moderate from today's perspective, would have been rejected as unthinkably radical and revolutionary at the time by almost all whites as well as by many blacks. To have tried to implement such demands too quickly would thus have inevitably resulted in violent conflict and repression rather than constructive social amelioration. Paton's awareness of this dilemma may be deduced from some of the emendations he made to the original manuscript, such as the downplaying of the mine workers' strike (Oppenheimer collection, Brenthurst Library, Johannesburg). Whatever the source of the problem, it ought not to be allowed to deflect attention away from the central thrust of the novel, namely, that the country must be restored, and that this restoration should take place at a number of different levels.

In fact, Paton's awareness of the difficulties involved in the regeneration of his society is again underlined when he raises a further thorny problem by linking the literal, agricultural restoration of the land with the political question of land ownership. Paton successfully weaves the issue into the story through the character of the young, politically conscious agricultural demonstrator, Napoleon Letsisi, who is hired by James Jarvis to teach the Ndotsheni community more modern farming methods. In response to Kumalo's praise of Jarvis, Letsisi remarks,

> Umfundisi, it was the white man who gave us so little land, it was the white man who took us away from the land to go to work. And we were ignorant also. It is all these things together that have made this valley desolate. Therefore, what this good white man does is only a repayment. (228)

This deeply problematic question of second-generation rights and the redistribution of the wealth is clearly too much for the old man, however, and, indeed, it is not brought to any definite resolution in the novel. For instance, though James Jarvis is to leave his farm to live in Johannesburg, Paton stops short of suggesting that farmers like Jarvis should relinquish their land, or that they should be encouraged to sell off part of their farms in order to equalise land ownership. This tension between property rights and economic equality remains a problem to this day, however (see Simkins 1986), and Paton could hardly have been expected to resolve it in *Cry, the Beloved Country*. It is to his credit, in fact, that he presents the issue in all its difficulty, and that he refuses to offer any glib or facile proposals for its solution.

It could well be argued that one of the distinctively liberal features of the novel is its willingness to confront complex problems and to present a variety of competing viewpoints on the subject rather than a rigid, monolithic ideological perspective. In this novel, as opposed to the typical social realist text, one encounters what a critic like Edward Callan (1982, 35) has called "a multitude of voices":

> South African voices talking incessantly about problems—problems of race, problems of language, and problems of separate living space.

As Callan (33) points out, one of the great advantages of this multifaceted perspective is that it provides both an understanding of individual experiences as well as an "overall point of view" on South Africa "and the struggles of its diverse peoples as a whole": it is

> a dramatic manifestation of the agony of a country in which the spirit of South Africa hovers always on stage and dominates the human actors.

A similar argument has recently been advanced by the Italian critic, Armando Pajalich (1992, 223), who has described the novel's narrative mode as "dialogic," in that it is made up essentially of a continuous dialogue between a variety of voices in conflict. Although he suggests (1992, 227–228) that Paton does not express a truly comprehensive spectrum of black opinion, he maintains, like Callan, that the novel derives several major benefits from its "polyphonicity" (his term for a "multitude of voices"). In particular, he believes that this sophisticated narrative strategy permits a variety of problems to be confronted "objectively and dialectically," while avoiding the inevitably simplistic bias of "a definite or univocal closure."

This readiness to express divergent ideas, and this refusal to offer facile utopian solutions to complex problems, represents some of the greatest strengths of liberalism, and may well help to explain the remarkable success of the novel. Far from descending into crude propaganda or arid theorisation, the novel manages to expose and explore some of the central social concerns of South Africa in a way which is moving, honest and enlightening. Moreover, while it remains deeply aware of the intensity and extent of the problems it identifies, it retains a sense of hope, however tentative, for the future, based not upon naïve idealism, but upon a fundamental belief in the power of humankind's innate desire for freedom and justice to prevail.

In *Cry, the Beloved Country*, Paton reveals himself to be keenly aware of the complex debates going on about South Africa's social, political and economic problems. As a liberal, however, he is interested not merely in general social theory but also in the individuals who make up the society. As such, his principal concern in the novel is to explore how these problems and their possible resolution are experienced at the level of the individual, of ordinary human beings. This he does especially through the characters of Stephen Kumalo and James Jarvis.

At the beginning of the novel, Stephen Kumalo and James Jarvis, though technically neighbours, live in totally different worlds, each utterly ignorant of the other. For example, Kumalo reveals to Father Vincent that he knows of Jarvis "by sight and name," but has never spoken to him (65); and Jarvis, in conversation with Mr Harrison, vaguely remembers the mission at Ndotsheni and its old parson, but can recall little about them (123). By the end of the novel, however, the two men have grown significantly closer together, and have established meaningful human contact, if only briefly and haltingly. Paton traces the gradual but steady development of their relationship through a number of carefully depicted incidents. Their first actual meeting, as noted earlier, occurs by chance at Springs, but the mutual respect they reveal to each other then lays the foundation for their future association. Their next meeting takes place during Jarvis's efforts to aid the Ndotsheni community, when, in a scene heavy with significance, they shelter from the drought-breaking rain in the local church. Later still, their communication continues through the wreath for Mrs Jarvis and the sympathy note which Kumalo organises and sends from Ndotsheni; and through Jarvis's letter of thanks, which, incidentally, convinces the bishop to allow Kumalo to stay on in Ndotsheni.

Finally, they meet fortuitously at the end of the story as Kumalo is on his way to his vigil for his son, and this last encounter provides some measure of how far the two men have come in their relationship (231–232). This meeting occurs in solitude and, as it were, on common ground—literally the mountain near the village but symbolically the holy mountain of Isaiah (11, 6–9) where "the wolf shall lie down with the lamb":

> They shall not hurt or destroy
> in all my holy mountain;

for the earth shall be full of the
  knowledge of the Lord
as the waters cover the sea.

The symbol of the holy mountain held great significance for Paton, and recurs throughout his work, most notably in the title of his first volume of autobiography. In one sense, it represents the teleological hope of the Judaeo-Christian tradition, but in another, Paton uses it to suggest the ideal of a just society, particularly in the South African context (see Paton 1975, 288, for example). Thus, the setting of this final meeting between Kumalo and Jarvis is not accidental but carefully chosen to betoken the possibility of the real and meaningful reconciliation of the races in South Africa. Paton is particular, however, to avoid rendering the scene implausible, and so the white man remains mounted while the black man stands on foot and there is no physical contact for "such a thing is not lightly done" (232). Nevertheless, despite the gathering darkness, the two men find the words to thank each other for their kindness and to console each other for their loss, and, in so doing, to confirm the potential for true human interaction that they have established. Such potential is reinforced by the fact of the generations coming after them: Jarvis's "bright" young grandson who has clearly inherited some of his father's best qualities; Kumalo's promising young nephew and daughter-in-law; and the child about to be born to take the place of the father who is about to die.

These details are clearly meant to provide some of the "comfort in desolation" that has been proposed in the narrative. However, while Paton seems adamant in this novel that there is, indeed, "hope for South Africa" (see Paton 1958), he is also at pains to emphasise that it is by no means certain how or when that hope will be actualised. Hence, in the last pages of the novel, the pervasive theme of fear is repeated, particularly Msimangu's great fear that when the whites finally turn to loving, they will find the blacks responding only with vengeful hatred. The famous final paragraph captures the complex mood of the novel perfectly:

But when that dawn will come, of our emancipation, from the fear
of bondage and the bondage of fear, why, that is a secret. (236)

The implication is that just as the literal dawn comes at the end of the book, so this political dawn must, of necessity, occur, even though it is difficult to predict precisely when this might be. As such, the novel may be said to end on a clear, if restrained, note of expectancy, a sentiment which seemed, perhaps, quite justified in 1946. After all, South Africa seemed to be on the verge of a political liberalisation. South African servicemen had recently returned from victory over the forces of Nazism and Fascism, and had been exposed to more enlightened international attitudes. Prime Minister Jan Smuts himself had composed the Preamble to the United Nations Charter, which had been ratified by the South African Parliament on 7 February 1946. And the liberal-minded Jan Hofmeyr seemed set to take over from Smuts as Prime Minister of the country. As it turned out, however, D. F. Malan's National Party won a shock election victory in May 1948, just a few months after the publication of *Cry, the Beloved Country*, and plunged the country into more than forty years of apartheid rule.

IV

The fact that the note of muted optimism sounded at the end of *Cry, the Beloved Country* proved to be unfounded, at least for many years, should not detract from the overall value and significance of the novel. Throughout the apartheid period, *Cry, the Beloved Country* represented a source of humane political principles and served as a powerfully influential document of social protest in South Africa. Although it is true that several novels up to that time had dealt with what was rather loosely referred to as "the native question"— most notably William Plomer's *Turbott Wolfe* (1925) and Peter Abrahams's *Mine Boy* (1946)—none had done so in as comprehensive, insightful and moving a fashion. Christopher Hope (1985, 41) has rightly termed *Cry, the Beloved Country* "the great exemplar" of protest novels in South Africa, of "powerful works which lay bare the evil of apartheid." Jack Cope (1970, 13), moreover, has claimed that *Cry, the Beloved Country* ushered in "a new period" in South Africa's literary history and that "with this book, South African fiction really came into its own," not least of all because "there is a new awareness in it of the man on the other side of the barbed wire, a true fellow-feeling between white and black as we had never had before."

Following the demise of apartheid, the popularity and influence of *Cry, the Beloved Country* and Paton's work in general has, if anything, increased. A new film version of *Cry, the Beloved Country*, directed by Darryl Roodt, was released in 1995; his short stories and autobiographical account of Diepkloof were turned into a television series by Roy Sergeant in 1997; his collected poems were published under the title *Songs of Africa* in 1995; Peter Alexander wrote his biography, *Alan Paton*, in 1994; and increasing numbers of theses and articles appear each year. There are several reasons for the continued interest in Paton and especially his first great novel. The most obvious is that *Cry, the Beloved Country* is a fine work of art, in which vital social and political issues emerge organically and coherently from vivid, moving details of plot and characterisation. Another is that many of the problems and debates raised in the novel persist in the South Africa of today as the country struggles to throw off the injustices of the past and to normalise itself. Problems such as unemployment, poverty, insufficient housing, inadequate educational opportunities, as well as, most evidently, the unacceptably high crime rate, remain crucially pertinent. In fact, reading the novel today inspires the uncanny feeling that, in terms of its portrayal of social ills, it might have been written in 1998 rather than 1948.

The one great difference, of course, is that South Africa has managed to transform itself into a constitutional liberal democracy. Had Paton lived, he would no doubt have been deeply gratified that his vision of a just political dispensation had been achieved and that it had come about through peaceful negotiated means. On the other hand, he would also, no doubt, have spoken out against corruption and the seeming inability of the government to deal effectively with many of the social problems identified above. His wise counsel and insight are preserved, however, in his books, especially in *Cry, the Beloved Country*. Above all, the continuing relevance of the novel lies in the principles and values which underpin it: the courage to confront social problems honestly and openly; the resolve to take action to alleviate such problems; and a faith in the power of ordinary individuals to take responsibility for themselves and their communities in improving the quality of life. The example set by Stephen Kumalo and James Jarvis remains no less relevant and important today than it was half a century ago.

Works Cited

Abrahams, Peter. 1946. *Mine Boy*. London: Faber.

Alexander, Peter F. 1994. *Alan Paton: A Biography*. Oxford: OUP.

Anonymous. 1957. *Times Literary Supplement* No. 2894 Special Insert: A Sense of Direction: being an examination of the efforts of writers to keep or regain contact with the everyday realities of life in terms of modern literature ("South African Conflicts"). 16 August: xxxvi.

Bright, John. 1980. *A History of Israel* (3rd ed.). London: SCM.

Callan, Edward. 1968. *Alan Paton*. Boston: Twayne.

———. 1982. *Alan Paton* (revised edition). Boston: Twayne.

———. 1991. *Cry, the Beloved Country: A Novel of South Africa*. Boston: Twayne.

Cope, Jack. 1970. "A Turning Point in South African English Writing." *Crux* 4.4: 10–20.

Davenport, T. R. H. 1987. *South Africa: A Modern History* (3rd ed.). Johannesburg: Macmillan.

Hope, Christopher. 1985. "The Political Novelist in South Africa." *English in Africa* 12.1: 41–46.

Morphet, Tony. 1983. "Alan Paton: The Honour of Meditation." *English in Africa* 10.2: 1–10.

Mphahlele, Ezekiel. 1962. *The African Image*. London: Faber.

Pajalich, Armando. 1992. *Una Litteratura Africana Coloniale di Lingua Inglese*, excerpt from chapter 10, "Alan Paton e la Narrativa 'Liberal'," translated as: "Alan Paton and the 'Liberal' Narrative," by J. A. Kearney; personal communication.

Paton, Alan. 1943a. "Punishment and Crime: False Reasoning in Society's Attitude Towards the Offender." *The Forum* 6.25: 5, 6, 34.

———. 1943b. "Society Aims to Protect Itself: How Effective Is Severity of Punishment as a Deterrent Against Crime?" *The Forum* 6.29: 25–27.

———. 1943c. "Significance of Social Disapproval." *The Forum* 6.36: 25–27.

———. 1944a. "Real Way to Cure Crime: Our Society Must Reform Itself." *The Forum* 6.44: 24–26.

———. 1944b. "A Plan for Model Prisons." *The Forum* 6.52: 24–26.

———. 1944c. "Let's Build Model Prisons: Enlightened Reform Would Result in a Vast Saving in Human Material." *The Forum* 7.6: 5, 6, 24.

———. 1945a. "The Prevention of Crime." *Race Relations* (Special Crime Number) 12.3–4: 69–77.

———. 1945b. *The Non-European Offender* (Penal Reform Series No.2). Johannesburg: South African Institute of Race Relations.

———. 1945c. "Who Is Really to Blame for the Crime Wave in South Africa?" *The Forum* 8.37:7–8.

———. 1957. *South Africa and Her People*. London: Butterworth.

———. 1958a. *Hope for South Africa*. London: Pall Mall.

———. 1958b. "Church, State and Race." *Christian Century* 75.1: 248–249; 75.2: 278–280.

———. 1958c. "The Archbishop of Cape Town Views Apartheid." *Contact* 1.3:11.

———. 1961. "A Deep Experience." *Contrast* 1.4: 20–24.

———. 1965. "John Harris." *Contact* 8.4: 2.

———. 1967. "Dr. Hendrik Verwoerd: A Liberal Assessment." *Natal Daily News*.

———. *The Long View*. London: Pall Mall.

———. 1971. *Case History of a Pinky* (Topical Talks No.28). Johannesburg: South African Institute of Race Relations.

———. 1973a. *Apartheid and the Archbishop: The Life and Times of Geoffrey Clayton, Archbishop of Cape Town*. Cape Town: David Philip.

———. 1973b. "On Turning 70." *Sunday Tribune* 7 January.

———. 1975. *Knocking on the Door: Shorter Writings*. Ed. Colin Gardner. Cape Town: David Philip.

———. 1980. *Towards the Mountain: An Autobiography*. Cape Town: David Philip.

———. 1988a (1948). *Cry, the Beloved Country*. Harmondsworth: Penguin.

———. 1988b. *Journey Continued: An Autobiography*. Cape Town: David Philip.

———. 1995. *Songs of Africa: Collected Poems*. Comp. Anne Paton. Ed. Peter Kohler. Durban: Gecko Books.

Plomer, William. 1925. *Turbott Wolfe*. Johannesburg: Donker.

Rich, Paul. 1985. "Liberal Realism in South African Fiction 1948–1966." *English in Africa* 12.1: 45–81.

Robertson, Janet. 1971. *Liberalism in South Africa 1948–1963*. Oxford: Clarendon Press.

Roodt, Darryl (director). 1995. *Cry, the Beloved Country* (Film).

Sargeant, Roy (director). 1997. *The Principal*. SABC–TV.

Simkins, Charles. 1986. *Reconstructing South African Liberalism*. Johannesburg: South African Institute of Race Relations.

Watson, Stephen. 1982. "*Cry, the Beloved Country* and the Failure of Liberal Vision." *English in Africa* 9.1: 29–44.

HERMANN WITTENBERG

Alan Paton's Sublime: Race, Landscape and the Transcendence of the Liberal Imagination

In the analysis of South African writing, the concept of the sublime[1] has thus far played a limited role, reflecting a critical consensus that discourses of the sublime are more properly at home in the European eighteenth century and the Romantic movement. If the sublime appears at all in colonial writing, the argument goes, it takes the form of belated, derivative and degraded variants of metropolitan aesthetic models. Thus, according to J M Coetzee, the sublime emerges in a "late, tentative, and stunted way in South Africa" (1988:61). In *White Writing*, his classic study of the politics and poetics of the South African landscape, Coetzee investigates the complex question "as to why the sublime did not flourish in nineteenth-century South Africa" (1988:55) and argues that the picturesque rather than the sublime became a more dominant mode in colonial 'white writing'.

A closer look at some major texts in South African literature, informed by newer, radical theoretical interpretations of the sublime reveals, however, a different story. A re-reading of Alan Paton's *Cry, the Beloved Country* (first published in 1948), in what I think is an unexplored light, suggests that non-metropolitan discourses of the sublime, far from being an outmoded rhetoric, could manage and contain the contradictions inherent in the aesthetic appreciation and appropriation of contested colonial landscapes. Indeed, in the classical philosophical foundations laid by Edmund Burke and Immanuel

From *Current Writing* 17, no. 2 (2005): 3–23. © 2005 by *Current Writing*.

113

Kant, the sublime is founded on problematic assumptions of racial difference. Rereading colonial discourses of the sublime in the light of the racial underpinnings that inform Burke's and Kant's aesthetic theories and philosophies can allow us to develop insights into the dynamics of the simultaneous disavowal and foregrounding of race that is present in much of South Africa's colonial and postcolonial writing.

The current lack of critical interest in the manifestations of the colonial sublime is not surprising, given the unpopularity, generally, of aesthetic approaches to literature in the aftermath of the poststructuralist turn in criticism. In the last decade, however, the field of cultural theory has seen a resurgence of critical interest in aesthetics. Terry Eagleton's major revisionist study, *The Ideology of the Aesthetic* (1990), is only one of numerous radical interventions in a field which Berthold Brecht thought was supremely reactionary. Brecht's question "Shouldn't we abolish aesthetics?", deriving from his modernist and Marxist distrust of ideological realms above or beyond social realities, is an index of the discredit into which formal aesthetics had sunk (Regan 1992:3).

In recent criticism, there has been a shift from analysing the sublime as a type of rhetoric or model of text (Weiskel 1976) to seeing it as a model of the Enlightenment subject (De Bolla 1989) or as a model of ideology (Eagleton 1990). A cursory look at recent critical and theoretical writing shows that indeed aesthetics, and notably the sublime, has made a substantial comeback in a number of fields. Particularly in postmodernist and feminist theory, the sublime occupies an increasingly important role in contemporary cultural debate. Jean-François Lyotard's theoretical work, for instance, is a sustained engagement with Kant's *Critique of Judgement*, leading him to declare that the "sublime is perhaps the only mode of artistic sensibility to characterise the modern" (1993:247). In *Critical Aesthetics and Postmodernism* (1993) Paul Crowther pursues a similar, if more reductive, analysis aimed at demonstrating that the sublime, despite being intellectually "out of fashion" at present, is nevertheless a precursor of postmodern cultural modes. Similarly, in *Postmodern Sublime*, Joseph Tabbi decries the fact that mainstream literary theories afford "little room for the un-ironic, expansive gestures that are traditionally associated with the sublime" despite the fact that the sublime persists as "a powerful emotive force in postmodern writing, especially in American works that regard reality as something newly mediated, predominantly, by science and technology" (1995:ix).

Further interest in the sublime has been advanced by a number of feminist studies which have critiqued the sublime as positing a gendered model of the subject that occludes women and serves to establish a masculine epistemology. Indeed, all classical theories of the sublime, including those of Kant and Burke, rely on the fundamental opposition between the beautiful and the sublime, where these opposites correspond to female and male sensibilities. As Kant puts it, "the fair sex has just as much understanding, but it is a beautiful understanding, whereas ours should be a deep understanding, an expression that signifies identity with the sublime" (1991:78). In revisionist feminist studies, the sublime is not read as a purely aesthetic category nor merely as a rhetorical style, but is seen to function, more generally, as an ideological mode of domination, a gendered structure of power, in which a male subject asserts his rational supremacy over an excessive and unrepresentable experience, leading to a triumphantly enhanced sense of identity. As Barbara Freeman puts it, the sublime involves a sexually coded dominance of "male spectatorship" over "objects of rapture" (1995:3). Similarly for Jacqueline Labbe, the sublime involves the masculine "power of the eye and a proprietary relationship to the landscape" (1998:37).

"The ill effects of black" on the Imagination

While theories of the sublime have been used to re-examine phenomena as divergent as sadomasochism, tourism and hypermedia computer technology,[2] surprisingly little attention has been given to the sublime in postcolonial literary criticism and theory. Gayatri Spivak's close attention to Kant's theories of the sublime in the introductory chapter of *Critique of Postcolonial Reason* (1999) is a rare exception. Her analysis of the sublime is a launching pad for a broader deconstruction of the authoritative narratives of Western philosophy which are posited as "universal" but are at the same time "unmistakably European" (1999:8) as they occlude non-western people. Receptiveness to and delight in the sublime becomes, in Spivak's reading of Kant, the touchstone for this "universal", rational, educated European subject, whereas for the uneducated and uncultured man (Kant's "*rohen Menschen*") overwhelming and immense natural phenomena are merely terrible. Capacity for the sublime is thus a marker of civilization that distinguishes enlightened subjects from aesthetically less developed peoples. In Kant's philosophical project, Spivak concludes, the "subject as such is geopolitically differentiated" (1999:26–7) and the sublime is thus imbricated in the "axiomatics of imperialism" (1999:19).

Spivak does not however use these critical insights to move beyond Kant, to develop a deconstructive reading of Kant's "Analytic of the Sublime" (1951) into a theory for analysing how manifestations of the sublime have shaped discourses in the colonial and postcolonial arena. She appears to be more interested in the sublime as a highly specialised philosophical argument than as a discursive practice that has left its mark on colonial culture. Her argument hinges substantially on Kant's single throwaway remark about the "*rohen Menschen*" and ignores a wider body of writing on the sublime, such as the troubling racial disavowal in Burke's celebrated *Philosophical Enquiry into the Origin of Our Ideas of the Sublime and the Beautiful.*

In this treatise Burke famously defined the sublime as "delightful horror" (1757:52) and associated it repeatedly with chaos, blackness and abyssal immensity in which "all is dark, uncertain, confused, terrible, and sublime to the last degree" (1757:42). When it comes however to the darkness of black bodies (in Burke's example, a black woman seen by a previously blind child), feelings of sublimity are blocked by "the ill effects of black on his imagination" and give rise merely to "great horror" (1757:145). Blackness, when associated for example with the body of the native in a colonial context, emerges as the weak spot that short-circuits the aesthetic mechanism of the sublime. Burke describes the sublime more fully as follows:

> What ever is fitted in any sort to excite the ideas of pain, and danger, that is to say, whatever is in any sort terrible, or is conversant about terrible objects, or operates in a manner analogous to terror, is a source of the Sublime; that is, it is productive of the strongest emotion which the mind is capable of feeling. (1757:13)

He solves the philosophical problem of how "pain", "danger" and "terrible objects" can produce the exalted delights of sublime rapture, by arguing that pain and pleasure are not binary opposites; that the presence of pain does not automatically mean absence of pleasure and *vice versa*, but that both pain and pleasure are positive qualities, independent of one another: "Many people are of the opinion, that pain arises necessarily from the removal of pleasure; as they think pleasure does from the ceasing or diminution of some pain" (1757:3). The sublime arises when the subject is presented with the prospect of pain and danger (conventionally, a towering mountain or a powerful storm), yet in such a manner that there is no actual physical harm but only the thrilling proximity of peril:

> The passions which belong to self preservation, turn on pain and danger; they are simply painful when their causes immediately affect us; they are delightful when we have an idea of pain and danger, without actually being in such circumstances. . . . What excites this delight, I call Sublime. (1757:32)

This theory neatly presents the sublime as a mode of containing and managing the terror that arises out of the subject's experience of alterity. The delight of the sublime is however but a thin veneer that barely manages to contain the horror of difference and excess that always threatens to erupt out of the real; and as Burke's telling example of the black woman shows, the sublime fails in the face of racial difference and gives way to absolute terror. Burke's sublime, already an unstable and ambivalent category of feeling that seeks to represent and contain the unrepresentable, unravels in the face of blackness.

Spivak's omission of Kant's own earlier, politically much more revealing *Observations of the Feeling of the Beautiful and Sublime* (first published in 1764), is even more surprising than her overlooking Burke's *Enquiry* (1757). As the title indicates, Kant's treatise was also founded on the by then conventional opposition between the beautiful and the sublime, and as in Burke's work this binary opposition serves as the governing logic for an aggressive, sustained differentiation between male and female. Furthermore, the distinction between the sublime and the beautiful functions as a template of taste that can be used beyond the aesthetic domain in order to judge the merits of various national traits and evaluate the respective worth of ethnic groups. Kant deploys the binary opposition between the sublime and the beautiful as an ethno-racial categorisation to differentiate between self and other. He proceeds by evaluating the national and ethnic entities of the world according to their predisposition for either the sublime or the beautiful: the effeminate Italians and the French are distinguished by feelings for the beautiful, but the virile Germans, English, Spanish have a keen capacity for the sublime. The notable exception among European nations is the Dutch who apparently have no aesthetic capacity whatsoever, neither for the sublime nor the beautiful. Kant's scathing comment is: "Holland can be considered as that land where the finer taste becomes largely unnoticeable" (1991:97).

His judgement becomes even more aggressive when it moves into the colonial field: the capacity for higher aesthetic judgement is singularly lacking outside of Europe. The only "savage race" that displays a "sublime mental character" is the North American Indian who supposedly has a strong feeling for honour and "seeks wild adventures hundreds of miles abroad" (1991:111). Kant reserves his lowest esteem for Africa:

> The Negroes of Africa have by nature no feeling that rises above the trifling. Mr Hume challenges anyone to cite a single example in which a Negro has shown talents, and asserts that among the hundreds of thousands of blacks who are transported elsewhere from their countries, although many of them have been set free, still not a single one was ever found who presented anything great in art or science or any other praiseworthy quality, even though among the whites some continually rise aloft from the lowest rabble, and through superior gifts earn respect in the world. (1991:110–111)

In Kant's normative judgement, his quick pronouncement on supposedly innate aesthetic capabilities ("by nature no feeling that rises above the trifling") was used to evaluate matters of character, intellect and the capacity for learning and self-improvement. Equally significant and telling is Kant's equation of "Negro" with "slave". In relying on and *repeating* the argument of Hume, Kant's pronouncements are an exemplary instance of the fixity and stability of racial stereotyping that has occupied postcolonial critics such as Frantz Fanon and Homi Bhabha. Kant's sublime is, then, a preserve (with minor exceptions) of the European master races as they alone have the rational mind that can transform baser feelings of fear and abjection into a triumph of the imagination.

This brief discussion of Kant's and Burke's philosophical writing is not intended to explore their philosophical argument fully, but merely to show that ideas of racial difference underpin their classical theories of the sublime. While it would be absurd to argue that the sublime is reducible to a theory of race, or even that racial difference underlies loco-descriptive Romantic poetry (for example Wordsworth's numerous evocations of the sublime), it would seem inappropriate to read colonial manifestations of the sublime without regard to the way both Kant and Burke sought to define sublimity by using the images of racial others as deficit models. Furthermore, both writers repeatedly invoke distant and exotic locales—often terrains of European colonial expansion—as privileged spaces for sublimity. In colonial discourse, I suggest, the sublime is less a mode of rhetorical grandeur and loftiness (as in the original Longinian analysis), and more a highly specialised technique of the imagination in which a subject attempts to master and contain a form of alterity (frequently coded as blackness) that is initially excessive, overwhelming, threatening and incomprehensible. The discursive operations of the sublime allow a paradoxical mastery of the subject over such excessive and threatening experience, leading to a triumphantly enhanced sense of identity. It is this understanding of the sublime that I will now use as a lens for an analysis of Paton's *Cry, the Beloved Country*.

"A Story of Beauty and Terror"

The sublime, as Burke tells us, is "productive of the strongest emotion which the mind is capable of feeling" and in this broad sense, the creative conditions that gave rise to *Cry, the Beloved Country* can be described as sublime. Emotion is a key term in assessing the novel. Its origins in the dark cathedral of Trondheim arose, as Paton puts it, from "the grip of a powerful emotion" (1986:268) and in the following three months of travel across Europe and the USA he was "in a fever to write" (1986:271) while the story "continued to possess" him (1986:272). Paton refers also to the "tumult of my emotions"

(1986:269). Upon rereading his own novel twenty-five years later, this same emotion "mastered" him (1986:272) and he suggests, somewhat hubristically, that it must have evoked "the same emotion in hundreds of thousands, perhaps millions of readers" (1986:272). Paton never details the exact nature of this passionate and overpowering emotion, as if it is itself beyond discourse. That the novel was able to evoke powerful feelings in many of its readers is without doubt, and even harsh critics such as Stephen Watson, who condemns it as a sentimental, politically naive "tear-jerker" (1982:39), confirm the novel's emotive force. In J M Coetzee's somewhat uncharitable judgment, *Cry, the Beloved Country* only works because of "the intensity of the driving passion" since Paton "had no particular gift for narrative" and his novels "are statically constructed, depending for their effect on character and emotion" (2001:325).

Not only is the novel entirely suffused with an overpowering affect that sublimely overwhelms its author, but the very nature of this emotion is, as in the classical Burkean sublime, a peculiar amalgam of simultaneous delight and terror. Many critics have noted the contradictory and ambivalent nature of the novel's emotive force without, however, using the term "sublime". As Tony Morphet puts it, the overpowering emotion which pervades the novel is a strangely paradoxical kind of fear which

> is a powerful unifying force in the novel, acting almost as a kind of connective tissue within which the shapes and pattern of experience are lodged ... It is the structural unifier, the common emotion felt and shared by everyone and present in everything, but it is also the destroyer, the cancer which eats away and breaks down the will to do good. The medium in which the story lives is itself destructive. (1983:4)

Similarly, Andrew Nash's analysis avoids the term "sublime" but describes Paton's emotional ambiguity in precisely the ambivalent and contradictory language that is widely associated with sublimity: "The 'beloved country' was to become a source of anguish as well as a source of delight, the threat to its enjoyment was anguish to endure" (1983:18). Both Morphet and Nash recognise the paradoxical and conflictual nature of this emotion, and what they observe can, I propose, best be understood by invoking a postcolonial theory of the sublime. As Paton himself puts it in the new Foreword to the 1987 edition, it "is a story of the beauty and terror of human life" (1988:5–6). The governing tension of the text, already encapsulated in its title, is an overwhelming love for the beauty of the land and a simultaneous fear that destruction and racial violence are imminent. In its primary form, Paton's sublime involves the simultaneous presence of contradictory and contesting affective forces: an evocation of the rapturous and thrilling delight of the African landscape, and, at the same time, the looming presence of the blackness and racial retribution that threatens to destroy the colonial settler order.

An exemplary instance of how the disturbing facts of racial displacement and difference structure Paton's sublime evocation of the land is found in the well-known opening passage of the novel. It warrants closer analysis:

> There is a lovely road that runs from Ixopo into the hills. These hills are grass-covered and rolling, and they are lovely beyond any singing of it. The road climbs seven miles into them, to Carisbrooke; and from there, if there is no mist, you look down on one of the fairest valleys of Africa. About you there is grass and bracken and you may hear the forlorn crying of the titihoya, one of the birds of the veld. Below you is the valley of the Umzimkulu, on its journey from the Drakensberg to the sea; and beyond and behind the river, great hill after great hill; and beyond and behind them, the mountains of Ingeli and East Griqualand.
>
> The grass is rich and matted, you cannot see the soil. It holds the rain and the mist, and they seep into the ground, feeding the streams in every kloof. It is well-tended, and not too many cattle feed upon it; not too many fires burn it, laying bare the soil. Stand unshod upon it, for the ground is holy, being even as it came from the creator. Keep it, guard it, care for it, for it keeps men, guards men, cares for men. Destroy it and man is destroyed.
>
> Where you stand the grass is rich and matted, you cannot see the soil. But the green hills break down. They fall to the valleys below, and falling, change their nature. For they grow red and bare; they cannot hold the rain and the mist and the streams are dry in the kloofs. Too many cattle feed upon the grass, and too many fires have burned it. Stand shod upon it, for it is coarse and sharp, and the stones cut under the feet. It is not kept, or guarded, or cared for, it no longer keeps men, guards men, cares for men. The titihoya does not cry here any more. (1988:7)

Paton's narrative presents the Natal midlands as a landscape deeply invested with affect, as a space intensely charged and suffused with feeling to the point that the capacity of language breaks down—signalled by the word "beyond". In this characteristic, sublime moment there is a simultaneous expansion and collapse of discourse, leaving the narrator's lyrical reverence, in the form of an extended loco-descriptive praise song, insufficient to express the fullness of the sentiment. In the narrator's passionate homage, the overwhelming beauty of the landscape exceeds representation and is "beyond any singing of it".

At first glance, this sublime moment presents a classical colonial prospect: the authorial narrative performs a survey of the surrounding landscape from a position of elevation. The sweep of the eye first travels across objects of close proximity ("About you there is grass and bracken"), then takes in the far distance ("the mountains of Ingeli and East Griqualand"), but simultaneously, in a panoramic, consciousness-expanding moment typical of sublime discourse, it moves beyond the visible ground to include imaginatively the unseen but known landscape of the entire region ("from the Drakensberg to the sea"). Following numerous postcolonial studies (Bunn 1988, Pratt 1992, McClintock 1995), prospect passages such as this could readily be interpreted as staging imaginative colonial mastery and control over a pliant, subjugated colonial terrain, particularly when we remember that the as yet unnamed vantage point that provides the platform for this expansive gaze will later be identified as "the farm and dwelling-place of James Jarvis, Esquire" (1988:112), the English-speaking white farmer protagonist of the novel. Aptly named "High Place", it is one of the settler farms commanding the high ground that adjoins the "native reserve" in the valley below and it is from here that the landowners can look out in control of the land from "the long verandas drinking their tea" (1988:113).

But Paton's use of prospect rhetoric is not easily readable as a triumphalist imperial gesture; in fact the text's already muted deployment of the romantic sublime is rapidly undercut by a change in direction of the gaze. It abandons the expansive horizontal axis with its views of the far-off mountains and instead follows the vertical plane downward. In almost cinematic fashion, the initial sweeping pan shot cuts to a high-angle shot that then zooms in to a close-up examination of the valley far below. The narrative first describes the condition of the grass and soil on the up-lands, and then the gaze descends into the valley below to reveal the degradation and poverty of the over-grazed land in the "native reserve". What unsettles the moment of sublime delight is the reality of the valley, requiring the eye to abandon the high and lofty prospect and examine the landscape and ground below ("the stones cut under the feet"). The stark socio-political realities of rural Natal undermine, literally from below, the grandiose, sweeping views which the settler farmers might enjoy.

An assessment of the passage and indeed of the novel as a whole suggests, then, that Paton's use of the sublime is complex and contradictory. The awe-inspiring and overwhelming, sublime effect of the landscape does not arise merely from the natural beauty of the land, but is always accompanied by, or rather *produced* by, the underlying facts of blackness and racial difference. The structure of Paton's sublime, effectively a lamination of "beauty and terror", heightens the loveliness and poignancy of the landscape by imagining its loss in the racial conflict that threatens to engulf South Africa. This juxtaposition of "beauty and terror" becomes a structuring motif in the novel, for example when the narrator asks:

> Who can enjoy the lovely land, who can enjoy the seventy years, and the sun that pours down on the earth, when there is fear in the heart? Who can walk quietly in the shadow of jacarandas, when their beauty is grown to danger? (1988:67)

In the striking image of the jacaranda, Paton shifts the focus from brightness and comforting sunshine to darkness and danger. The jacarandas, exotic trees whose purple blooms are conventionally associated with white urban landscapes on the highveld, are no longer merely beautiful, leafy avenues that provide delight for the eye and cool shade for residents. Paton sees them as avenues of fear and their shade is less a refuge than a dark place of danger.

This analysis is confirmed in an untitled article, written by Paton at Anerley on the Natal South Coast soon after the publication of *Cry, the Beloved Country*. In it, he sketches the troubling racial landscape of South Africa, and ends with a quotation from his own novel:

> We white South Africans, are a conscience-troubled people. Not all our colourful fruits and birds, our beauties of mountain and plain, our long hours of sun, our mineral and other wealth, can distract us from graver, deeper, more anxious thoughts. What I wrote in *Cry, the Beloved Country* is the plain and simple truth: 'The sun pours down on the earth, on the lovely land that man cannot enjoy. He knows only the fear of his heart.' (n.d.: PC 1/8/1/1/16)

The structure of denied joy and fearful beauty arising from "graver, deeper, more anxious thoughts" can also be discerned in one of the signal passages in the novel that can be read as almost an anti-sublime, repudiating the rapturous delight in the "beauties of mountain and plain" of the South African landscape:

> Cry, the beloved country, for the unborn child that is the inheritor of our fear. Let him not love the earth too deeply. Let him not laugh too gladly when the water runs through his fingers, nor stand

too silent when the setting sun makes red the veld with fire. Let him not be too moved when the birds are singing, nor give too much of his heart to a mountain or a valley. For fear will rob him of all if he gives too much. (1988:72)

Although the narrative compellingly foregrounds the dangers of giving oneself to the seductive aesthetic pleasures of the land, there is, in the act of disavowal, a simultaneous passionate evocation of this very same landscape. Even here, a lingering Romantic sense of love and delight in the land is not completely obliterated by the underlying threat of a racial cataclysm. The facts of black rural poverty and dispossession, and the potentiality of racial retribution and violence are always inherent in Paton's imagination of the landscape. Paton's sublime, to use Tony Morphet's words, "keeps the full force of contradiction alive" (1983:6).

Youthful Ecstasies

The degree to which a political awareness in Cry, the Beloved Country intrudes on and disrupts a more innocent romantic vision of the land is remarkable if one considers that only five years before Paton had, as he admits, still "clung to the irrational idea that one could maintain white supremacy and yet be just" (1986:240). This political stance, as we shall see, is not entirely absent from the novel. Indeed, traces of Paton's politically "irrational idea" conceal themselves in the sublime moments of the text, perhaps precisely because the sublime itself exceeds the rational.

When Paton started to abandon his supremacist political position, partly due to his experiences at Diepkloof reformatory and serving in the Anglican commission that had been tasked "to define what it believed to be the mind of Christ for South Africa" (1986:238), this change had irrevocable and painful consequences for the way he could imagine the South African landscape. Paton's growing awareness and intense emotional response to the racial problems of South Africa are, in effect, the motor driving the shifts in his aesthetic appreciation of the "beloved country". His capacity to write and evoke sublimity shifts from its roots in an initially romantic, youthful and politically innocent rapture and delight in the landscape to a more complex aesthetic response that reflects a growing maturity and a sustained engagement with the politics of the land, in particular the traumatic question of race.

The development of Paton's youthful sublime is described in some detail in his autobiography, Towards the Mountain:

I cannot describe my early response to the beauty of the hill and stream and tree as anything less than an ecstasy. A tree on the horizon, a line of trees, the green blades of the first grass of spring, showing up against the black ashes of the burnt hills, the scarlet of the fire-lilies among the black and the green, the grass birds that whirred up at one's feet, all these things filled me with an emotion beyond describing. . . . I was much older before I responded, and no less intensely, to the beauty of the plain and sky and distant line of mountains. (1986:4–5)

Paton refers to two distinct aesthetic modes that shaped his earlier responses to the landscape. The first, corresponding to the period of his boyhood rambles in the veld around Pietermaritzburg, revels primarily in the textures and minute details of nature, an impulse that would continue to shape his later amateur interests in ornithology and botany, fields in which he would become highly competent. Traces of this aesthetic mode also repeatedly influence the descriptions of nature in *Cry, the Beloved Country*. It is also an aesthetic that was shaped, from early childhood, by a sustained and intense exposure to romantic literature, especially Robert Burns and R L Stevenson. Later, while studying at Natal University College, he would imbibe the larger English canon of poetry. Together with a group of "boy-men" (1986:63) he would read the poetry of "Shakespeare, Milton, Wordsworth, Coleridge, Keats, Shelley, Byron, Tennyson, Browning" (1986:63) and recite verse while rambling romantically through the Natal midlands.

The second and later sublime of "the beauty of the plain and sky and distant line of mountains" involves a grander, more expansive vision that goes beyond the minutiae of natural details and the self-absorbed recitation of verse. It is more directly a source of the landscape descriptions in *Cry, the Beloved Country*, as in the novel's opening paragraphs. We can trace the development of this sublime to the late 1920s, the period of Paton's teaching in Ixopo, where the recently graduated young man fell in love with Dorrie, a married woman who was later to become his wife. On their excursionary walks in the surrounding hills, Paton's passion for his first true love must have fused with the ardour he already felt for the landscape of Natal. "I was in love with the countryside and its bracken and its mists", Paton writes, and was "[w]alking the hills with an energy that is limitless" (1986:101,102). Again he writes of "the intensity of response to this magic country. . . . The Ixopo countryside laid me under a kind of spell" (1986:85). But this landscape, as it is initially described in *Towards the Mountain*, is not yet the truly sublime space that it would become in *Cry, the Beloved Country*. While undoubtedly inspiring passion and delight, it lacks the elements of imagined fear and traumatic loss to give it its sublime pathos. As Paton concedes, his youthful ardour was completely devoid of any political awareness around the question of land ownership and a social concern about the people whose land it once was: his "great love of the country … was in those days not a love of its peoples, of whom I knew almost nothing" (1986:56). It is only Paton's later political understanding that would introduce the painful idea that the beauty of the landscape was threatened by the facts of racial injustice. Indeed, the rolling hills of Ixopo could only be recuperable by the imagination as a sublime space after they had, in reality, become a lost landscape. The language of the following passage, fed by this sense of loss and yearning, is instantly recognizable as part of the sublime discourse of *Cry, the Beloved Country*:

> Much of the beauty of the Ixopo countryside has gone, because the grass and the bracken and the rolling hills and farms have in large part given way to the endless plantations of gum and wattle and pine, and the titihoya does not cry there anymore. (1986:86)

The landscape of Ixopo, as Paul Rich has pointed out, is written out of nostalgia as it was even then "written on the crest of a profound economic and social transformation in rural Natal which had important consequences for the landscape" (1985:56).

An unfinished and unpublished story written by the younger, largely unpoliticised Paton offers us another intriguing glimpse into the pre-sublime Ixopo landscape. "Secret for Seven" (written in the early 1930s) deals with the marriage of Mary Massingham, daughter of an old, genteel, landed Natal family, who falls in love with and marries Charles Draper, son of a carpenter. The problem set up in the narrative is not so much one of violating class distinctions (landed money marrying working class), as the matter of Draper's swarthy mother whose racial identity is dubious ("A dark-skinned woman about whose descent kindly tongues did not enquire").[3] The theme of miscegenation and race is clear in the moment of crisis: Mary gives birth to their first child, who turns out to be black skinned. Major and Mrs Massingham arrive and Draper, who must break the news to them, resolves to disown the child and give it to Catholic nuns. The story is unfinished, as if Paton is unable to resolve the intractable problem of race.

Of more interest to my argument is the setting of the story. It is, prototypically, the same spatially and racially divided colonial landscape of *Cry, the Beloved Country*, which contrasts the high ground occupied by white settlers with the low-lying reserve of the Zulu people:

> A world apart; for when the mists came down over the mountain, they cut off white from black with their level line. Up here the swirling mist, & wattles dripping eerily in it, & gates looming

suddenly out of it; down there clearness & stars, & the cries of natives from kraal to kraal, & lights here & there from but and hut. Up here the farms of white people, houses, wireless, mist; down there the lands of blacks, huts, singing, & stars.... She [Mrs Massingham] and her daughter would sit on the verandah of 'Emoyeni', looking down on the valley below at a different world. For there lived the natives in their reserves, a land where no mist came & no bracken grew & no titihoyas called; where the earth was red, & the thorn-tree and the aloe flourished, a hot country where colours were more vivid & sounds more loud.

The similarities to *Cry, the Beloved Country* are striking, but so are the differences. 'Emoyeni' is Zulu for 'High Place', but the low-lying "reserve" is not yet recognised by Paton as the degraded land that speaks of dispossession and racial injustice. Compared to the white farms that are isolated from each other in the cold, swirling mists of the uplands, the reserve is a scene full of song, warmth and vibrant life. It is a happy, exotically colourful locale as opposed to the hunger-stricken, rural labour-pool of Ndotsheni in the novel. It is clear that "Secret for Seven" cannot achieve the sublime juxtaposition of *Cry, the Beloved Country*: the urgency of human suffering and tragic awareness of racial oppression is missing from a scene that is more akin to a tourist postcard.

"Unspeakable sorrow and unspeakable joy"

In *Cry, the Beloved Country* Paton is fully aware of the stark, racialised divisions of colonial space which produce, on the one hand, elevated settler landscapes of transcendent and wholesome beauty, and on the other, environmentally degraded lowlands of African poverty, malnutrition and social dysfunction. The novel diagnoses the causes of rural poverty and environmental degradation as being rooted in the wholesale colonial dispossession of Africans from their land. As the novel puts it through Arthur Jarvis: "We set aside one-tenth of the land for four-fifths of the people" (1988:127).

The problem however is that despite the novel's trenchant analysis of the colonial land question, settler farms such as Jarvis's "High Place" are presented as benign, custodial spaces that somehow respectfully combine agribusiness with the preservation of the edenic, natural or imaginary pre-colonial wholeness of the land, keeping it "even as it came from the Creator" (1988:7). Such an account cannot but validate the right to continued ownership. So, even as Paton's novel eloquently exposes the injustice of colonial land dispossession and indeed foregrounds the intrinsic structural connections between white wealth and black poverty, his sharp critique of the colonial land question results in at best paternal, ameliorative interventions (supplying milk to malnourished children), or gradualist environmental upliftment which can only fail to change the basic inequitable racial structure of land ownership. Although the novel incorporates and even validates a more radical political critique gesturing towards revolutionary systemic change (John Kumalo and the agricultural demonstrator), these voices can ultimately not shake the affective force of Jarvis's love for his land that dominates the novel. Owning and retaining the "High Places" is non-negotiable in Paton's liberal vision of South Africa. Through the figure of Jarvis's orphaned grandchild, who is allowed to recuperate from the menace of Johannesburg's racial violence, the novel can indulge in the fantasy of continued patrilineal inheritance of white colonial property in Africa. It is an escapist agrarian political solution that nostalgically seeks to validate and revitalise a vanishing paternal rural order of just and strong, but compassionate, gentlemen farmers, and loyal, simple and honest African folk.

In his sublime, Paton is thus able to admit and contain the disturbing facts of blackness, but in such a manner that the overall sense of identification with the land and colonial ownership is not displaced. Thus Paton's sublime, as it finds expression in *Cry*, is less about the rapturous effect of indescribable natural beauty, but rather represents that tenuous and illusionary moment in the white liberal imagination at which an impossible oneness with the beloved land can be imagined. In a transport away from the trauma of social and political realities, South African white guilt and responsibility are temporarily suspended in a purely affective space in which the subject can be momentarily redeemed in the presence of God's creation.

In 1948, such sublime moments of settler transcendence were becoming less sustainable in the contested landscape of South Africa and so Paton's other expressions of sublimity invoke political and social utopian fantasies of a "promised land", rather than the land itself. Indeed, in the most powerful deployment of sublimity in Paton's *oeuvre*—the description of the funeral of Edith Rheinallt-Jones—the sublime has shifted completely away from the landscape and founds itself in a social event that gives a glimpse of a possible future non-racial society:

> Black people, white people, Coloured people, European and African and Asian, Jew and Christian and Hindu and Moslem, rich and poor, all came to honour her memory, their hates and their fears, their prides and their prejudices all for this moment forgotten. . . . As for me, I was overwhelmed, I was seeing a vision, which was never to leave me, illuminating the darkness of the days through which we live now. To speak in raw terms, there was

some terrible pain in the pit of my stomach. I could not control it.
I had again the overpowering feeling of unspeakable sorrow and
unspeakable joy. (1986:252–3)[4]

The opposites that structure South African politics, here conceived of primarily in terms of race and religion, merge into a sublime Kantian *Aufhebung*. But here it is primarily racial difference and the illusionary moment ("a vision") of its dissolution into an imaged oneness that is the primary emotive force in Paton's imagination, for he can conclude that he "was no longer a white person but a member of the human race" (1986:253). Paton's use of the sublime, as we can clearly see in this passage, is founded on a simultaneous recognition of racial difference (he writes not of 'people' but defines them as "Black", "white" and "Coloured") and the collapse of these racial categories. The result is an ecstatic and painful loss of identity that is "unspeakable" and resists full representation. Paton's sublime, as we can see, has fully shifted from the evocation of a beloved landscape to the thrilling vision of the promised land of racial harmony. Of course, the multiracial homage to Jones that gives rise to Paton's sublime feelings reaffirms the centrality of the good white liberal who selflessly "gave her money, her comforts, her gifts, her home, and finally her life" (1986:253) in the service of black upliftment. The liberal, political vision of South Africa is ultimately affirmed rather than challenged.[5]

"Africa dark and savage"

But this mode of transcendence—which we might call Paton's utopian sublime—is but one mode of sublimity. It is also counterbalanced by another form of rapturous transcendence, a sublime that replaces the vision of racial harmony with the terror of racial retribution. As the novel's narrative moves from the degraded, yet orderly world of rural Natal to the modern urban setting of Johannesburg, we encounter John Kumalo's powerful black African voice:

> There are those who remember the first day they heard it as if it were today, who remember their excitement, and the queer sensations of their bodies as though electricity were passing through them. For the voice has magic in it, and it has threatening in it, and it is as though Africa itself were in it. A lion growls in it, and thunder echoes in it over black mountains. (1988:158)

Kumalo's voice, like the vast, rolling expanses of the African landscape of the novel's opening paragraphs, has the capacity to achieve sublime effect.

His voice *is* the landscape, "Africa itself". His consummate oratorical skill is, in the words of a white security policeman "like the great stop of an organ. You can see the whole crowd swaying. I felt it myself" (1988:161). But what is Kumalo saying? His speech pleads for economic justice, for higher wages for workers on the rich goldmines: "We ask only for those things that labouring men fight for in every country in the world, the right to sell our labour for what it is worth, the right to bring up our families as decent men should" (1988:159). He also suggests that workers should use their only weapon, namely withholding their labour. This is hardly a revolutionary message, in fact Arthur Jarvis's treatise spells out much the same: "It is not permissible to mine any gold, or manufacture any product, or cultivate any land, if such mining and manufacture and cultivation depend on their success of keeping labour poor" (1988:126). But in revealingly illiberal moments, the narrator twice contemptuously describes Kumalo as a man lacking intelligence, a "bull voice" without brains. So what is it about John Kumalo that makes him the target of aggressive, racist disparagement? Why is he depicted as the stereotypical uppity black man whose rhetorical accomplishments are but a thin veneer over a primitive mind? The key is not in what Kumalo actually says, but what he could say should he want to. Inherent in Kumalo's oratorical mastery is the threat of powerful racial incitement and native uprising: his voice could "paint for them pictures of Africa awaking from sleep, of Africa resurgent, of Africa dark and savage" (1988:158).

If John Kumalo's speech-making contains the germs of a violent black uprising, the archetypal stuff of white settler fears, it also holds the promise of future black liberation, a goal Paton was publicly committed to. Indeed, it is at this very political objective that the entire thrust of the novel is ostensibly directed. But Kumalo's brand of ethnically defined, worker-led liberation is fundamentally at odds with Paton's paternal Liberalism that still sees responsible and enlightened whites (such as Edith Rheinallt-Jones) as the central agency for effecting change in South Africa. In the "white man's burden" argument of Arthur Jarvis's treatise, white colonisation destroyed the old African tribal system and "[o]ur civilisation has therefore an inescapable duty to set up another system of order and tradition and convention" (1988:127). White leadership is thus ultimately required to repair the ill-effects of colonisation and lead black Africans into an orderly and rational South African modernity. In such a political vision, revolutionaries such as Kumalo must necessarily be represented as a threatening and destabilising force. In the figure of Kumalo, Paton allows us to imagine a form of transcendence that conjures up images of a future mass uprising and of black freedom—a revolutionary sublime that simultaneously appals and fascinates.

Conclusion

Although the term "sublime" is itself not used in *Cry, the Beloved Country*, it is a key discursive structure that shapes the text's complex and ambivalent representation of South Africa's politicised landscape. Paton, reread through this critical lens, emerges perhaps more creditably as a writer intensely alive to the complex politics of race than was allowed by his numerous critical detractors in the late 1970s and 1990s. Paton's imaginings of transcendence do not evade the racial and colonial trauma of South Africa, but rather embody these very tensions and shape them into an ambivalent and contradictory affective force that can, I think, be best understood in terms of the sublime. Put differently, Paton's sublime that so powerfully pervades his "story of beauty and terror" is unthinkable without the spectre of racial violence as its driving force.

Paton evokes sublimity in different ways in his writing, ranging from a youthful, innocent rapture in the face of the beauties of the land to a more mature and complex compound of overwhelming terror and exultation that accompanies visions of either racial harmony or racial cataclysm. Racial difference and its political consequences are the forces that produce Paton's sublime, but paradoxically, these sublime moments in the text manage and contain the very fears that have produced sublimity in the first place, and do so in a way that intensifies the affective force of his love for the land into an ecstatic affirmation of belonging.

NOTES

1. At a very basic level, two rather simplistic 'definitions' of the sublime may provide a provisional conceptual map. Firstly, the sublime is that which moves one: an affective force with power to transform the subject, usually in a manner that is elevating and uplifting, but also potentially terrifying. Secondly, such sublime experience cannot be represented, or at least not fully represented. Any discourse of the sublime also embodies, paradoxically, its own representational failure as the immensity of the sublime object or experience exceeds the capacity of language to represent it.

2. See, for instance Bell and Lyall (2001) and Spivak's observation: "The Internet has . . . domesticated the sublime, somewhat like the cultivated ruins and wilderness two centuries ago" (1999:325).

3. "Secret for Seven" is an unpaginated and undated manuscript.

4. Paton uses very similar terms for an earlier occasion, also a memorial service, where he was "near to being overwhelmed by a feeling of unspeakable sorrow and unspeakable joy" (1986:235). This memorial service honoured the fallen soldiers of St John's College, Cambridge.

5. Paton drew on this scene in *Cry, the Beloved Country* too, but the sublime force of the autobiography's narrative is curiously dissipated in the novel. Instead of Edith Rheinallt-Jones, it is the funeral of Arthur Jarvis. Both the fictional Jarvis (a character most closely modelled on Paton himself) and Jones share a similar

liberal philosophy and are engaged in philanthropic projects that seek to uplift the "natives". The fictional funeral also brings together "[w]hite people, black people, coloured people, Indians" (1988:128), but this multiracial gathering fails to become a moment of transcendence for the grief-stricken James Jarvis. His handshakes with black people afterwards, "the first time he had ever shaken hands with black people" (1988:129), also have little effect on him.

REFERENCES

Alexander, Peter. 1994. *Alan Paton: A Biography*. Oxford: Oxford University Press.

Bell, Claudia and John Lyall. 2001. *The Accelerated Sublime: Landscape, Tourism and Identity*. Westport: Praeger.

Bunn, David. 1988. "Embodying Africa: Woman and Romance in Colonial Fiction." *English in Africa* 15(1):1–28.

Burke, Edmund. 1757. *A Philosophical Enquiry into the Origin of Our ideas of the Sublime and the Beautiful*. London: R & J Dodsley.

Coetzee, J M. 1988. *White Writing: On the Culture of Letters in South Africa*. Johannesburg: Radix.

———. 2001. *Stranger Shores. Essays, 1986–1999*. London: Secker & Warburg.

Crowther, Paul. 1993. *Critical Aesthetics and Postmodernism*. Oxford: Oxford University Press.

De Bolla, Peter. 1989. *The Discourse of the Sublime. Readings in History, Aesthetics and the Subject*. Oxford: Basil Blackwell.

Eagleton, Terry. 1990. *The Ideology of the Aesthetic*. Oxford: Blackwell.

Freeman, Barbara. 1995. *The Feminine Sublime: Gender and Excess in Women's Fiction*. Berkeley: University of California Press.

Kant, Immanuel. 1951 (1790). *Critique of Judgement*. Trans. J H Bernard. New York: Hafner.

———. 1991 (1764). *Observations of the Feeling of the Beautiful and Sublime*. Trans. John Goldthwait. Berkeley: University of California Press.

Labbe, Jacqueline. 1998. *Romantic Visualities: Landscape, Gender and Romanticism*. London: Macmillan Press.

Lyotard, Jean-François. 1993. "The Sublime and the Avantgarde". In: Thomas Docherty (ed). *Postmodernism: A Reader*. New York: Harvester Wheatsheaf: 244–256.

———. 1994. *Lessons on the Analytic of the Sublime*. Stanford: Stanford University Press.

Mansfield, Nick. 1997. *Masochism: The Art of Power*. Westport: Praeger.

McClintock, Anne. 1995. *Imperial Leather: Race, Gender and Sexuality in the Colonial Context*. New York: Routledge.

Morphet, Tony. 1983. "The Honour of Meditation". *English in Africa* 10(2): 1–10.

Nash, Andrew. 1983. "The way to the Beloved Country: History and Individual in Alan Paton's *Towards the Mountain*." *English in Africa* 10(2):11–27.

Paton, Alan. 1988 (1948). *Cry, the Beloved Country*. Harmondsworth: Penguin.

———. 1949. "South Africa's Racial Problems of an intensity and complexity unknown to any other country". Alan Paton Centre, University of KwaZulu-Natal: PC 1/8/88/12.

———. 1986. *Towards the Mountain*. Harmondsworth: Penguin.

———. n.d. "Secret for Seven". Alan Paton Centre, University of KwaZulu-Natal: PC 1/3/4/6.

Pratt, Marie Louise. 1992. *Imperial Eyes: Travel Writing and Transculturation*. London: Routledge.

Regan, Stephen. 1992. *The Politics of Pleasure: Aesthetics and Cultural Theory*. Buckingham: Open University Press.

Rich, Paul. 1985. "Liberal Realism in South African Fiction, 1948–1966". *English in Africa* 12(1):47–81.

Spivak, Gayatri Chakravorty. 1999. *A Critique of Postcolonial Reason: Toward a History of the Vanishing Present*. Cambridge (Mass.): Harvard University Press.

Tabbi, Joseph. 1995. *Postmodern Sublime: Technology and American Writing from Mailer to Cyberpunk*. Ithaca: Cornell University Press.

Watson, Stephen. 1982. "*Cry, the Beloved Country* and the Failure of Liberal Vision." *English in Africa* 9(1):29–44.

Weiskel, Thomas. 1976. *The Romantic Sublime: Studies in the Structure anti Psychology of Transcendance*. Baltimore: John Hopkins.

ANDREW VAN DER VLIES

Whose Beloved Country?
Alan Paton and the Hypercanonical

I do not remember precisely when I first read Alan Paton's novel, *Cry, the Beloved Country: A Story of Comfort in Desolation*, although it was probably late in my primary-school career. I do, however, have vivid memories of two later engagements with the novel which speak to this chapter's attempt to account for its remarkable biography. I bought a copy of the new Penguin Twentieth-Century Classics edition at Fogarty's Bookshop on Main Street, in downtown Port Elizabeth, in late 1991. Before leaving the store, I recognised another customer, an elderly black man, as the recently released political prisoner Govan Mbeki (father of President Thabo Mbeki), and asked nervously for his autograph, which he gave graciously. I pasted it into my copy of *Cry, the Beloved Country*. The novel's emotional energies clearly worked on a white youth of 17, attuned to the politics of the interregnum—Mandela had been released, negotiations were underway, the television news reported violence engineered by mysterious 'third forces'—but feeling marooned (in hindsight, self-righteously) in white suburbia. Had I been identifying Mbeki with the long-suffering Stephen Kumalo, and myself with Arthur's child, the young white boy pleased with his contact with a real African? I remember recalling that encounter when the post-apartheid City Council renamed Main Street as Govan Mbeki Avenue.

From *South African Textual Cultures: White, Black, Read All Over*, pp. 71–105. © 2007 by Andrew van der Vlies.

The second memory is of my first train journey to Johannesburg, in January 1996. Initially, I shared a second-class compartment with a former Umkhonto we Sizwe (the ANC's armed wing) cadre, but he disembarked at Bloemfontein to rejoin his National Defence Force unit, and with the compartment to myself, I opened the blinds as the train crossed the Vaal River and read Paton's description of Kumalo's train journey to Johannesburg. Despite my 21-year-old self's cynicism about Paton's Christian paternalism, I still found the novel immensely moving: two years into the New South Africa, it seemed we hadn't all turned to hating, as Stephen Kumalo, at the end of the novel, recalls his friend Msimangu fearing.

These two moments attest to the strange and enduring power of *Cry, the Beloved Country*, despite many of the justifiable criticisms levelled against it. They support Dan Jacobson's claim, in a tribute on Paton's death, that the book had achieved a 'proverbial' status, that for South Africans it evaded adequate assessment in exclusively political or aesthetic terms, instead becoming 'part of a common stock of reference and of modes of self-recognition'.[1] At the time of Paton's death in 1988, his most famous novel had sold 15 million copies in 20 languages, and was still selling some 100,000 a year.[2] Repackaged in book club, college and school editions, sometimes in shortened or simplified 'versions', serialised and abridged, filmed, dramatised and staged as a jazz opera on Broadway, *Cry, the Beloved Country* qualifies as what Rob Nixon calls 'the only blockbuster in the annals of anti-apartheid literature'.[3]

Its remarkable afterlife continues, it seems fair to say, because it has satisfied an array of ever-changing context- and period-specific desires. Its model of Christian humanism, trusteeship and reconciliation spoke to white, middle-class, American readers, anxious about racial tensions in their own country. Paton's novel seemed to offer something to many in post-war Labourite Britain, too, capitalising on interest in social conditions across the Commonwealth, while touching on a sense of crisis in white British identities as the Empire ebbed away. In a letter in May 1948, Paton mused about the possible reception of the novel in South Africa, fearing that it would 'be very different from the American', that it would 'arouse unconscious antagonism' and that, 'instead of attacking the cause of their antagonism', his critics would 'attack … its art'.[4] While there was immediate scorn for the novel's politics from activists and writers on the left of the political spectrum in South Africa, hostile to Paton's apparent answers to the country's racial injustices, he need not have worried.[5] Readers there, their sense of cultural nationalism both encouraged and piqued by the fact of the novel's Anglo-American publication and the nature of its reception abroad, encountered a text whose local pre-publication advertising declared it already a masterpiece, a classic-in-the-making. Only a very few dared comment on its 'art', and then, usually, only to praise what had already been validated by critical acclaim in the capitals of northern aesthetic judgement. The coincidence of the novel's appearance in the same year as the May 1948 election victory of the National Party, with its programme of apartheid policies, created a climate in which Paton's prognostications on the country assumed near prophetic status.[6]

Endorsements by prominent South African public figures (significantly, both white) on the back cover of a recent Penguin edition suggest its continuing national and international construction: Nadine Gordimer calls it the 'most influential South African novel ever written'; the late Donald Woods thought that '[n]o book since *Uncle Tom's Cabin*' had a comparable impact 'on international opinion on the issue of race'.[7] Both comments indicate the extent to which *Cry, the Beloved Country* has come to be revered both as an important—and specifically 'South African'—social *document* and also a work of *literature*. It has been and remains a multimedia phenomenon unparalleled in the history of the country's literary and cultural production, undoubtedly its best example of the demands and dividends of *canonisation*; one might call it 'hypercanonical', following Jonathan Arac's description of the mid-twentieth-century contestation and elevation of Mark Twain's *Huckleberry Finn*, which is both among the most banned texts by American school boards, but also a premiere text in discourses about American national literary identity.[8] Paton's novel continues to be taught in schools around the world, its most recent film adaptation was as late as 1996 and, in 2003, it was featured on Oprah Winfrey's Book Club, touted by no less than Bill Clinton, Alicia Keys and Charlize Theron.[9] In this chapter I seek to account for some of the ways in which the novel's political energies have been modified or elided by the material conditions of different instances of publication. I consider its reception in the USA, Britain and South Africa after publication in 1948, some exemplary appropriations of the novel published during the 1950s and 1960s and its promotion as an educational text from the 1960s to the 1980s.

The 'exquisite pleasure' of 'moral indignation': America Reads *Cry, the Beloved Country*

Paton was serving as warden of Diepkloof Reformatory, a borstal for young, black, male offenders, when he began his novel. At the time, September 1946, he was on a brief visit to Trondheim in Norway during a study tour of reformatories and prisons in Europe and North America. The manuscript was completed in California during the same trip, in late December, and sample chapters dispatched to a dozen American publishers. Several expressed interest, but Paton chose Charles Scribner's Sons in New York. In February 1947, the firm's Maxwell Perkins accepted the novel for publication, and it appeared on 1 February 1948.

It is chiefly to its reception in the USA that *Cry, the Beloved Country* owes its remarkable success. Six impressions of the Scribner's edition appeared within three months of first publication, and sales since have been consistently impressive.[10] Early success was not an accident: Scribner's sent advance copies to the *New York Times* and *New York Herald Tribune*, where the novel would be noticed by book club editors, and library and school advisers. A favourable notice from the *Christian Herald* was sent to forty religious bookshops, too, to excite attention from retailers thought likely to respond well to Paton's message.[11] Advertisements in the trade journal *Publishers' Weekly* quoted ringing endorsements from three constituencies—critics, clergy and booksellers—suggesting the qualities which Scribner's sought to emphasise, and which would be rehearsed repeatedly in the novel's very many American reviews: its 'strong inspirational appeal', its nature as a 'penetrating and timely study of a pressing social problem' and its 'unique, beautiful, and moving writing'.[12] The tone of the blurb on the first edition's cover expressly invokes all three categories of judgement: Kumalo's journey to Johannesburg is to 'the city of evil', his search for 'his only son' is 'long and sorrowful', reaching a 'height of tragedy which has seldom been equalled in contemporary fiction', and although it is 'a sad book', it is also 'beautifully wrought with high poetic compassion'; it is 'the story' of South Africa's 'landscape, its people, its bitter racial ferment and unrest'.[13] Whether in mass circulation dailies or rural weeklies, *Cry, the Beloved Country* was read as all of these things: an affecting narrative, a documentary and also a work of art.

On the day preceding publication, the Sunday edition of the *New York Times* carried an advance notice by Richard Sullivan calling it 'beautiful', a 'rich, firm and moving piece of prose' and 'poetic and profound spiritual drama' which 'in other hands might have made merely an interesting sociological document'.[14] The Monday edition of the same newspaper carried Orville Prescott's description of it as 'creative fiction of a high order' demonstrating that 'a thesis novel' need not sacrifice 'artistic integrity'. Paton did not mount a 'soap box to orate at the expense of his novel as a work of fiction', Prescott argued: the novel was a documentary record *and* a work of art.[15] Harry Hansen's review in New York's *Survey Graphic* in March 1948, 'A Gentle Protest', commended it, too, as an 'outstanding example of a creative effort embodying social comment', expressly not 'propaganda', 'a word that novelists detest'.[16]

The discussion of the novel's characters both as dignified individuals and as types acting out a psycho-drama, the universal resonances of which prevented the novel from being viewed as propaganda, was widespread. Adrienne Koch's suggestion in New York's *Saturday Review of Literature* that Kumalo's 'pilgrimage' was an 'objective correlative for one of the central problems of our time—how to resolve belief in the dignity and integrity of the individual with the needs of modern industrialized society'is exemplary.[17] Kumalo was seen as 'a complete human being' and the white characters as representative of 'white colonials anywhere'.[18] A reviewer in the African-American journal *Phylon* called it 'as ironic and detached as a fine Greek tragedy' and commended Paton's 'moving, human drama, that lifts this novel to the plane of great social vision, and, simultaneously, to the plane of great art'.[19] In its apparent representation of universal human values, then, the novel was regarded in the USA as having avoided the pitfalls of social protest literature, in a period in which 'protest' was widely distrusted in literary circles. In a 1939 *Partisan Review* symposium, for example, Lionel Trilling called 'protest' damaging; despite legitimately intending to arouse 'pity and anger', as a genre it was merely a form of 'escapism', 'subtle flattery by which the progressive middle-class reader is cockered up with a sense of his own virtue';[20] 'moral indignation', Trilling observed in his 1947 essay 'Manners, Morals and the Novel', 'may be in itself an exquisite pleasure'.[21] The public was not convinced by the aesthetic merits of works which held up 'some image of society to consider and condemn', he argued, and, if 'the question of quality' was raised, readers were likely to declare these books 'not great . . . not imaginative . . . not "literature"'.[22] Jonathan Arac also identifies Trilling—particularly his Introduction to Rinehart's 1948 college edition—as the most important critical voice whose endorsement precipitated the hypercanonisation of Twain's *Huckleberry Finn* in the latter half of the twentieth century.[23] I suggest that, while there is no similarly identifiable, single, authoritative, critical intervention in the reception of *Cry, the Beloved Country*, liberal critical discourses of the type of which Trilling's is exemplary explain, at least in part, the widespread celebration of the novel in America, a celebration which set the scene for the novel's positive British and South African reception.

   Cry, the Beloved Country was, of course, amenable to this reading. A response which absolves the state of the responsibility to eliminate discrimination is mystificatory and encourages a revisionist history of oppression; reading Paton's novel as a tale with universal appeal and application by focusing on individual characters as representative human types marginalised the novel's undeniable critique of institutionalised racial discrimination, no matter how retrograde Paton's representations of black characters would, in themselves, be regarded by some more radical readers. It should be noted that not all critics were so easily won over, however. The reviewer in the *Chicago Tribune* agreed that *Cry, the Beloved Country* was valuable as a 'revelation of conditions in South Africa', but suggested that it was 'unfortunately . . . more of a tract than a novel', its characters 'simply dummies pushed around for the sake of the plot', 'types without any individuating traits whatever'.[24]

It is clear, however, that Paton's novel played to a particular anxiety in the USA. A review by Aubrey Burns, in whose home in California Paton had finished the manuscript, suggests its clear parallels for America: Burns called *Cry, the Beloved Country* 'a mirror in which the American South may be seen reflected in dispassionate perspective', and claimed that it offered 'the most acceptable and effective expression on the subject of race relations for American readers'.[25] Cannily, perhaps, or perhaps inadvertently, the jacket blurb of the Scribner's edition refers to James Jarvis having a 'great plantation', a southern term by then current across America (especially after *Gone With The Wind*), but a term which is not used in the same way in South Africa. It comes as no surprise that Paton came to enjoy the status of a sage in the USA on the issue of racial conflict, touring the country for *Collier's Magazine* in 1954 to write two articles on the position of African-Americans.[26] *Cry, the Beloved Country* received the Ebony Award 'for the best book improving racial understanding' in 1948, and won $1,000 in the Anisfield-Wolf Awards for Books on Racial Relations in 1949.[27]

Paton's novel suggested to an American audience that a non-confrontational, non-communist solution could be found also for that country's racial inequalities and discrimination. Lesley Cowling suggests that it 'allowed for a collective imagining of a narrative of race, trauma and Christian reconciliation in an imagined world (the beloved country) that was not [Americans'] own', that the 'thorny problem of racism in their own context could be displaced and resolved in the imagined world of the book'.[28] It was right for its time. Diana Trilling confessed, tellingly, in *The Nation* in 1948: 'I suppose if Alan Paton had written about the American Negro or even about the American Indian in the idyllic vein in which he writes about the Zulus, I would be quick to dismiss him as a sentimentalist.'[29] Paton's is not the only South African writing which has appealed in this way to American audiences, of course: Athol Fugard's plays have proved consistently popular over the past thirty years precisely because they, too, can be construed as participating in the ongoing 'agonized conversations about race in America', Fugard's white South African characters seeming, American academic Jeanne Colleran suggests, 'like long-lost cousins who have reappeared just in time to remind us that despite our tepid political response to both apartheid and to domestic racism, our capacity for moral outrage is still intact'.[30]

A Novel Guide: Britain Reads *Cry, the Beloved Country*

Not long after Scribner's had accepted the manuscript, British publisher Jonathan Cape, on business in New York, called on Maxwell Perkins and was offered the British rights to the novel.[31] Paton always claimed that Cape accepted *Cry, the Beloved Country* without hesitation, and that Plomer, the firm's chief reader, was 'immediately enthusiastic' about the manuscript.[32] This, however, was not the case. The reader's report, long presumed lost, actually survives among Paton's papers and shows that Plomer was far from confident that the novel was worthy of the firm's list. His report, dated 12 March 1947, also shows that he thought the author to be 'English by birth and South African by adoption', which might explain his less than glowing assessment that Paton had not been successful in 'the difficult task of trying to describe the natives from the inside'.[33] He was unable to portray convincing characters, Plomer suggested, because his was 'essentially a propagandist novel, intended to show the native in as favourable a light as possible and to influence white opinion'. While the novel had 'considerable merits' as a social commentary, it was unlikely to succeed, he felt: 'I have known better books of the kind flop, though they have had respectful reviews.'[34] It is ironic, of course, that Plomer's *Turbott Wolfe* and the stories in *I Speak of Africa* had been similarly construed by many British reviewers.

While Plomer had some difficulty deciding whether serious purpose should outweigh doubts about the novel's artistic merit, and concerns about it being propaganda, short reports from two other readers were more positive. Daniel Bunting noted that, while 'disposed to resist the urgent propaganda appeal' and the biblical style of the prose, the narrative was compelling, and readers would find 'its unusual theme and treatment . . . of great interest'.[35] He reinforced that reading when reviewing the novel (as Daniel George) in the *Daily Express* in late September, describing it as having 'literary merits which must command universal respect'.[36] Bunting had recommended Orwell's *Animal Farm* to Jonathan Cape—in vain, it turned out—in 1944, and was clearly receptive to novels engaging with political issues.[37] Cape finally accepted Paton's novel, but post-war paper shortages meant it was unlikely to appear in Britain or South Africa, where Cape held the rights, before 1949. The novel's warm reception in America, however, encouraged Cape to hurry it out, and the British edition appeared on 27 September 1948.[38]

There are some differences between the British and American editions. Scribner's edition is dedicated to Aubrey and Marigold Burns (in whose Californian home Paton completed the manuscript), the Cape edition to Paton's wife and his mentor, United Party politician and jurist J. H. Hofmeyr.[39] Apart from the American and British English spelling variations, the American edition is divided into three 'books' with chapters numbered consecutively throughout, while chapter numbers in the British edition begin anew in each book.[40] There are several minor textual variations: one notable difference occurs in the passage in which Reverend Kumalo discusses his future with the bishop (the fifth chapter in Book Three) and a letter arrives from James Jarvis, acknowledging Kumalo's message of sympathy at his wife's death, and offering to build a new church. Kumalo declares it 'from God' but the bishop reads the letter and, in the American edition, declares gravely: 'That was a foolish jest. This is truly a letter from God.' The Cape and subsequent Penguin editions omit the final sentence, altering the tone of the bishop's response from that of a mild rebuke which affirms the divinely inspired providence of the help Jarvis offers to severe displeasure at Kumalo's insolence in suggesting that Jarvis is God-like (it reads, too, as pique at being excluded from unfamiliar cooperation between black and white).[41]

British reviewers repeated the anxious American representation of *Cry, the Beloved Country* as both social document *and* literature—and by virtue of being literary, more than mere social document, or propaganda. *Current Literature* called Paton 'too good an artist to descend to partisanship'.[42] The *Daily Telegraph's* reviewer called it 'that rare treat, a novel with a social purpose which is also a good story and an artistic whole'.[43] The *British Weekly* ('A Journal of Christian and Social Progress') thought it 'social history in the form of great literature', and the *Manchester Guardian* called it 'as remarkable . . . for its facts as for its truth', suggesting that truth was a function of the art which made the novel more than a presentation of fact.[44] Francis Brett Young—a prolific English writer and critic who lived in South Africa from 1945 until his death in 1954 and a passionate advocate of the country—wrote in the *Sunday Times* that *Cry, the Beloved Country* was 'not only a work of art but a "novel with a purpose"', 'sincere' and with 'moments of beauty and pitiful emotion' which marked it as 'a work of art'.[45] Extracts from that review were reproduced on the front inside jacket-flap of later impressions of the Cape edition, replacing the first British edition's more narrative blurb, which had stressed Paton's 'wide knowledge of local conditions', and his 'religious sense'.[46] For the few critics mildly sceptical of Paton's literary abilities it was the availability of universal themes in the novel which they chose to emphasise. Walter Allen in the *New Statesman and Nation*, for example, thought *Cry, the Beloved Country* 'amateurish' in some respects, but noted that in Stephen Kumalo Paton had created a 'moving and wholly acceptable symbol of human goodness'.[47] The *Tribune's* reviewer found 'overwritten rhetorical musings', but suggested that, while it had 'weaknesses as a novel', it was 'a morality story, of course'.[48]

Some reviewers likened the purpose and potential impact of the novel to the work of Victorian condition-of-England novelists: the *British Africa Monthly* ventured that, 'like *Oliver Twist* and the other social tracts of the great Victorian novelist', it might 'let light into dark corners'.[49] In a similar vein, many regarded it as a kind of report on the situation in South Africa, but as more significant—and 'true'. In South Africa, the Government's Fagan Commission's report had also been published in February 1948, addressing many of the same issues as Paton's novel. It came too late to offer impetus for real change to the jittery United Party Government of Prime Minister Jan Smuts, soon to lose elections to D. F. Malan's revitalised National Party, but nonetheless raised the possibility of changes of which Paton would have approved: that black workers be allowed to bring their families with them to the cities; that more humane conditions be created on the new Orange Free State goldfields; that landlessness and deprivation in the tribal reserves be addressed and the pass system ameliorated.[50] The *British Africa Monthly* was no doubt correct in supposing that *Cry, the Beloved Country* would have greater appeal than a government report, but its suggestion that Paton's novel contained essentially the same material, possibly to greater effect, is intriguing. 'May it not be that Alan Paton in clothing the problem in flesh and blood by the creation of Africans and Europeans of goodwill has done something that will help to make it possible to keep alive the liberal spirit in South Africa', the reviewer asked.[51]

The third impression of Cape's edition had appeared in Britain within a month of publication. There were 18 Cape impressions by 1951, although each was of only 5,000 copies. At least half of these, about 45,000 copies, were sold in South Africa. There were 31 Cape impressions between 1948 and 1977, amounting to 178,000 copies, and the novel also sold 158,000 copies in the Reprint Society World Books series.[52] Exceptionally large sales of the novel in Britain and South Africa were achieved in its Penguin edition; Penguin had been anxious to acquire rights to the novel for several years before Cape decided to license a paperback edition in 1958, and there were new editions in 1959, 1988 and 2001.[53] Sales figures are sketchy, but the Penguin edition, for example, sold in excess of 30,000 copies in the 6 months to the end of December 1972 and the same number in the 6 months following.[54] Penguin's licence was extended regularly, earning Paton a considerable amount.[55]

'A great book in any [other] country': South Africans and *Cry, the Beloved Country*

The *Cape Times* noted on 24 March 1948 that American critics were praising *Cry, the Beloved Country* 'so enthusiastically that it [was] likely to move up into the ranks of the best sellers in that country', while South African readers had to 'wait impatiently for a British edition, available to booksellers in the Union, to be published'.[56] Once it had arrived, most English-language reviews in mainstream white papers were positive. A review in the *Daily Dispatch* in early October 1948, for example, agreed that while it was 'often not possible to rely too closely upon foreign opinion in estimates of their worth of books upon South Africa' ('works that might impress outside

observers do not always stand up to the searchlight of local knowledge'),
Paton's novel was indeed 'entitled to be called a great book in any country,
anywhere'.[57] Advance advertisements in the country had drawn heavily on
American notices and reviews, often repeating them almost exactly (as in the
Central News Agency's advert in the *Rand Daily Mail* on 18 September).[58]
This quoted 4 American endorsements, 3 directly from the *New York Times*
advertisement, and encouraged readers to obtain a copy of a 'timeless story
of modern South Africa'. The description draws on American endorsements
which discover a universal appeal, while also suggesting that the novel was
a document of contemporary, specifically South African, circumstances.

A review in the *Natal Mercury*, published in Paton's home province,
echoed those sentiments, confirming that the novel was widely *expected* to
become a best-seller. It claimed, too, that while foreign readers had judged
it 'an outstanding piece of literature', South African readers would 'look at
it differently' and be impressed chiefly by Paton's 'realistic understanding of
some of the indigenous problems of this country'.[59] These by now familiar terms of engagement are clear from the *Daily Despatch* review: Paton's
novel 'has deep truth, and simplicity and directness' which spoke of 'profound
understanding'; it was not mere reportage. Furthermore, it suggested 'a force-
ful message that is concealed in the writing of it and that emerges indirectly
and not at the insistence of the author'.[60] An anonymous reviewer in *Jewish
Affairs* grappled with a concern that the novel was not great literature even
if it seemed important documentary work. The novel was noticed in all the
major South African *Jewish* papers, all of which were very aware, in the early
post-Holocaust years, of the urgent need to extend to other races in South
Africa the recognition and tolerance which Jews demanded themselves.[61]
Echoing in order to dismiss the suggestion that anyone with Paton's experience of 'African conditions' could have written the novel, the *Jewish Affairs*
reviewer argued that '*Cry, the Beloved Country* looks so much like a document,
so much like a presentation of facts, merely edited, that its literary merit tends
to be overlooked', but literary merits it had, the reviewer thought. Paton 'contrived to import to what is essentially a work of fiction, an authenticity which
gives it the validity of a document', the reviewer noted, but, while certainly a
document, it was also 'a piece of creative art'.[62] For *Femina*, too, Paton's novel
was a technically accomplished 'tour de force' as well as (or on account of
being also) 'a statement, a documentary'.[63]

Operating with a limited conception of the category of 'the literary',
one effected in large measure by metropolitan assumptions about a (British)
literary standard, the horizon of expectations for many South African critics was challenged by Paton's novel—as it had been in a different manner by,
for example, Schreiner's *The Story of an African Farm* and Plomer's *Turbott*

Wolfe. To read the novel was 'to undertake a new step in our own education', declared the *Rand Daily Mail's* reviewer, who suggested further that a 'very good preparation for reading it intelligently [was] to go down to Johannesburg station at nine o'clock in the morning and watch the Natal train come in and pour its passenger-load of problems on the platform'.[64] The veracity of Paton's representation of the problems attendant on urbanisation and detribalisation—which the reviewer uncomfortably, and perhaps tellingly, anthropomorphises in the persons of their victims—might be ascertained through social observation: 'This stream of humanity is so vividly heterogenous that you cannot fail to be shocked by it into a sudden, sharp realisation of the extent of Johannesburg's impact upon these people, and it is precisely this impact which is the theme and impulse of the book.'[65] Once again, discourses of the literary and the social documentary complement and qualify each other.

Almost all such reviews mirrored the paternal attitude to 'these people' which, many have argued, informed Paton's approach. The *Daily Despatch* reviewer called the novel 'a message of sympathy and kindliness towards a childlike people groping in the darkness'.[66] Joseph Sachs claimed in *Trek* that the reader of *Cry, the Beloved Country* witnessed 'the Natives whom we know as a people and a problem, shed their anonymity and emerge as . . . human beings with feelings, passions, dimensions'.[67] But his discussion of Paton's representation of the cadences of the vernacular Zulu militated against any presentation of Africans as other than undifferentiated members of a primitive, pre-linguistic community: 'their discourse has the animistic flavour of the primitive; their ideas run to metaphor and personification', it is 'redolent of a primal symbolism', it 'vibrates with the living rhythms that stir their childlike minds'.[68] It was this portrayal of black characters which invited trenchant criticism on political grounds from black South African intellectuals.

A reviewer in the Cape Town-based periodical *The Torch*, which served a largely Coloured readership and was the mouthpiece of the Non-European Unity Movement (and so allied with South Africa's Trotskyist Left), took issue with the politics of *Cry, the Beloved Country* soon after its arrival in the country, rejecting what it took to be the novel's suggestion that the '[b]lack man's answer to oppression' ought to be 'long-suffering humility and gratitude for small mercies'. Such 'time-worn answers' were 'no longer acceptable to the Non-Europeans', *Torch* declared; they had rejected 'Christian trusteeship' and Paton's message had 'no validity for them to-day'.[69] There was a lively debate about the novel in *Torch*. A letter published on 29 November 1948 took issue with those who praised the 'humanity' of *Cry, the Beloved Country*. They ran into trouble, the correspondent suggested, because the 'politics of emancipation' was the only critical standard by which to measure 'the ideological side' of such a novel, and, in the final analysis Paton stood 'condemned' for 'preaching regressive policies in the name of progress'.[70]

Paton's novel gives little idea of any effectively organised black political opposition. Reverend Stephen Kumalo is quick to chide Napoleon Letsitsi, the agricultural instructor brought to Ndotsheni by James Jarvis, for suggesting that blacks should aspire to self-sufficiency, to refuse handouts from conscience-stricken whites.[71] John Kumalo is an inefficient, selfish, cowardly manipulator, and black South Africans are represented as incomplete: of the three important local black politicians, Msimangu tells Stephen, Tomlinson 'has the brains', John Kumalo 'the voice', while Dubula 'has the heart'. All lack something, and the intelligent one is Coloured—'brown'—rather than black.[72] Predictably, Msimangu is full of praise for a white liberal who, of course, combined the talents of all three: 'Professor Hoernlé . . . was the great fighter for us', with, significantly, 'Tomlinson's brains, and your brother's voice, and Dubula's heart, all in one man'.[73]

For Lewis Nkosi, Stephen Kumalo was a 'cunning expression of white liberal sentiment', his forbearance, humility and resignation suggesting that whites could evade responsibility for racial injustice. Paton's novel could envision only a 'distorted, sentimental' solution 'in which reconciliation consists of liberals supplying milk and helping build a dam in a Bantustan'.[74] For Ezekiel Mphahlele, too, Paton 'sentimentalized his black characters in order to prove the effectiveness of a liberal theory that he posed'.[75] Nat Nakasa dismisses the novel for its black characters' 'naïve confidence in the potential goodness of the next man and his religion'.[76] As Rob Nixon notes, *Cry, the Beloved Country* was a 'cardinal counter-text for the Sophiatown set—it was the book they wrote against'.[77] Their distaste for Paton's representation of black characters was given form in Lionel Rogosin's seminal film *Come Back, Africa* (1959), in which Blake Modisane, Can Themba and others 'expound on the inadequacy of Paton's account of urban African life'.[78]

Left-wing white critics were also generally dismissive of the novel. Murray Carlin, writing in Rhodes University's *Review*, declared that Paton's supposedly simple style was in fact 'highly artificial', and, the novel as a whole 'too unskilled in technique and too false in feeling to be considered at all highly as a literary work'.[79] Some reviewers grounded a judgement of the novel's apparent literary merit in an appreciation of the manner in which Paton conveyed the impression of a transposed and translated Zulu idiom.[80] The *Daily Despatch* reviewer suggested that through its use Paton achieved 'an atmosphere of realism and effect that would probably not be secured in any other way'.[81] Interestingly, J. M. Coetzee would repeat many of Carlin's criticisms of the novel's artifice in *White Writing*, even uncannily using the same examples of Paton's unnecessarily awkward and childlike Zulu usage.

This language, Coetzee asserts, is a 'phantom Zulu', less a medium through which characters speak than 'part of the interpretation Paton wishes us to make of them', marking them as belonging to an 'old-fashioned context of direct (i.e. unmediated) personal relations based on respect, obedience, and fidelity'.[82] Carlin found *Cry, the Beloved Country* wanting as a 'social document'. He called Paton's 'the Christian viewpoint', but remarked that it was 'also the sentimental, the compliant, and, worst of all, the ignorant viewpoint'; the novel glossed over 'the real savagery of the situation in South Africa', a failing which, Carlin noted sharply, was undoubtedly a reason for the novel's success.[83]

Carlin claimed that other reasons for its popularity included the 'reigning artistic-patriotic fervour'—'whereby anything South African [was] automatically good'—and 'confusion in loyal minds between literary and political standards, between Paton the novelist and Paton the Liberal'.[84] It is certainly true that the real subject of appreciative—and defensive—South African reviews was 'Paton the Liberal', rather than his novel. Liberal assumptions are paramount, for example, in Sachs's review in *Trek*, which casts Paton as speaking for the speechless. Yet it was this interpellation which Nkosi and his contemporaries found most disturbing, and its assumptions evidence what Bhabha and others have usefully described as '*processes of subjectification* made possible (and plausible) through stereotypical discourse', processes which are part of the 'productivity of colonial power', and which construct colonial subjects—in this case the black characters in Paton's novel and, by extrapolation, black South Africans in general—as paradoxically both *other* and *knowable*.[85] Said suggests that the 'general liberal consensus that "true" knowledge is fundamentally non-political (and conversely, that overly political knowledge is not "true" knowledge) obscures the highly if obscurely organized political circumstances obtaining when knowledge is produced'.[86] Paton's *artful* representation of socio-political conditions in South Africa had the appearance of document for many reviewers, but masked a clear political programme: Christian, liberal, humanist trusteeship.

'White Man, Do Not Deceive Yourself': Paton and the *African Drum*
Given the hostility to the novel among black intellectuals, what are we to make of the fact that *Cry, the Beloved Country* was serialised, in 1951 and early 1952, in the first thirteen issues of *The African Drum*, a journal aimed at a black readership?[87] The changing content of the magazine provided a context which commented on Paton's novel in oblique but fascinating ways: where the first instalment appeared alongside African-American poet Countee Cullen's 'Heritage', a poem expressing a similar Christian idealism and nostalgia for a rural, archaic, African identity and similarly able to be

adduced to a non-confrontational political ethic, later installments appeared alongside reports on rival conferences of African liberation organisations and an article on forced removals under the Group Areas Act.[88]

An editorial in the second issue quoted a letter from a reader, Mr Zondi, approving of the young magazine's disavowal of politics. While 'as black as ebony and an African of the first water', Zondi wrote, he had been sceptical of the magazine, which he initially expected to be another 'call to arms for our political rights', a cause on which he was reluctant to 'waste time'. He had expected 'photographs of gargantuan political gatherings and doubtful patriots with corpulent tummies delivering orations with voices that shake the very air and sway the masses', but was delighted to find that the magazine's editors had 'decided to shun the political field which is strewn with partisanship, hate and controversy'.[89] The second issue also included, unabridged, Chapters Six, Seven and Eight of Book One of *Cry, the Beloved Country*, including Stephen Kumalo's meeting with his brother John, the latter portrayed in Paton's description and in the accompanying illustration, as every bit one of the corpulent demagogues Mr Zondi despised.[90] John had 'grown fat', his brother notices, and sits 'with his hands on his knees like a chief', suggesting that he is acting above his station. He is dangerously beguiling, swaying 'to and fro' as if addressing an absent crowd, and speaks in a 'strange voice'. Paton's is a distinctly unflattering portrait, and one which was in accord with *The African Drum*'s dismissal of 'dubious patriots' who stirred up violence.[91]

By contrast, later in 1951, the October issue included, with English translation, a Zulu poem, 'Mlung' Ungazikhohlisi' (White Man, Do Not Deceive Yourself), which invited the 'white man' to consider that education and acceptance of Western dress and habits did not mean that a black person had been subjugated or assimilated. The poem was by 'Bulima Ngiyeke', a pseudonym which can be translated as 'stupidity leave me alone'. Cutting sarcasm suggests an ironic and knowing mimicry, which, in Bhabha's formulation of the positive tension of mimicry as a strategy to subvert oppression and stereotype, turns the 'gaze of the discriminated back upon the eye of power'.[92] The speaker warns in conclusion:

> If I pretend to be like you, Prince,
> Apeing you, I know what I am about
> I know what I brought with me
> I know what I will take away with me
> I know well what is in my gourd,
> How could I forget, this is my birthright
> White Man, do not deceive yourself.[93]

Deference and submission to the multiple indignities of segregationist legislation, and apparent adoption of, or aspiration to adopt, the trappings of Western civilisation, did not negate a black African identity, the poem suggests. Paton's young Johannesburg priest Theophilus Msimangu, marked by his name as loving (the white man's) God, by consciously and sincerely mimicking the 'European' in dress and metaphysics, does not, however, apparently intend to return the gaze of the oppressor: Paton has him state explicitly that he is grateful that missionaries brought his 'father out of darkness'.[94]

Edited initially by whites who wholly endorsed Paton's novel's (apparent) model of humanitarian trusteeship, *The African Drum* did not sell well, although those who bought it thought highly of the novel: it received the most nominations in a poll to rank regular features, with nearly 2,000 'votes' compared with 1,360 for the least favourite feature, 'Music of the Tribes'. The editors wondered, in response to the latter item's poor showing, whether 'the African of to-day [is] too much concerned with the 20th century and . . . juke boxes to be interested in his tribal antecedents and environment'.[95] Paranoia about detribalisation constantly exercised the magazine's white managers, but articles on tribal customs and music did not appeal to an increasingly sophisticated, urbanised readership, and within a year the magazine was transformed into *Drum* under a new editor, Anthony Sampson. With talented writers and polemicists like Nat Nakasa, Can Themba, Ezekiel Mphahlele, Todd Matshikiza and Lewis Nkosi, *Drum* soon became the mouthpiece of vibrant, black, Johannesburg culture, publishing articles on crime, jazz, sports and celebrities.[96] Early installments of Paton's novel appeared under a banner illustration juxtaposing a rural scene with the city. Under the new team, drawings casting the city in a negative light and romanticising the country gave way to photographs of the actors starring in the 1951 London Films version of the novel.[97]

Early installments of *Cry, the Beloved Country* were unabridged, but as the tone and editorial direction of the magazine changed, Paton's novel was no longer the only fiction it published. The issue for September 1951 included other fiction for the first time: a short story by Bloke Modisane, 'The Dignity of Begging', involving a courtroom scene which, unlike those the reader was still to encounter in the serialisation of *Cry, the Beloved Country*, was satirical, humorous at the expense of whites.[98] By early 1952, under its new editor, *Drum*'s pages were crammed with popular culture stories, competitions and photo essays, and there is a very real sense that Paton's text was outstaying its welcome; the serialisation continued only because it was so nearly completed, one suggests, but the final installments are heavily abridged. In the issue for September 1951, all but the final two sentences of the excerpt which

James Jarvis reads from his son's essay (in Chapter Twenty-One), are omitted, significantly shortening Arthur's bitter indictment of the hypocrisy of a
supposedly religious white society.[99] Much of the twenty-third chapter (the
discovery of gold at Odendaalsrust) and all of the chapter following (Jarvis
re-visiting his son's study) are omitted from the October issue, reducing further the extent to which Arthur Jarvis's liberal dilemma is dwelt on in the
Drum text.[100]

    Both of these installments appeared under the old editorial team, and
their care to ameliorate, or circumscribe, potentially negative representations of whites is clear. In the February 1952 instalment, which included the
first chapter of Book Three (Kumalo's return to Ndotsheni), the section in
which the new schoolteacher wishes to sing *Nkosi Sikelel' iAfrika*, a prayer for
Africa and an anthem long associated with black South African nationalism,
but finds the people do not know the words, is omitted. This appeared after
Sampson's assumption of the editorship, and he may have thought that the
villagers' ignorance ought not to be represented.[101]

    The March 1952 instalment omits the faintly comical portrait of the
chief's attempts to help the surveyors mark out the site for the dam, in the
third chapter of Book Three.[102] Restricting representation of the chief's slow-
ness to understand the advances planned for the valley effectively circum-
scribes implied criticism of traditional leadership structures (which *African
Drum* had been keen to promote). In the context of its new editorial policy, it
may have been that this portrayal was excluded as a negative and potentially
politically reactionary presentation by a white writer of a black character (as
excessively naïve). Many of the omissions work to limit Paton's criticism of
black political activity. In the final instalment, the novel's penultimate chapter is omitted in its entirety, and all of Kumalo's discussion with Letsitsi,
and Paton's implicit critique, through Kumalo, of Letsitsi's pan-Africanism,
are consequently lost.[103] These tensions between the abridged text of Paton's
novel and its context in *Drum* suggest both how amenable the work was to
appropriation by liberal attitudes of trusteeship and how it was received scep-
tically by a sophisticated, politicised, urban, black readership.

Condensed and Digested: Abridging *Cry, the Beloved Country*
The serialised and abridged version of Paton's novel in *Drum* was not its
only appearance in such a highly charged context. In the wake of the early
success of Scribner's edition in the USA, and the positive tone of almost
all the American reviews, *Cry, the Beloved Country* had been selected as an
alternative choice for the American Book-of-the-Month Club as early as
April 1948.[104] Janice Radway suggests that judges for the Club's list were
especially keen on texts which appeared to them 'to combat despair with

sympathy and affiliation'.[105] A similar endorsement of individualism and forbearance was propagated by the *Reader's Digest* magazine which, from its inception in 1922, but particularly during the Cold War, played a significant role in the construction of a popular American national identity through accessible, widely read, 'middlebrow' publications, its flagship magazine consistently presenting itself as a guardian and promoter of the 'American' virtues of individualism and optimism.[106] In 1950, *Reader's Digest* launched its 'Condensed Books' series and the very first volume, which went on to sell half a million copies by 1957, contained an abridged version of *Cry, the Beloved Country*. This abridged text was included, in 1956, in the second volume of the Canadian 'Condensed Books' series, and, with some variations, in a British 'Condensed Books' volume of at least 250,000 copies, also marketed in Australia and South Africa, in early 1958.[107]

The other abridged texts in the American volume had a popular appeal and emphasised similar values of individual perseverance in the face of adversity: *The Show Must Go On*, by prolific dramatist Elmer Rice; Morton Thompson's *The Cry and the Covenant*, about a Hungarian medical innovator; and the autobiography of the much-loved cowboy entertainer Will Rogers. Other abridgements in the Canadian and British 'Condensed Books' volumes were similarly popular 'middlebrow' novels: in Canada, Herman Wouk's best-selling war novel *The Caine Mutiny* and Irving Stone's *The President's Lady*; and in Britain *The Enemy Below*, *Minding Our Own Business* and Edna Ferber's *Giant*, which partially dealt with white–Mexican contact in Texas, the film adaptation of which, starring James Dean, had been released by Warner Brothers in 1956.

Publication in a series aimed at the 'middlebrow' readers of a culturally and politically conservative magazine in the early years of the Cold War constitutes a revealing appropriation of Paton's text in a fascinating *local*, but globally conscious, context. Joseph Grigely prefaces an analysis of a simplified and abridged *Reader's Digest* version of *Tom Sawyer* with the observation that while 'few people would consider a *Reader's Digest* condensed text an important text worth scholarly attention', the existence and popularity of such items witness to the fact that 'the vicissitudes of culture are not in the end dictated by the intentions of artists alone'.[108] The text of the *Reader's Digest* version of *Cry, the Beloved Country* is even more amenable than Paton's original to being read as a Christian morality tale of the corrupting effects of the city on *simple* peoples, with potentially universal application.

A prefatory note, surrounded by a border featuring sketches of black workers with spades and other implements, and Zulu warriors brandishing shields and assegais, describes the narrative as moving from 'semi-primitive tribal life in the green hills of Natal to the Shanty Town warrens of Johannesburg's slums,

breeding ground of racial tensions and violent crime'.[109] Attention is drawn
thematically and visually to the contrast between the corrupting city and rural
life, although in the text itself much of the original novel's detailed descriptions of rural and urban conditions is omitted, with the cumulative effect of
lessening the novel's constant emphasis on the disparities between the social
conditions of whites and blacks.[110] Many passages containing material which
could be read as critical of whites, or which detail political injustice or repression, are cut from the *Reader's Digest* text.[111] Chapters Nine and Thirteen are
omitted in their entirety; the absence of the first lessens the novel's indictment
of appalling township conditions and eliminates the multiple voices of the
nameless black residents who act in Paton's original text as a kind of chorus.
By contrast Chapter Twelve, which presents numerous voices of *white* Johannesburg residents, is significantly retained largely unchanged.[112]

Several chapters in Book Two are omitted in their entirety, of which the
ninth, in which John Kumalo addresses a gathering in support of the 1946
miners' strike, is the most significant. The conversation about politics between
Stephen and John in Book One (Chapter Seven) is also severely edited, but
the representation of John as a demagogue, corpulent and duplicitous, remains
relatively unaffected, although Msimangu's subsequent discussion of his fail-
ings (in the same chapter) is shortened to omit a critique of blacks who break
the law, however unjust or immoral.[113] The *Reader's Digest* version appears,
then, to mitigate what many have read as Paton's implicit dismissal of black
political activists, by omitting negative portrayals of those activists. The original text is, however, more complex than is sometimes acknowledged. Often
overlooked descriptions of John's effective self-censoring, lost in the omission
of the ninth chapter in Book Two (chapter twenty-six in consecutive num-
bering), may appear redundant, but offer a notional point of comparison with
another kind of black political aspiration which Paton's novel posits, even
if perhaps unintentionally. In the original text of the novel, the experienced
policemen listening to John's speech know he is 'afraid' of his own rhetoric,
and that he does not address his audience on pan-African resistance. Paton
could be argued implicitly to be acknowledging the force of this alternative
politics in stressing John's failure to exploit its possibilities.[114] As such, the
omission of these passages from the *Reader's Digest* text might be regarded
as marginalising all black political opinion more comprehensively than Paton
can be accused of doing.

A similar subtext of pan-Africanism is to be found in the original text's
numerous references to the singing of *Nkosi Sikelel' iAfrika*. With one exception, all references to it, and so (obliquely) to pan-Africanist discourse, are
omitted from the *Reader's Digest* text. In Paton's novel, it is sung in the shantytown scene, while in the first chapter of Book Three the new teacher calls

for it to be sung, but is rebuked by the old teacher, who dislikes politics and is ashamed at not knowing the words. In the penultimate chapter, when Kumalo asks why Letsitsi insists that all who are intent on regenerating the land must work for *Africa*, not South Africa, he replies: 'We speak as we sing . . . for we sing *Nkosi Sikelel' iAfrika*'.[115] Kumalo's extreme disquiet at Letsitsi's attitude to Jarvis's magnanimity, and Letsitsi's claim that white largesse is the least that is owed by whites for having stolen the land, are also omitted. All criticism of Jarvis is removed, and Paton's powerfully ambivalent portrayal of the conflicting imperatives of Kumalo's Christian humanism and Letsitsi's pan-Africanist socialism is lost. Paton's original text does, at least, admit of the complexity of socio-political alternatives. The one reference to *Nkosi Sikelel' iAfrika* which is retained occurs in the final chapter of the novel. Alone on the mountain on the morning of his son's execution, Kumalo prays 'for all the people of Africa, the beloved country. *Nkosi Sikelel' iAfrika*, God save Africa.' The British (but not Canadian and American) *Reader's Digest* text adds brackets, arguably depoliticising the reference by making the Xhosa title merely the translation of a prayer, '(God save Africa)', rather than the name of the anthem of black nationalism.[116]

Similarly, extensive excisions from the courtroom scenes render Paton's emphasis on the importance of the rule of law considerably less qualified than in the original text, which highlights, not entirely unintentionally, the precarious inscrutability of the court. There are many other omissions. Some are likely to have been informed by the abridgers' sense of the likely audience's religious sentiments—for example those emphasising Stephen Kumalo's virtue by removing all reference to 'flaws' in his character (including his cruelty to Absalom's girlfriend, the religious doubts and anger he expresses to Father Vincent, and the lie he tells to hurt his brother).[117] Others mediate the complexities of the South African situation for the intended audience of the abridged version, the average American reader not conversant with many facts about the country or its history, and subsequently similar readerships in Canada and elsewhere in the Commonwealth. Consequently, many of the subtleties of the South African situation depicted with considerable care in Paton's novel are lost. More significantly, the author's implied socio-religious programme for addressing the disparities between a first world and (not inconsequentially) largely white society, on the one hand, and an intentionally undeveloped or under-developed black population, on the other, would have appealed to white American readers in an age in which, Ralph Ellison argues, America's 'so-called race problem' had 'lined up with the world problems of colonialism and the struggle of the West to gain the allegiance of the remaining non-white people who [had] thus far remained outside the Communist sphere'.[118]

'Preferably a bit simple': Paton in the Classroom

If a process of therapeutic identification (or displacement) operated in the *Reader's Digest* abridgement of *Cry, the Beloved Country*, the novel's serialisation in the *African Drum* evidences modes of self-recognition as interpolated by a paternalistic, white, editorial regime, endorsed, then challenged, and ultimately displaced by the local demands of a black readership. The novel's wide uptake in school curricula in the USA and across the Commonwealth displays some of the same kinds of displacements, but also altogether more *local*—and economic—decisions.

The novel's suitability for American schools and colleges was discussed in educational magazines, including those concerned with African-American schools, as early as 1949. Gertrude Rivers wrote that year in the *Journal of Negro Education* that it was a 'guide book' and an indictment of injustice, and compared it favourably with Richard Wright's *Native Son* and Lillian Smith's *Strange Fruit*, two influential studies of the injustices suffered by African-Americans.[119] Harold R. Collins suggested in *College English* in 1953 that *Cry, the Beloved Country* was a 'capsule history' of South Africa.[120] He argued that the novel's primary theme was detribalisation and the attendant 'loss of the old African moral order that gave purpose and meaning to African lives', but that it did 'what no discursive work in political science, sociology, economics, or anthropology could': it conveyed 'the "form and pressure" of life' in the country.[121] Both Rivers and Collins, then, advanced a reading of the novel as a guide to actual social conditions in South Africa, in much the same manner that many reviewers in Britain and America had done. School and college sales increasingly amounted to a large proportion of the novel's American sales. By 1959, it was selling between 6,000 and 8,000 copies annually to colleges, and around 3,000 a year in bookstores, and Scribner's published a paperback edition in 1959 to increase sales, particularly to colleges, where, as Charles Scribner Jr wrote to Paton, the novel had 'acquired the status of a classic'.[122]

Other interventions confirmed that part of the novel's attraction for many American readers was its Christian humanist message. Sheridan Baker argued in *College English* in 1957 that a specifically Christian 'moral geography' (valleys of despair, mountains of hope) mirrored the novel's depiction of 'the salvage of evil through love and suffering'.[123] He went on to edit an edition of *Cry, the Beloved Country* in the Scribner 'Research Anthology' series, billed as providing access to 'the Novel, the Critics, the Setting', in 1968. In addition to the full text of the novel, this volume included responses to the work (including Collins's and Baker's essays) and a range of documents, by Paton and others, on social and political conditions in South Africa, including extracts from anthropological studies and discussions of the effects of apartheid (including crusading anti-apartheid British cleric Trevor Huddleston's memoir, *Naught for Your Comfort*, and the defensive riposte by the Director of Information at South Africa's British Embassy).[124]

Baker claims in his Introduction that *Cry, the Beloved Country* is 'an important twentieth-century novel' which merits 'close analysis in its own right'. But its value is also that it 'evokes a specific time and place, South Africa in 1946', and opens 'a world outside the novel for investigation'. The criterion of literariness hovering on the edges of Baker's discourse is that the literary 'springs from a deep private response to the social sense', that 'particulars must convey some universal implications'; Paton's novel satisfies this requirement, demonstrating 'uncommonly well the fundamental nature of literature'.[125] Confirming an implicit recognition in many earlier reviews and assessments, Baker concedes tellingly that the 'most significant reason for the novel's strange power' over American readers is that it 'speaks with immediacy to analogues within our own society and our individual experience'.[126] Universality opens eyes to the world, and to the world at home. The date of this volume's publication, 1968, is significant, too, coinciding with the Reverend Martin Luther King Jr's assassination and the Democratic National Convention riots in Chicago, in the midst of a heated period of protests for civil rights and against the Vietnam War.

The earliest example of the effect of a judgement about the suitability of Paton's novel for use in the classroom in Britain and the Commonwealth is an abridged and 'very lightly' simplified edition published by Longmans, Green & Co. in 1953. This was the first of several school editions or versions of the novel published by the firm and its successors over the next forty years. Each made intriguing decisions about the presentation of the work and sometimes revealing changes to its text. Some of these are now considered in turn.

The 1953 series aimed to provide reading material for students with a limited vocabulary and little grasp of '*English* thought and ways of life', and who had completed a simplified course in the language.[127] All titles in the series—which included *Nicholas Nickleby*, *Great Expectations*, Sherlock Holmes stories, selections of one-act plays and various prose anthologies—started from a 3,000-word vocabulary, introducing suitably glossed new words to a limit of 7,000 words.[128] There are many omissions from Paton's original text, most simplifying the novel's politics and emphasising its presentation of black South Africans' conditions as tragic—rather than the result of the white rulers' policies or neglect. Relatively few words in the remaining text appear to have been changed. In the opening paragraphs, for example, 'matted' is changed to 'thick', 'well-tended' becomes 'well looked after', 'unshod' becomes 'barefoot' and 'kloof' is translated as 'small valley'.[129] The Afrikaans *kloof*—like *koppie*, in its Dutch form *kopje*—had almost certainly become familiar to British readers from nineteenth- and early twentieth-century colonial adventure stories and reportage from the Anglo-Boer War, but the simplified abridgement (and the series as a whole) was clearly intended for a different set of readers: second-language speakers, many in the same kind of social and economic circumstances as Paton's novel's poor rural and shanty-town black communities.

This simplified version did well enough for Longmans, Green & Co. to publish an abridged edition of the original text in 1962, aimed at younger native speakers or older, more accomplished students of English, in Britain and the Commonwealth, in a series which included established set texts like *A Tale of Two Cities*, *Wuthering Heights* and *Pride and Prejudice*. An introduction argued that *Cry, the Beloved Country* had universal appeal, and sought to position it in the context of 'big problems that hit the headlines of the world: colonialism, the colour problem, bad farming', and 'swift and careless industrialism'; it also suggested that the novel was a guide to the 'helpless confusion of African affairs'.[130] Almost every reference to prostitution, pregnancy out of wedlock and common-law marriage—sensitive topics in a text aimed at a school market across the Commonwealth—is omitted from the abridged text. One can only speculate on whether it was cultural and religious sensibilities that prompted the omissions or a paternalistic concern for morals amongst likely readers who were often constructed in imperial and liberal discourse as childlike and easily influenced.[131] The novel's political discourse is also radically circumscribed: selective editing of the judge's summation at the end of Absalom's murder trial curtails discussion of the concepts of the *law* and *justice* in an unjust society; all representations of rural ignorance or naïvety are cut, as are many of the chorus-like passages conveying the anonymous and politically inflected voices of black and white Johannesburg. The novel's moral, as paraphrased by the editor, is clearly served by all of these changes: 'If the greed and hatred could be turned to love and co-operation, Paton believes the land could be nursed to an abundant fertility and every human enterprise could flourish.'[132]

Longman published an unabridged edition of *Cry, the Beloved Country* for school use, primarily in Britain, in 1966, in its 'Heritage of Literature' series. The apparatus provided in this edition presents it as a social-problem novel: the Introduction discusses urbanisation and the effects of industrialisation, describing detribalised Africans problematically, as having crowded into cities, 'where they were responsible for some of the social problems described in *Cry, the Beloved Country*'.[133] Themes of personal tragedy and the triumph of personal faith are highlighted, as is Paton's 'style', which is described as biblical and as conveying the 'symbolic, poetic quality of the Zulu language'.[134] The editor reinforces the novel's depiction of John Kumalo as one of 'those Africans who have learnt from the Europeans but who have abandoned the ideals and traditions of their own people and found nothing to put in their place'.[135] Young readers are encouraged to read the novel as an endorsement of trusteeship, as exactly the kind of text black South African intellectuals criticised.

Cry, the Beloved Country was widely prescribed by Britain's domestic examining bodies in the 1970s and 1980s. It appeared on many approved reading lists for schools, and many will have used Longman's 1966 edition, which went through sixty-six impressions and had never been out of print when the company included it in another series, 'Study Texts', aimed at the 'O' and 'A' levels market and launched in 1983.[136] The fact that Longman could reprint the novel seems largely to explain why it did so: there being no pattern for selecting set texts, publishers generally played to the sets of books teachers already had in their book cupboards. The series editor, Richard Adams, a chief examiner for the Oxford Board, invited Mark Spencer Ellis, an English master at the independent Forest School in London, to provide new prefatory and paratextual material to accompany the 1966 typesetting for the 'second wave' of titles in the series, in 1986.[137] Ellis's Introduction situates the novel specifically in the history of South African protest literature, providing extensive context for students to evaluate the veracity of Paton's portrayal of legalised injustices, and placing it in perhaps the most overtly political context of all the novel's editions to date. Paton had to approve new editorial matter, which he did, doubtless flattered at the political incisiveness attributed to his work nearly forty years after its first appearance.[138]

Ellis seeks to negotiate a means of reading *Cry, the Beloved Country* less as a novel of liberal reaction than a text remade through an act of perceptive reading. He attempts, in effect, to save Paton from his own book, suggesting that if one's 'assessment of *Cry, the Beloved Country* is that it reveals a world which can only be put right through revolution', then it appears to be 'a revolutionary text, irrespective of the peaceful humility of the principal characters'. Ameliorating Paton's presentation of black political activists, Ellis argues that an 'assessment of John Kumalo's personality' should not 'affect the way we see his views on society'; after all, he notes, 'people we dislike can be right while those we are fond of can talk nonsense'.[139] The emphasis on the difference between the logic of Paton's text and its perception and reconstruction by the reader, paying less attention to construed authorial intention, are clearly functions of contemporaneous movements in critical theory, and Ellis freely admits that, like many schoolteachers of the time, he was increasingly interested in ideas being promoted by the likes of Catherine Belsey.[140] The South African authorities would not allow that edition to be used in the country, but, as so often with apartheid-era censorship, not for the reasons one might have expected: Longman South Africa informed Ellis that it was his description of Paton's novel as representing entrenched discrimination against women in South Africa which was found especially objectionable.[141]

Just as Paton's novel was the target of much radical reappraisal in South Africa in the 1980s, so its suitability for teaching in British schools was also questioned. Teacher David Evans offered a critique in 1986, arguing that there was 'something suspicious' about a writer 'belonging to a power elite (however marginally) enjoining the powerless to eschew power', and something 'offensive' in his use of 'one of the powerless to convey the message of restraint'.[142] Just as Lewis Nkosi had done thirty years previously, Evans called the Reverend Kumalo an 'unrepresentative figure, even from the perspective of 1946–48', merely 'a white man's construct: too simple, too moral, too innocent'. Paton's novel appealed 'to the liberal-conservatism, the paternalism and the latent racism' of the British 'educational establishment', he charged: 'Revolutionary, autonomous blacks are not wanted in either Britain or South Africa, in fact or fiction. What is wanted is blacks who are cooperative, apologetic, servile and preferably a bit simple.'[143] As if responding to Ellis's Introduction, which he may well have been doing, Evans declared that, 'whatever its author's intentions', *Cry, the Beloved Country* was a 'dated, deeply paternalistic and even reactionary book' which ought to be replaced by another 'which upsets, not reinforces, white half-way house compassion and milky complacency'. A better choice might be made from work by Nadine Gordimer, Athol Fugard, Alex La Guma, Bessie Head or any of the new black authors being published by Ravan Press, he suggested.[144]

Despite this criticism, *Cry, the Beloved Country* continued to be set for examinations. The 1986 edition proved moderately successful in Britain, until the introduction of the GCSE examinations (when, in Ellis's assessment, educational publishers began aiming at a mass market). The 'Study Text' series books 'were seen as too difficult for GCSE', while 'A' level boards do not prescribe editions.[145] Nonetheless, the market for Paton's novel did not dry up completely: Longman reprinted the 1966 typesetting again in 1991, in a new series, 'Longman Literature', with new introductory and explanatory material, an additional glossary, study programme with questions and a list of further reading—including several South African novels: *The Story of an African Farm*, Gordimer's *July's People*, Mbulelo Mzamane's *Children of Soweto* and Beverley Naidoo's *Journey to Johannesburg*. This edition, aimed primarily at British schools and English-speaking schools in Anglophone Africa and the Caribbean, has had sixteen impressions to date and is still in print.[146] Longman has also republished the text of Wear and Durham's 1953 simplified version—in 1996, and again as a Penguin Level Six Reader aimed at the international second-language English teaching market, in 1999. The firm is reluctant to provide information on sales figures, but the Reader is currently in its second impression: Pearson Educational has consolidated the Longman and Penguin imprints; it remains open to speculation whether it continues to publish this text merely because it has the rights to it.

Paton and the Global Mediascape

Not only has Paton's novel sold in large numbers in multiple trade, book club, school and college editions, as well as in serialised, abridged and simplified print versions, it has also long been a multimedia phenomenon. In the decade following its publication and early reception, that extended originary moment of February to September 1948, dramatic, musical and cinematic adaptations, a self-propelling momentum as a best-seller, abridgement in school and *Reader's Digest* editions, and consistent investment at school level kept Paton's novel in the global public imagination.[147] Within a month of publication in the USA, rights were being negotiated to adapt it for the stage and for film. Kurt Weill and Maxwell Anderson's Broadway musical *Lost in the Stars*, based on the novel, opened in October 1949 and had 273 performances. It was revived by the Boston Lyric Opera in 1992, and a filmed version, loosely adapted by Alfred Hayes, appeared in the American Film Theatre series in 1974.[148] There have been at least two filmed adaptations of *Cry, the Beloved Country*. The first, produced by the famous Korda brothers' London Film Corporation and directed by Zoltan Korda, was filmed in South Africa and at London's Shepperton Studios in 1951 and released in 1952. The second, directed by Darrell Roodt and produced by Anant Singh, was released by Miramax in 1995.[149] In addition to these musical and film adaptations, there was a British verse drama adaptation by Felicia Komai, first performed at St Martin-in-the-Fields in London in February 1954. Roy Sargeant produced a 'new' stage adaptation at the South African National Arts Festival in Grahamstown in 2003 (reviewed as 'art that can heal').[150] Each adaptation has, without fail, emphasised the novel's universal themes or exploited its resonances for foreign audiences (and even, increasingly, for a new generation in the 'new' South Africa, for whom its problematic 'liberalism' is historical).

Set in an unrecognisable South Africa, *Lost in the Stars* draws on stereotypical representations of African-American culture to depict both Johannesburg and Zululand, confirming the reading of Paton's work as speaking to American anxieties about race. Maxwell Anderson's book alters the South African historical contexts of the novel, too: the letter which summons Kumalo to Johannesburg (sent in the play by John Kumalo rather than Msimangu) is dated 9 August 1949, setting the action of the musical in its audience's immediate past, but at least three years later than in Paton's novel and, significantly, *after* the National Party victory in South Africa in 1948.[151] The reconciliation between James Jarvis and Stephen Kumalo also involves a greater change of heart than in the novel, as Jarvis is initially portrayed as being extremely racist (this was to be repeated in the 1951 film).[152] Among many changes in *dramatis personae*, the musical introduces a chorus with a 'Leader' and an 'Answerer' to comment on the play's action, in the manner of a Greek tragedy (and in the call-and-response form of much traditional African-American music), exemplifying the widespread perception of the novel's plot as allegorical and archetypal (and speaking to American audiences in particular). Like *Lost in the Stars*, Komai's dramatic adaptation made use of representative, chorus-like figures ('Black Man' and 'White Man'), and developed Kumalo's analogy of 'a man / Sleeping in the grass', over whom 'is gathering / The greatest storm of all his days', into a strategically repeated motif.[153] The verse attempts to capture the biblical cadences of Paton's supposedly translated Zulu idiom, and these figures and symbols invite a reading of racial injustice as a tragedy, enacted by vast, inhuman agents. Both *Lost in the Stars* and Komai's version exaggerate—and thereby foreground—the novel's amenability to be read as making the causes of the novel's tragic events seem 'the function of some Fate or divinity', obscuring 'the real reasons (and hence possible solutions) for the tragic incidents' (in the words of Stephen Watson's critique).[154]

Zoltan Korda had previously made imperial adventures like *The Four Feathers* (1939) and justifications of imperial rule like *Sanders of the River* (1935). Always more left-wing than his brother Alexander, he had long looked for a vehicle for a more nuanced representation of Africa, and felt he had found it in Paton's novel.[155] Despite casting mostly Americans in the lead roles (the young Sidney Poitier played Msimangu), Korda nonetheless took risks, jeopardising American distribution by casting the African-American actor Canada Lee, blacklisted in Hollywood for his communist sympathies, as Stephen Kumalo. American distributors further 'infuriated Korda', Peter Davis notes, by renaming the film *African Fury*, and so removing possible association with the novel and implying 'a totally different character for the film, changing it to the jungle genre'.[156] The film was not a commercial success, and Paton claimed that he received little more than the £1,000 for which his agent had sold the film rights.[157]

Others have written at greater length about both filmed adaptations. As Mark Beittel observes, both are clearly products of their times and intended audiences. The 1951 film draws on conventions of early documentary film and *cinema verité* (the shantytown scenes really were filmed in townships), and emphasises the universality of the film's (and novel's) themes by avoiding all references to dates, thus making its historical present deliberately vague: it casts 'the story in a symbolic mode as part of an indefinite present and emphasizes the struggle against evil and the hope for a better day'.[158] The 1995 version, appearing a year after the first democratic elections in South Africa, focused less on the symbolic hope of the first film, producing an account of injustice and so 'historici[sing] Paton's parable of good versus evil'.[159] Nelson Mandela's speech at the 1995 film's premiere in New York City endorsed that reading, calling the film a historical representation of 'the terrible past from which South Africa has just emerged', as well as a 'monument to'—or for—'the future'.[160] Once again, emphasising the film's intention to appeal to a global audience, the leads were played by non-South Africans: James Earl Jones as Stephen Kumalo and Richard Harris as James Jarvis.

The history of the novel's global reception recently took a strange turn, as I intimated earlier: in late 2003, it was the second novel to be featured on Oprah Winfrey's revamped Book Club, 'Traveling with the Classics'. Winfrey's phenomenally successful Book Club made her, for a time, arguably 'the most powerful literary tastemaker' in American history; her choices for the first club made the best-seller list twenty-eight times in a row by the end of 1999.[161] She cast Paton's novel as both expressly the 'personal and political story of a nation' (especially the 'new' nation—Winfrey offered three readers a chance to visit the country and has herself adopted South African charities with remarkable dedication and vigour)—and, once again, as a novel with powerful universal resonances for a global audience.[162] The symbolism of its endorsement by a black media figure whose cachet transcends racial divisions in the USA is profoundly telling, too; such an endorsement could not, one feels, have come from a black South African media figure without considerable dissent from black intellectuals. Rita Barnard, an expatriate South African academic at the University of Pennsylvania, acted as the Book Club's online 'literary expert' for several months in late 2003, answering (mostly American) readers' questions about the novel, sketching an admirably nuanced picture of the novel's reception and continuing resonance by reminding readers that 'in South Africa, *Cry, the Beloved Country* is not as beloved as it is overseas. The novel has been vulnerable to criticism, especially on the basis of its liberal and paternalistic view of race relations.'[163] In an assessment of her engagement with the Book Club, Barnard suggests that the complex implications of Oprah's endorsement of *Cry, the Beloved Country* challenges notions of the 'political' in judgements of literary value and processes of reputation and reception. It is possible, she suggests polemically, that if interest in South African writing abroad was, in the past, 'fed and financed to the degree that it provided a vicarious sense of indignation, or moral *frisson*, in countries where politics seemed less urgent and dramatic' (or, as I have suggested, where it was easier to concentrate on problems far from home), future interest in the country's literary and cultural production may now depend 'on the degree that it provides images and narratives of suffering and its overcoming'.[164] *Cry, the Beloved Country* thus seems eminently well placed for an even longer afterlife.

Notes

1. Jacobson, 'Nostalgia', 830.
2. Callan, *Cry*, 17; Iannone, 'Tragic Liberalism', 442; see Alexander, *Paton*, 222.
3. Nixon, *Homelands*, 26.
4. Alan Paton Centre, Pietermaritzburg (APC), PC1/1/1/6–3, Paton to Juta. All unpublished Alan Paton correspondence quoted with permission, Mrs Anne Paton and the Alan Paton Centre.
5. See, for example, Nkosi, *Home and Exile*, 3; Nixon, *Homelands*, 26–7.
6. Paton, *Cry, the Beloved Country* (Scribner's 1948) and (Jonathan Cape, 1948), hereafter *Cry* (S) and (C). On the significance of the novel's success and the National Party's victory, see Paton's *Kontakion*, 82, and *Journey Continued*, 8; see also Van der Vlies, 'Alan Paton', 501–11.
7. Paton, *Cry, the Beloved Country* (Penguin, 2001), rear cover. Woods was editor of the *Daily Despatch* from 1965 to 1977, and famously a friend and supporter of Steve Biko.
8. Arac uses the term 'hypercanonization': *Idol and Target*, vii, 6.
9. See Barnard, 'Oprah's Paton', 94.
10. Alexander, *Paton*, 221.
11. APC, PC1/1/1/5, Dunn to Paton.
12. Scribner's, Advertisement.
13. Paton, *Cry* (S), dust-jacket cover blurb.
14. Sullivan, 'Fine Novel', 6.
15. Prescott, 'Books of the Times', 17.
16. Hansen, 'A Gentle Protest'.
17. Koch, 'Comfort in Desolation'; see also T. M. O., 'Without Fanfare'; Gardiner, 'On Saying "Boo!"', 662.
18. Gross, 'South Africa Presented'.
19. Locke, 'Dawn Patrol', 6, 7.
20. Quoted in Arac, *Idol*, 128.
21. Trilling, *The Liberal Imagination*, 220; see 205–22.
22. *Ibid.*, 214, 215.
23. Arac, *Idol*, vii, 7, and chapter 5; see Trilling, *The Liberal Imagination*, 104–17.
24. Nims, 'Grim View'.
25. Burns, 'Mirror to the South', 408–10.
26. See Paton, 'Negro in America Today' and 'Negro in the North'. *College English* noticed Paton's articles with the observation that 'he sees with a fresh eye and a sense of perspective almost impossible to a native American': Anon., 'News and Ideas', 192. Paton's photographer on this tour, Dan Weiner, later collaborated with him on a journey around South Africa which resulted in *South Africa in Transition* (1956). Paton's output of writing on race relations and related issues was prodigious: Alexander, *Paton*, 294–5, 493–8.

27. See 'Ebony Awards for 1948'; APC, PC1/1/1/5, Canby to Paton.

28. Cowling, 'The Beloved South African', 89.

29. Quoted in *ibid.*, 89.

30. Colleran, 'South African Theatre', 228; see Kruger, 'Apartheid on Display'.

31. APC, PC1/4/1/2, Paton to Howard; see Howard, *Jonathan Cape*, 214.

32. Alexander, *Paton*, 223. Alexander's biography of Plomer cites Paton as the source for the claim that Plomer was delighted by the success of Paton's novel, which he 'had highly recommended to Cape's when he first read it in manuscript': Alexander, *Plomer*, 292, 377; see Alexander, *Paton*, 463.

33. APC, PC1/1/1/5, Plomer, 'CRY, THE BELOVED COUNTRY', 1, 2.

34. *Ibid.*, 2.

35. APC, PC1/1/1/5, D.G. and L.L., 'Two Readers' Reports'. On Bunting, see Howard, *Jonathan Cape*, 178–83. Lamplugh also recommended the novel.

36. George, 'Evil City'.

37. Cape had been discouraged by the Ministry of Information from publishing Orwell's book lest it offend Russia, Britain's wartime ally. Secker and Warburg published it after the war: Howard, *Jonathan Cape*, 179.

38. In April 1948 Margot Barkham, an expatriate South African in New York City, reporting on the novel's American success, noted that 'Paton's London publisher' did not expect to have enough paper for publication until 1949: Barkham, 'South African's FIRST NOVEL', 77; see APC, PC1/1/1/5, Paton to Scribner, and Paton to Meyer.

39. Paton, *Cry* (S), v; (C), 5.

40. The fourth chapter of the second book in the American edition is thus Chapter 21, while in the British edition it is Book Two, Chapter 4. Chapters are cited hereafter as, e.g., 2:21/2:4, for *Cry* (S)/(C).

41. Paton, *Cry* (S), 257; see also (C), 239.

42. Street, 'Displaced Persons', 176.

43. Anon., 'Some New Novels', 3.

44. Herron, 'A Great Novel Comes Out of Africa'; Fausset, 'New Novels'.

45. Young, 'Out of Africa Something New'; see Hall, *Francis Brett Young*.

46. Paton, *Cry* (C), inside front cover flap of 1948 first edition and 1952 twentieth impression.

47. Allen, 'New Novels', 445, 446.

48. Bain, 'Four New Novels', 18.

49. Green, 'Grave and Sombre Words'. Comparison with social reformer-novelists like Trollope, Reade, and, pre-eminently, Dickens, was made by 'Castor', 'In Darkest Johannesburg', 581.

50. See Davenport and Saunders, *South Africa*, 360–1.

51. Green, 'Grave and Sombre Words'.

52. The 1977 Cape edition cites S reprints in 1948, 7 in 1949, 5 in 1950, one in 1951, 2 in 1952, one each in 1953, 1954, 1955, 2 again in 1957, and one a year in 1959, 1961, 1965, 1967, 1970 and 1977.

53. APC, PC1/4/1/1, Howard to Paton (1956), and Paton to Howard. In 1959, Penguin incorporated the note Paton wrote for Cape's 1959 edition. In 1988 the novel appeared in Penguin's Twentieth-Century Classics series, with Paton's note for the 1987 Collier Macmillan (New York) edition. It was repackaged for the Penguin Classics series at the turn of the new century.

54. APC, PC1/4/1/2, Poulton to Paton.

55. In 1976, the five-year extension of their licences earned Paton £6,000 for *Cry, the Beloved Country*, and £5,000 for the short story collection *Debbie Go Home* and his second novel, *Too Late the Phalarope*. Renewals in 1982 earned him £30,000 for *Cry, the Beloved Country*, in addition to a 12.5 per cent royalty (less Scribner's and Cape's shares). Further 5-year renewals, from 1987, earned £58,000, £55,000 of which for *Cry, the Beloved Country*: APC, PC1/4/1/4, Poulton to Paton, and Logan to Paton.

56. Aschman, 'Distinguished New South African Novel', 8.

57. Anon., 'New Books'.

58. Compare Scribner's, 'A Best-Seller Is Born!', and Central News Agency, 'A Best-Seller Is Born!'; see figs 4.1 and 4.2.

59. Anon., 'S.A. Novel Meets With High Praise'.

60. Anon., 'New Books'.

61. See Anon., 'Ein Buch', 4–5.

62. Anon., 'Alan Paton's Significant Scrutiny', 53, 55.

63. Anon., Review of *Cry, the Beloved Country*, 19.

64. S., Review of *Cry, the Beloved Country*.

65. *Ibid.*

66. Anon., 'New Books'.

67. Sachs, 'Books of the Month', 25.

68. *Ibid.* Lithuanian-born Sachs (1908–68) arrived in South Africa as a boy. He contributed widely to English-language newspapers and journals in the country: Herzberg, 'Dr. Joseph Sachs', 17.

69. S. C., '"Cry, the Beloved Country": Another View'; on *Torch* see Adhikari, *Not White Enough*, 96–116; and for my use of 'Coloured' see *ibid.* generally.

70. J. M., 'The Reviewer Reviewed', 5.

71. Paton, *Cry* (S), 262–3; (C), 244–5.

72. Paton, *Cry* (S), 43; (C), 45; (S), 39; (C), 41.

73. Paton, *Cry* (S), 45–6; (C), 47–8.

74. Nkosi, *Home and Exile*, 5.

75. Mphahlele, 'What the South African', 175; he repeated much the same analysis in *African Image*, 157–60.

76. Nakasa, 'Writing in South Africa', 38.

77. Nixon, *Homelands*, 26.

78. *Ibid.*, 261.

79. Carlin, '*Cry, the Beloved Country*', 10, 11.

80. For example, Young, 'Out of Africa', 3. Paton's language was imbued with cadences of the Authorised Version from childhood. Other influences include Steinbeck's *Grapes of Wrath*, Hamsun's *Growth of the Soil*, and Bunyan's *Pilgrim's Progress*. See Alexander, *Paton*, 198; Paton, *Towards the Mountain*, 267–72.

81. Anon., 'New Books'.

82. Coetzee, *White Writing*, 129; see 126–9, and compare with Carlin, '*Cry, the Beloved Country*', 10; see also Morphet, 'Stranger Fictions', 54–5.

83. Carlin, '*Cry, the Beloved Country*', 11.

84. *Ibid.*, 10

85. Bhabha, *Location of Culture*, 67.

86. Said, *Orientalism*, 10.

87. For more on *Drum*, see Chapman (ed.), 'More than Telling a Story'.

88. Anon., 'At Bloemfontein Africans Choose'; Anon., 'The Story of Bethal'; Xuma, 'Black Spots or White Spots?'; see Nixon, *Homelands*, 25–6. On the ANC and AAC, see Davenport and Saunders, *South Africa*, 327, 361–6, 383.

89. Anon., 'Opinion', *African Drum* 1.2, 1.

90. See fig. 4.3.

91. See Paton, 'Cry', *African Drum* 1.2 (April 1951), 5, 6; and compare *Cry* (S), 35–8; (C), 38–41.

92. Bhabha, *Location of Culture*, 112.

93. Ngiyeke, 'Mlung' Ungazikhohlisi', 11.

94. Paton, *Cry* (S), 25; (C), 30. The voicing of the humility and forbearance of Paton's black characters might also be read as (unconscious) subversive mimicry: Bhabha, *Location of Culture*, 36–7.

95. Anon., 'Opinion'.

96. Lindfors, 'Post-War Literature', 51, 52. 'While we were preaching tribal culture and folk-tales, they were clamouring to be let into the Western world', Anthony Sampson recalled: *Drum*, 21. The title on the contents page remained '*The African Drum*', but from late 1951 the cover, and each page, referred to the journal as *Drum*.

97. The photographs are of Canada Lee, who played Stephen Kumalo, relaxing off set, and of Paton and Korda (in vol. 1.9, 30–1) and of the glamorous Ribbon Dhlamini, who played Gertrude Kumalo (in vol. 2.1, 31).

98. Modisane, 'The Dignity of Begging'. Sanders discusses Modisane's intention (which he described in *Blame Me On History*) to have the beggar in the story represent black South Africans in a society 'which has determined that black is the condition of being dependent on white charity': Sanders, *Complicities*, 110.

99. Compare *Cry* (S), 151–2; (C), 143, 145; and 'Cry', *African Drum* 1.6 (September 1951), 36.

100. See Paton, 'Cry', *African Drum* 1.7 (October 1951), 18.

101. Compare *Cry* (S), 220, 221, and *Cry* (C), 206, 207 with 'Cry', *African Drum* 2.2 (February 1952), 30. For a political essay which drew on Paton's novel as evidence for 'Native' South Africans singing *Nkosi sikelel' iAfrika* see Deutsch, 'The Growth of Nations', 189.

102. Compare *Cry* (S), 238, 242, and *Cry* (C), 222, 226 with 'Cry', *African Drum* 2.3 (March 1953), 31.

103. See Paton, 'Cry', *African Drum* 2.4 (April 1952), 20.

104. APC, PC1/1/1/5, Scribner to Paton; see Alexander, *Paton*, 230.

105. Radway, *Feeling for Books*, 279.

106. Sharp, *Condensing the Cold War*, vii–xiv; see 43–4, 165–7.

107. Sales figure are quoted in APC, PC1/4/1/1, Howard to Paton (1957).

108. Grigely, *Textualterity*, 2.

109. References to the text of the North American abridgement are to the 1956 Canadian volume; the British volume is *Condensed Books* (1958). Paton, *Cry, Condensed* (1956), 196 and (1958), 346.

110. For example, passages are omitted in Chapter Eighteen—*Cry* (S); or (C) 2:1—in which James Jarvis is shown to know about poor agricultural practices and food shortages in the tribal reserves: *Cry* (S), 127; (C) 121, and compare *Cry, Condensed* (1956), 259; (1958), 416.

111. Including Msimangu's account of how John Kumalo and his followers call the Bantu Press the 'Bantu Repress', and the description of Stephen Kumalo's

shock at conditions in Claremont. Compare *Cry* (S), 28; (C), 32 and *Cry, Condensed* (1956), 212; (1958), 263.

112. See Paton, *Cry* (S), 49–62; (C), 51–62 and *Cry, Condensed* (1956), 228; (1958), 378.

113. Compare Paton, *Cry* (S), 39; (C), 42 and *Cry, Condensed* (1956), 220; (1958), 372.

114. Compare Paton, *Cry* (S), 180–1; (C), 169–70 and *Cry, Condensed* (1956), 291; (1958), 452).

115. Paton, *Cry* (S), 264; (C), 245; see *Cry* (S), 58; (C), 58; (S), 220; (C), 206.

116. Compare Paton, *Cry* (S), 271; (C), 252; *Cry, Condensed* (1956), 334; (1958), 499.

117. The passages omitted are from 1:16, 1:15, 2:29/2:12, 3:36/3:7 respectively.

118. Ellison, 'Art of Fiction', 212, 223–4.

119. Rivers, '*Cry, the Beloved Country*', 51.

120. Collins, 'Broken Tribe', 379.

121. Ibid., 380, 385.

122. APC, PC1/4/2/1, Scribner (Jnr) to Paton (1961); and see Scribner (Jnr) to Paton (1959).

123. Baker, 'Paton's Beloved Country', 56, 60.

124. Baker (ed.), *Paton's Cry, the Beloved Country*. Other titles in the series included volumes on Hemingway and editions of *Julius Caesar*, James's *Daisy Miller*, and Wharton's *Ethan Frome*. The text of the novel appears on pages 7–132 (with pagination from the Scribner's first edition in parentheses). See Huddleston, *Naught for Your Comfort*; Steward, *You Are Wrong*.

125. Baker, Introduction, 1.

126. *Ibid.*

127. Bright. 'The Bridge Series', v.

128. *Ibid.*, vi.

129. Paton, *Cry* (19.53), 3.

130. Blacksell, Introduction, 5, 6.

131. The omissions are too numerous to cite here, but for one example, compare the treatment of the original text's introduction of Absalom's pregnant girlfriend: see Paton, *Cry* (C), 65, 66 and this 1962 abridgement, 47.

132. Blacksell, Introduction, 6.

133. Clark, Introduction, 255.

134. *Ibid.*, 260.

135. *Ibid.*, 265.

136. See Evans, *Novel as Political Tract*, 1, 12. Not all new examining bodies have maintained their archives, and it has proved impossible to trace precisely when and where *Cry, the Beloved Country* was prescribed and examined, or to obtain copies of all relevant examination questions. Edexcel, whose examination papers are used by many schools in the south of Britain, has not prescribed *Cry, the Beloved Country* for some years (Davies to Van der Vlies, private correspondence). The Cambridge Local Examinations Syndicate archive confirms that the novel was set for British CSE examinations, but the CSE examining boards which merged with UCLES—the southern regional and west midlands boards—passed on very few records, and UCLES holds little examination material (Emerson to Van der Vlies,

private correspondence). Jonathan Cape told Paton that the 1966 Longman edition had sold well 'and never been out of print': APC, PC1/4/1/4, Mossop to Paton.

137. Ellis to Van der Vlies, private correspondence, and Ellis, Interview.

138. Ellis, Interview. Paton approved this material in due course: APC, PC1/4/1/4, Paton to Mossop (January and July 1985).

139. Ellis, Introduction, xx.

140. Ellis, Interview.

141. *Ibid.*

142. Evans, *Novel as Political Tract*, 6.

143. *Ibid.*, 11.

144. *Ibid.*, 11, 13.

145. Ellis to Van der Vlies, private correspondence.

146. Timothy to Van der Vlies, private correspondence.

147. The novel has also been translated widely. Norwegian, Danish, Swedish, Dutch, Finnish, Czech and French translation were all first contracted in 1948, Portuguese and Italian in 1949, Japanese and Hebrew in 1950, and subsequently German (1951), Icelandic (1955), isiZulu (1957), Malayan (1959), Ovambo (1974), Spanish (1976; significantly, after Franco), Greek (1983), and Tsonga (1998). There have subsequently been new translations in some of these languages.

148. Alexander, *Paton*, 466; Paton, *Journey Continued*, 20, 23–4; Anderson, *Lost in the Stars*; Matlaw, 'Alan Paton's', 272. Paton, unimpressed with the Broadway production, was particularly upset by its tone of religious scepticism: Paton, *Journey Continued*, 20, 23–4.

149. Alexander, *Paton*, 221–2, 260–4, 266, 268; Beittel, '"What Sort of Memorial?"'.

150. Sargeant's production was directed by Heinrich Reisenhofer: Bothma, '"Cry' op die Verhoog' (online).

151. Anderson, *Lost in the Stars*, 11.

152. See *ibid.*, 18–20, 92–4.

153. Komai, *Cry*, 45, 65; see 6. Compare Paton, *Cry* (S), 105; (C), 101.

154. Watson, 'Failure of Liberal Vision', 32, 33; see also Parker, 'The South African Novel', 8.

155. Beittel, '"What Sort of Memorial?"', 73–4; Davis, *In Darkest Hollywood*, 39–42.

156. Davis, *In Darkest Hollywood*, 44.

157. Paton, *Journey Continued*, 54; see 17–19, 41–9, 53–5.

158. Beittel, '"What Sort of Memorial?"', 72.

159. *Ibid.*, 84.

160. Mandela, 'Remarks at the Miramax Films World Premiere' (online).

161. English, *Culture of Prestige*, 34.

162. Winfrey, Book Club e-mail; see Barnard, 'Oprah's Paton', 94–8.

163. Barnard, online answer.

164. Barnard, 'Oprah's Paton', 101.

Chronology

1903	Born on January 11 in Pietermaritzburg in the province of Natal, South Africa, to James Paton, a civil servant, and Eunice Warder Paton.
1919–22	Attends Natal University College (now the University of Natal).
1921	Publishes first poems in the college's magazine.
1925–28	Teaches at Ixopo High School in Ixopo, Natal, South Africa.
1928	On July 2, marries Doris Olive Francis.
1928–35	Teaches math, physics, and English at Maritzburg College, Pietermaritzburg, Natal.
1930	Son David is born.
1935–48	Principal of Diepkloof Reformatory, near Johannesburg, South Africa.
1936	Son Jonathan is born.
1946	Takes leave of absence and travels to Europe, the United States, and Canada to study penal and correctional facilities.
1948	Publishes *Cry, the Beloved Country*.
1949	Maxwell Anderson creates an adaptation of *Cry, the Beloved Country*. This musical tragedy, *Lost in the Stars*, with music by Kurt Weill, is produced on Broadway.

167

1953	Publishes *Too Late the Phalarope*.
1954	Tours the United States to write on race relations for Collieris.
1955	Publishes *The Land and the People of South Africa*.
1956	Publishes *South Africa in Transition*. A play version of *Too Late the Phalarope*, adapted by Robert Yale Libott, is produced on Broadway.
1958–68	President of Liberal Party of South Africa.
1958	Publishes *Hope for South Africa*.
1961	Publishes *Tales from a Troubled Land*.
1962	*Sponono*, a play he writes with Krishna Shah that is based on three stories from *Tales from a Troubled Land*, produced in Durban and Johannesburg.
1964	Publishes *Hofmeyr*, a biography. *Sponono* produced on Broadway at Cort Theatre.
1967	Wife dies of emphysema.
1968	Liberal Party of South Africa declared an illegal organization. Publishes *The Long View*, edited by Edward Callan.
1969	Publishes *For You Departed*. Founding editor of *Reality: A Journal of Liberal Opinion*. Marries Anne Hopkins.
1973	Publishes *Apartheid and the Archbishop: The Life and Times of Geoffrey Clayton, Archbishop of Cape Town*.
1974	A film, *Lost in the Stars*, is produced based on the musical.
1975	Publishes *Knocking on the Door*, a collection of his shorter writings, edited by Colin Gardner.
1980	Publishes *Towards the Mountain: An Autobiography*.
1981	Publishes *Ah, but Your Land Is Beautiful*.
1988	Dies of throat cancer on April 12, in Bothais Hill, Natal, South Africa. *Journey Continued: An Autobiography*, second volume of his autobiography, is published in November.
1995	*Songs of Africa: Collected Poems* published.

Contributors

HAROLD BLOOM is Sterling Professor of the Humanities at Yale University. Educated at Cornell and Yale universities, he is the author of more than 30 books, including *Shelley's Mythmaking* (1959), *The Visionary Company* (1961), *Blake's Apocalypse* (1963), *Yeats* (1970), *The Anxiety of Influence* (1973), *A Map of Misreading* (1975), *Kabbalah and Criticism* (1975), *Agon: Toward a Theory of Revisionism* (1982), *The American Religion* (1992), *The Western Canon* (1994), *Omens of Millennium: The Gnosis of Angels, Dreams, and Resurrection* (1996), *Shakespeare: The Invention of the Human* (1998), *How to Read and Why* (2000), *Genius: A Mosaic of One Hundred Exemplary Creative Minds* (2002), *Hamlet: Poem Unlimited* (2003), *Where Shall Wisdom Be Found?* (2004), and *Jesus and Yahweh: The Names Divine* (2005). In addition, he is the author of hundreds of articles, reviews, and editorial introductions. In 1999, Professor Bloom received the American Academy of Arts and Letters' Gold Medal for Criticism. He has also received the International Prize of Catalonia, the Alfonso Reyes Prize of Mexico, and the Hans Christian Andersen Bicentennial Prize of Denmark.

CHARLES R. LARSON is a professor at American University. His critical works include *The Emergence of African Fiction* and *The Novel in the Third World*. He also edited *Under African Skies: Modern African Stories* and has published novels and a collection of sketches.

J. ALVAREZ-PEREYRE has been a professor of English language and literature at Grenoble University, France. He is the author of *Poetry of Commitment in South Africa*, part of the Studies in African Literature series.

169

R.W.H. HOLLAND has taught in the English department at the University of Rhodesia, which later became the University of Zimbabwe.

STEPHEN WATSON is a professor at the University of Cape Town, where he also is Director of Creative Writing. He coauthored *Dante in South Africa*. He also is the editor of *A City Imagined*, a collection of pieces by South African authors about Cape Town.

CAROL IANNONE has taught at New York University's Gallatin School of Individualized Study. She is editor at large of Academic Questions on *The American Conservative* Web site.

DAVID MEDALIE teaches in the English department at the University of the Witwatersrand. He published *E. M. Forster's Modernism* and is the editor of *Encounters: An Anthology of South African Short Stories*.

ANDREW FOLEY has been a professor at the University of Witwatersrand's School of Education. He published *The Imagination of Freedom: Critical Texts and Times in Liberal Literature* and coauthored *Cowboys and Aliens*.

HERMANN WITTENBERG is a lecturer in the English department at the University of the Western Cape. He is the editor of the Paton travel narrative *Lost City of the Kalahari*. He was organizer of the Interaction project, a postgraduate conference and journal in the humanities.

ANDREW VAN DER VLIES teaches at the University of Sheffield. He is the author of *J. M. Coetzee's* Disgrace and an associate editor of the *Oxford Companion to the Book*, for which he was responsible for sub-Saharan Africa and postcolonial book cultures.

Bibliography

Adler, Tony. "Return to Paton's Place." From *American Theater* 10, no. 7 (July–August 1993).

Asein, Samuel O. "Christian Moralism and Apartheid: Paton's *Cry, the Beloved Country* Reassessed." *Africa Quarterly* 14, nos. 1–2 (1974): 53–63.

Baker, Sheridan. "Paton's *Beloved Country* and the Morality of Geography." *College English* 19, no. 2 (November 1957): 56–61.

Baker, Sheridan, ed. *Paton's* Cry, the Beloved Country: *The Novel, The Critics, The Setting.* New York: Scribner's, 1968.

Barnard, Rita. "Oprah's Paton, or, South Africa and the Globalization of Suffering." *English Studies in Africa: A Journal of the Humanities* 47, no. 1 (2004): 85–108.

Bloom, Harold, ed. *Alan Paton's* Cry, the Beloved Country. Bloom's Guides series. Philadelphia: Chelsea House, 2004.

Callan, Edward. "*Cry, the Beloved Country*: Forty Years On." *Four Quarters* 2, no. 1 (Spring 1988): 24–30.

———. Cry, the Beloved Country: *A Novel of South Africa* [a study]. Boston: Twayne Publishers, 1991.

Chapman, Michael. "African Popular Fiction: Consideration of a Category." *English in Africa* 26, no. 2 (October 1999): 113–26.

Chiwengo, Ngwarsungu. *Understanding* Cry, the Beloved Country: *A Student Casebook to Issues, Sources, and Historical Documents.* Westport, Conn.: Greenwood Press, 2007.

Clark, Roger S. "Cry, the Beloved Country." *Human Rights Quarterly* 14, no. 4 (November 1992): 653–56.

Coetzee, J. M. "Simple Language, Simple People: Smith, Paton, Mikro." In *White Writing: On the Culture of Letters in South Africa*. New Haven and London: Yale University Press, 1988.

Collins, Harold R. "*Cry, the Beloved Country* and the Broken Tribe." *College English* 14, no. 7 (April 1953): 379–85.

Cowling, Lesley. "The Beloved South African: Alan Paton in America." *Scrutiny 2* 10, no. 2 (2005): 81–92.

Dovey, Lindiwe. *African Film and Literature: Adapting Violence to the Screen*. New York: Columbia University Press, 2009.

Duncan, Robert L. "The Suffering Servant in Novels by Paton, Bernanos, and Schwarz-Bart." *Christian Scholar's Review* 16, no. 2 (January 1987): 122–43.

Ellis, Mark Spencer, ed. Cry, the Beloved Country: *A Story of Comfort in Desolation*. Harlow: Longman, 1986.

Foley, Andrew. "Christianity and Liberalism in *Cry, the Beloved Country*." *Alternation* 6, no. 2 (1999): 116–33.

———. "The First Page of *Cry, the Beloved Country*." *English Academy Review* 23 (2006): 34–47.

Fuller, Edmund. "Alan Paton: Tragedy and Beyond." In *Books with Men Behind Them*. New York: Random House, 1959.

Gailey, Harry A. "Sheridan Baker's 'Paton's *Beloved Country*.'" *College English* 20, no. 3 (December 1958): 143–44.

Gardner, Colin. "Paton's Literary Achievement." *Reality* 20 (July 1988): 8–11.

Hasluck, Nicholas. "Thought Crimes and Other Themes in Commonwealth Literature." *Quadrant Magazine* 52, no. 5 (May 2008): 36–43.

Hestenes, Mark. "To See the Kingdom: A Study of Graham Greene and Alan Paton." *Literature and Theology* 13, no. 4 (December 1999): 311–22.

Marcus, Fred H. "*Cry, the Beloved Country* and *Strange Fruit*: Man's Inhumanity to Man." *English Journal* 51 (1962): 609–16.

Martínez Lirola, María. "Exploring Predicated Themes from a Systemic Functional Point of View in Alan Paton's Novels." *Journal of Literary Studies/Tydskrif vir Literatuurwetenskap* 24, no. 1 (March 2008): 100–27.

Matlaw, Myron. "Alan Paton's *Cry, the Beloved Country* and Maxwell Anderson's/ Kurt Weill's *Lost in the Stars*: A Consideration of Genres." *Arcadia: Zeitschrift fur Vergleichende Literaturwissenschaft* 10 (1975): 260–72.

Mbeboh, K. W. "*Cry, the Beloved Country*: A Liberal Apology." *Cameroon Studies in English and French* 1 (1976): 71–77.

Monye, A. A. "*Cry, the Beloved Country*: Should We Merely Cry?" *Nigeria Magazine* 144 (1983): 74–83.

Ndlovu, Victor and Alet Kruger. "Translating English Terms of Address in *Cry, the Beloved Country* into Zulu." *South African Journal of African Languages/Suid-Afrikaanse Tydskrif vir Afrikatale* 18, no. 2 (May 1998).

Odumuh, Emmanuel. "The Theme of Love in Alan Paton's *Cry, the Beloved Country*." *Kuka: Journal of Creative and Critical Writing* (1980–1981): 41–50.

Rice, Linda J. "Racial Tensions, Injustice, and Harmony in South African Literature." In *Exploring African Life and Literature: Novel Guides to Promote Socially Responsive Learning*, edited by Jacqueline N. Glasgow and Linda J. Rice, pp. 207–28. Newark, Del.: International Reading Association, 2007.

Rive, Richard. "The Liberal Tradition in South African Literature." *Contrast: South African Literary Journal* 14, no. 3 (July 1983): 19–31.

Roson, Myriam. "Interview with Alan Paton." *CRUX: A Journal on the Teaching of English* 21, no. 1 (February 1987): 43–47.

Sharma, R. C. "Alan Paton's *Cry, the Beloved Country*: The Parable of Compassion." *Literary Half-Yearly* 19, no. 2 (1978): 64–82.

Smock, Susan Wanless. "*Lost in the Stars* and *Cry, the Beloved Country*: A Thematic Comparison." *North Dakota Quarterly* 48, no. 3 (1980): 53–59.

Tucker, Martin. "The Color of South African Literature." In *Africa in Modern Literature: A Survey of Contemporary Writing in English*. New York: Frederick Ungar Publishing, 1967.

van der Vlies, Andrew. "'Local' Writing, 'Global' Reading, and the Demands of the 'Canon': The Case of Alan Paton's *Cry, the Beloved Country*." *South African Historical Journal* 55 (2006): 20–32.

Williams, Kemp. "The Style of Paradox: Thematic and Linguistic Duality in *Cry, the Beloved Country*." *English Studies in Africa* 39, no. 2 (1996): 1–15.

Wren, Robert M. "*Cry, the Beloved Country* as Fantasy in New York." *Contrast* 8, no. 2 (1973): 55–60.

Acknowledgments

Charles R. Larson, "Alan Paton's *Cry, the Beloved Country* after Twenty-Five Years." From *Africa Today* 20, no. 4 (1973): 53–57. Copyright © 1973 by Indiana University Press.

J. Alvarez-Pereyre, "The Social Record in Paton's *Cry, the Beloved Country.*" From *Études Anglaises*, vol. 25, no. 2 (April–June 1972): 207–14. Copyright © 1972 by *Études Anglaises*.

R.W.H. Holland, "Fiction and History: Fact and Invention in Alan Paton's Novel *Cry, the Beloved Country.*" From *Zambezia: The Journal of the University of Rhodesia*, vol. 5, no. 2 (1977): 129–39. Copyright © 1977 by the University of Rhodesia.

Stephen Watson, "*Cry, the Beloved Country* and the Failure of Liberal Vision." From *English in Africa*, vol. 9, no. 1 (May 1982): 29–44. Copyright © 1982 by *English in Africa*.

Carol Iannone, "Alan Paton's Tragic Liberalism." From *American Scholar*, vol. 66, no. 3 (Summer 1997): 442–51. Copyright © 1997 by the author.

David Medalie, "'A Corridor Shut at Both Ends': Admonition and Impasse in Van der Post's *In a Province* and Paton's *Cry, the Beloved Country.*" From *English in Africa*, vol. 25, no. 2 (October 1998): 93–110. Copyright © 1998 by *English in Africa*.

Index

Abrahams, Peter, 3
  Mine Boy, 109
abridged/serialized version, 148–151, 153–154
Absalom Kumalo, 23, 59, 66
  execution of, 13, 40, 57
  murder by, 21, 22, 28, 30, 53, 56–57, 88, 92
  trial of, 21, 43, 75–76, 154
  wife to be of, 13, 56, 57, 151
Adams, Richard, 155
African Drum, The, 145–148, 152
African Fury (film), 158
African Image, The (Mphahlele), 5, 15, 95
African practices, traditional, 79
African Resistance Movement (ARM), 102–103
African Workers' Union, 74
Afrikaans, 15, 43–44, 61
Afrikaner Calvinist mentality, 48
Afrikaner nationalism, 33, 34, 60, 61, 63
Afrikaner republics, 50
"aftermath" function, 26
Ah, but Your Land Is Beautiful (Paton), 44, 45–46, 47
Alan Paton (Alexander), 109
Alexander, Peter F., 50
  Alan Paton, 109
  Journey Continued, 62
  Towards the Mountain, 62, 123–124
Alexandra Bus Boycott, 21–25, 28, 29
  bus fare and, 22–23, 31
Alexandra Township, 13, 23, 24
Allen, Walter, 140
alterity/blackness, 118
Alvarez-Pereyre, 9–17
ambiguity, 21, 75
anachronism, 73, 83
Analytic of the Sublime (Kant), 115
A.N.C., 104, 134
Anderson, Maxwell, 157
  Lost in the Stars, 4, 54
Anglican Diocesan Commission, 85
Anglo-Boer War, 154
Anisfield-Wolf Awards, 138
antiapartheid movement, 62, 134
apartheid, 4, 13, 62, 83, 135, 153
  demise of, 8, 109
  "grand apartheid," 53, 61
  policies of, 46, 47
Arac, Jonathan, 135
Archbishop Clayton, 97
Aristotle, 35
Arthur Jarvis, 14, 130
  murder of, 6, 13, 20–21, 28, 40, 53, 56, 72, 88
  papers by, 10, 11, 12, 13, 28, 39, 55, 74, 85, 93, 100
artificial literalism, 82

177

Atlantic Monthly, 3
author's note, 21, 30, 86
autobiography, 62
awards, 138

Baker, Sheridan, 152, 164
Bantu reserves, 9
Barnard, Rita, 159
Beatitudes, the, 99
Beittel, Mark, 158
Belsey, Catherine, 155
Berlin, Isaiah, 46
Bhaba, Homi K., 145
biographer, 50, 62
Black Beauty (Sewell), 4
black militants, 58
black nationalists, 105
blackness/racial difference, 118, 127.
   See also racial problems
black/white contact, laws against, 6
Bloom, Harold, 1
Bloom, Harry
   Transvaal Episode, 69
Bochabela incident, 45, 46
Boer War, 60
book clubs, 135, 159
boy's club, 40, 53, 57, 58, 94, 102
Brecht, Berthold, 38, 114
British rights/reading, 138–141
   British reviewers, 140
   textual variations and, 139–140
Brutus, Dennis, 59
Bunting, Daniel, 139
Burke, Edmund, 113–115, 117, 118
   Philosophical Enquiry into the
    Origin of Our Ideas of the
    Sublime and the Beautiful, 116
Burns, Aubrey, 138, 139
Burns, Marigold, 139
Burns, Robert, 124
bus boycotts, 19, 90, 104. *See also*
   Alexandra Bus Boycott
Buthelezi, Chief, 62

Callan, Edward, 58, 96, 106

Calvinist, 48
canonization, 135
Cape, Jonathan, 138–141
Carisbrooke, 120
Carlin, Murray, 144–145
"Case History of a Pinky" (Paton),
   85
censored books, 4
Centenary of the Great Trek, 61
central problem, 38–39
"Change from Within" vs. "Change
   from Without," 41–42
change of heart/atonement, 45, 59,
   66
Children of Soweto (Mzamane), 156
choric sections of book, 25, 104
Christianity, 15, 50, 63, 99–100
   colonialism and, 7, 74
   hypocrisy and, 7, 56, 62
   liberalism and, 39, 40–41, 100,
    145
   message of, 34, 55
   polemic against, 48
   racial discrimination and, 93
church, role of, 15, 100
classroom, Paton's work in, 152–157
Clayton, Geoffrey, 85
Coetzee, J. M., 35, 82, 119
   White Writing, 113, 144–145
collectivist politics, 68–69, 70, 71, 79
Colleran, Jeanne, 138–141
Collins, Harold R., 152
colonialism, 55, 125, 129, 130, 151
   Christianity and, 7, 74
   tribal legacy and, 71
Come Back, Africa (Rogosin), 144
"comfort in desolation," 108. *See also*
   subtitle
conflict, patterns of, 44
Congress of the People, 46, 61
Cope, Jack, 109
   The Golden Oriole, 69
Cowling, Lesley, 138
crime, 12–13, 39, 60
criminal justice, 13. *See also* law

Critical Aesthetics and Postmodernism
(Crowther), 114
criticism, 83, 140–141
of language/tone, 46–47
of liberal outlook, 95–109
of paternalism, 94–95
point of view and, 53
of sentimentality, 58
Critique of Judgment (Kant), 114
Cronin, J. F., 33
Crowther, Paul
*Critical Aesthetics and
Postmodernism*, 114
Cullen, Countee
"Heritage," 145–146
cultural authenticity, 80

Debbie Go Home (Paton), 13, 162
"Deep Experience, A" (Paton), 85
dehumanization, 71
delinquents, 95
democracy, 110
Dent, Railton, 50
determinism, social, 47
detribalization, 39
dialogic, 106
didacticism, 7
Diepkloof Reformatory, 10, 58, 90,
109, 135
freedom/rules at, 59–60
Principalship at, 16, 50–51, 85,
87, 95, 123
punishment at, 62
"Dignity of Begging, The"
(Modisane), 147
Down Second Avenue (Mpahlele), 10
Dr. Hendrik, 46

Eagleton, Terry, 38
The Ideology of the Aesthetic, 114
earnings, inequalities in, 12
Ebony Award, 138
economic disparity, 44–45
economic equality, 106
education, 7, 12, 56, 89–90

modernity and, 73
Paton's work in, 152–157
Eliot, T. S.
The Waste Land, 98
Elliott, S. H., 87
Ellis, Mark Spencer, 155–156
Ellison, Ralph, 151
emancipation, 58
English United Party, 34
equality, 41
estrangement effects, 38
Evans, David, 156, 164
Ezenzelini, 15, 69, 99

Fanon, Frantz, 118
Father Vincent, 14, 15, 20, 43, 90,
107, 151
fear, 8, 16, 42, 54, 58, 91
bondage and, 108
crime and, 12–13
racial fears, 45
federalism, 62
feminist studies, 114–115
fictional vs. historical time, 19–31,
20–21, 25
historical distortions, 30
historical Shanty Town, 27
nowness vs. aftermath function,
26, 28
timeless/timeful, 27
film version, 54, 58, 84, 86–87, 109,
147, 157
final scene, 40
Foley, Andrew, 83–111
Forum, 87, 88
Fountainhead, The (Rand), 1
Freedom Charter of the African
National Congress, 45–46, 61
freehold rights, 14
Freeman, Barbara, 115
Fugard, Athol, 138, 156
funeral scene, 6, 53

Gannett, Lewis, 58
Gertrude, 13, 29, 52, 53, 57, 88, 103

global mediascape, 157–160
gold mining, 10, 12, 13, 19, 42, 55,
    102, 129, 141, 148, 150
"Golden Age," 46
Golden Oriole, The (Cope), 69
Gordimer, Nadine, 3, 4, 34, 49, 135,
    156
Government's Fagan Commission's
    report, 140–141
Grace Kumalo, 53
Group Areas Act, 146

Hansen, Harry, 136
Hardy, Thomas
    Return of the Native, 4
Harris, John, 103
Harris, Richard, 159
Harrisons, the, 11
Hayes, Alfred, 157
Head, Bessie, 156
Hemson, David, 66
"Heritage" (Cullen), 145–146
hero, 5, 35, 37–38
"High Place," 121, 126, 127
historical time. *See* fictional vs.
    historical time
historicity, 20
Hofmeyer, J. H., 34, 50, 61, 63, 109,
    139
Holland, R.W.H., 19–31
holy mountain, symbolism, 107–108
housing, 12, 27, 37. *See also* Shanty
    Town
Huckleberry Finn (Twain), 135, 137
Huddleston, Trevor
    Naught for Your Comfort, 153
human condition, 64
humanism, 41, 134, 145, 151
Hume, David, 117, 118
Hunter and the Whale, The (Van der
    Post), 69

I Speak of Africa (Plomer), 139
Iannone, Carol, 49–64
idealist view, 43, 45, 58

identity, 69, 70, 118, 128, 135
ideological conflict, 40–41, 43
    materialist-idealist clash, 45
    pluralism and, 46
    poverty of ideology, 44
Ideology of the Aesthetic (Eagleton),
    114
In a Province (van der Post), 65–66,
    69
    Colonel of police in, 71–72
    communism/collectivism, 68–69
    CTBC, major difference and, 78
    Johan van Bredepoel in, 65–66,
        72, 73, 77–78, 80, 82
    Kenon Badiakgotla in, 65–66, 68,
        70, 72, 76–77, 78
    liberalism and, 79
    non-African affiliations in, 81
    old Africa in, 80
    Paulstad massacre in, 71–72, 77,
        80, 82
    Port Benjamin in, 65, 66, 68
    Rule of Law in, 76
inadaptability, 73
individual, rights of, 41
individual responsibility, 59, 69
industrialization, 53
inequalities, 11
Inhalavini, 11
inspirational tone, 7
institutions, 13–14
internal dissonance, 38
interracial love, 35
Ixopo district, Natal, 51–52, 124–
    125

Jacobsen, Dan, 134
Jacobson, Dan, 3, 33, 58
Jamba, Sousa, 59
James Jarvis, 11, 14, 34, 84, 88, 107,
    158
    "High Place" of, 121
    liberal change of heart by, 40
    loss of son, 40, 53, 91–91
    philanthropy of, 40, 43, 57, 94, 97

shaking black hands, 53, 131
  turning point for, 93
Jewish Affairs, 142
Johannesburg, 13, 29
  all roads lead to, 25–26, 67
  squalid conditions in, 10, 23,
    52–53, 87, 88
  white Johannesburg, 12–13
Johannesburg City Council, 22
Johannesburg Housing Committee,
  28
John Harrison, 92
John Kumalo, 53, 88, 127, 144, 150
  education and, 73
  hostility toward, 75
  modernity and, 81
  as political speechmaker, 41–43,
    55, 69, 70, 74, 80–81, 104,
    128–129
  on role of church, 15
Jones, James Earl, 54, 159
Journey Continued (Alexander), 62
Journey to Johannesburg (Naidoo), 156
July's People (Gordimer), 156

Kant, Immanuel, 118
  Analytic of the Sublime, 115
  Critique of Judgment, 114
  lowest esteem for Africa, 117–118
  *Observations of the Feeling of the
    Beautiful and Sublime*, 117
Kennedy, Bobby, 6
Kennedy, John F., 6
King, Martin Luther, Jr., 6, 153
Koch, Adrienne, 136
Koestler, Arthur
  "The Yogi and the Commissar,"
    41
Komai, Felicia, 157, 158
Korda, Alexander, 54, 158
Korda, Zoltan, 54, 157, 158

La Guma, Alex, 3, 156
Labbe, Jacqueline, 115
labor. *See* gold mining

land. *See also* sublime, the
  beauty of the, 119–120, 122, 123,
    125
  colonial land question, 126–127
  countryside, 11, 67–68
  paradisial/purgatorial, 45
  restoration of, 7, 98–99, 105–106
language, 46–47, 57, 70, 82
Language and Silence (Steiner), 35
Larson, Charles R., 3–8
law
  intention to kill, 56–57
  jurisprudence and, 47
  pass laws, 6, 87
  Rule of Law, 75–76, 77, 151
  segregationist legislation, 147
lawlessness, 38
Lee, Canada, 158, 163
Let My People Go (Luthuli), 10, 14
Liberal Party, 16, 17, 61, 100, 102,
  144
liberalism, 46, 72, 103
  beliefs, 40–41, 43, 45, 62–63, 84
  black people and, 70
  Christianity and, 39, 40–41, 100
  criticism and, 95–109
  white liberalism, 14, 34, 58, 128
Lincoln, Abraham, 92, 94
literary devices, sophisticated, 82
Longman unabridged edition,
  154–155
Lost in the Stars (musical version), 4,
  54, 157, 158
Louis Botha Avenue, bus boycott
  and, 23, 24
love, 6, 39, 101
  interracial, 35
  as solution, 39, 42, 58–59, 96
Lufafa, 11
Luthuli, Albert John
  Let My People Go, 10, 14
Lyotard, Jean-François, 114

Malan, Daniel F., 33, 58, 60, 61, 86,
  109, 141

Malcolm X, 6
Mandela, Nelson, 62, 133, 159
manuscript, writing of, 51
Marquard, Leo, 40–41
Marxism, 96, 104, 114
materialist-idealist clash, 42–43, 45
Matshikiza, Todd, 147
Maughan Brown, David, 69, 81
Mbeki, Govan, 133
Mbeki, Thabo, 133
Medalie, David, 65–82
migratory labor, 9
Mine Boy (Abrahams), 109
mining. *See* gold mining
Mission for the Blind, 29, 30
"Mlung" Ungazikhohlisi (Zulu
    poem), 146
modernity, 67, 72, 73, 75, 81–82, 129
Modisane, Bloke
    "The Dignity of Begging," 147
moral conscience, 43
moral degeneration, 10, 34, 38, 43
moral progress, 97
Morphet, Tony, 119, 123
Mpanza, Sofazonke, 27
Mphahlele, Exekiel, 3, 6, 59, 144, 147
    The African Image, 5, 15, 95
    dissatisfaction expressed by, 41
    Down Second Avenue, 10
    on writer's liberalism, 43, 96
Msimangu, 15, 54, 81, 82, 89, 104,
    144, 150, 158
    central problem and, 38–39
    famous statement of, 6, 63, 108
    as Kumalo's guide, 100–101
    love as solution, 39, 40
    sermon of, 57, 69–70, 91, 99, 101
    Shanty Town search, 29–30
multiculturalism, 63
mystification, technique of, 37, 38,
    48
Mzamane, Mbulelo, 156

Naidoo, Beverly (*Journey to
    Johannesburg*), 156

näiveté, 5, 40, 83, 96, 97
Nakasa, Nat, 144, 147
Napoleon Letsisi, 14, 78, 97, 105,
    144
Nash, Andrew, 119
Natal district, 29, 51–52, 67, 76, 91,
    94, 97, 120, 121, 122, 124. *See
    also* Ndotsheni
nationalism, 148
Nationalist Party, 15, 33, 102–103,
    135
    control of country by, 4, 6, 16, 17
Native Son (Wright), 152
natives, 27, 31. *See also* tribal systems
    the native question, 109
    tribal systems and, 13, 79–80
Naught for Your Comfort
    (Huddleston), 153
Ndotsheni, 10–11, 29, 52, 57, 67, 77,
    78, 88, 89, 97, 98, 105, 107, 126,
    144
New Guard, 45–46
Nixon, Richard, 7
Nixon, Rob, 134, 144
Nkosi, Lewis, 6, 145, 147
    Home and Exile, 5
Nkosi Sikelel' iAfrika (anthem), 148,
    150, 151
non–South African public, 16
nonviolent protest, 102, 103
nowness, 26

*Observations of the Feeling of the
    Beautiful and Sublime* (Kant), 117
Odendaalsrust, 10, 104, 148
old Africa, 80, 81
"On Turning 70" (Paton), 101–102
Oppenheimer, Sir Ernest, 14
Orange Free State goldfields, 141
oratory, 69
Orlando, 26

Pajalich, Armando, 106
pan-Africanism subtexts, 150–151
paradox, 75

Parliament, Native M.P.'s and, 14
pass laws, 6, 87
paternalism, 44, 62, 83, 134
    criticism of, 94–95, 97
Paton, Alan, 50–51, 73, 84–88
    Ah, but Your Land Is Beautiful,
        44, 51
    articles written by, 10, 85, 88, 93,
        101–102
    "Case History of a Pinky," 85
    Christian outlook of, 16
    death of, 134
    Debbie Go Home, 13, 162
    at Diepkloof Reformatory, 10, 16,
        50–51, 59–60, 61, 62, 85, 87,
        95, 123, 135
    enteric fever illness, 50, 85
    Liberal Party co-founding of, 16,
        61
    militant left and, 62
    objectivity used by, 15
    philanthropy of, 58–59
    politics/liberalism of, 60, 61–62,
        63–64
    Songs of Africa, 109
    South Africa and Her People, 102
    Tales from a Troubled Land, 4
    Too Late the Phalarope, 4, 48, 51,
        162
Paulstad massacre, 71–72, 77, 80, 82
peace, fear of change and, 16
period piece, 1, 8
Perkins, Maxwell, 51, 84, 135, 138
philanthropy, 40
*Philosophical Enquiry into the Origin
    of Our Ideas of the Sublime and the
    Beautiful* (Burke), 116
Phylon, 137
Pietermaritzburg, 124
Pimville, 12
Plomer, William, 138–139
    I Speak of Africa, 139
    Turbott Wolfe, 109, 139, 142–143
pluralism, 46
poetry, 118, 124

Poitier, Sidney, 54, 158
political situation, 60, 108, 144. *See
    also* apartheid; liberalism
polyphonicity, 106
Postmodern Sublime (Tabbi), 114
postmodernist theory, 114
poverty, 52, 123, 126
precolonial African society, 75
Prescott, Orville, 136
Professor Hoernlé, 14, 34, 144
publisher, 51, 84, 135

racial problems, 7, 45, 130. *See also*
    apartheid; poverty
    discrimination and, 56, 87, 93,
        137
    injustice/oppression, 125, 126,
        134
    racial moralism, 54–55
Radebe, Gaur, 24–25
radicalism, 62
Radway, Janice, 148–149
Rand, Ayn
    The Fountainhead, 1
Rand Daily Mail, 142, 143
Reader's Digest, 149–150, 156
reconciliation of blacks/whites, 40,
    44
reformist agenda, 78
religion, 7, 41. *See also* Christianity
religious tragedy, 35
reparations, 92, 105
restorative possibilities, 96–97. *See
    also* land
Return of the Native (Hardy), 4
reviewers, 140–141
Rheinalt-Jones, Edith, 34, 85–86,
    92, 127–128, 129, 130
Rich, Paul B., 79, 95
    "Secret for Seven," 125–126
Rive, Richard, 59
Rivers, Gertrude, 152
Robertson, Janet, 105
Rogosin, Lionel
    Come Back, Africa, 144

Rolo, Charles J., 3
Roodt, Darryl, 84, 109, 157
Roux, Edward, 27, 31
rural reserves, 79–80

Sachs, Joseph, 143, 145
Sampson, Anthony, 147
Sargeant, Roy, 157
Schreiner, Olive
    The Story of an African Farm, 142
Scribner, Charles, Jr., 152
Scribner's, 135–136, 138
"Secret for Seven" (Rich), 125–126
segregationist legislation, 147
sentimentality, 34, 43, 58, 95
separatism, 53
Sergeant, Roy, 109
serialized/abridged version, 148–151
setting of story, 125–126
Sewell, Anna
    Black Beauty, 4
Shanty Town, 27, 31, 149
    erection of, 9, 10, 14, 19, 26–30,
        104
signal passages, 122–123
Singh, Anan, 157
slave system, 14
Smith, Lillian
    Strange Fruit, 152
Smuts, Jan Christian, 33, 60, 61,
    109, 141
social engineering, 61
social problems, 7, 38, 96. *See also*
    apartheid
    built-in limitations, 62
    division, poverty and, 52
    social disintegration, 39, 89,
        90–91
    timelessness of, 26
social record, 30, 83–111
    details of in *CTBC*, 88
social reform/regeneration, 44,
    87–88, 105
Society and the Offender, 10
Songs of Africa (Paton), 109

Sophiatown, 29, 53
Sophoclean tragedy, 36, 40
South Africa and Her People (Paton),
    102
South African Institute of Race
    Relations and the Wayfarers, 85
South African public, 16, 34. *See also*
    social problems
South African reviews, 141–145
Spivak, Gayatri, 115
Steiner, George, 37
    Language And Silence, 35
Stephen Kumalo, 20, 34, 52–53, 59,
    82, 84, 88, 95, 103, 107, 136, 140,
    158
    leaky church of, 97, 98
    leaving Ndotsheni, 29, 52
    loss of son/lost son, 23, 29, 40, 99
    as minister-hero, 5, 67
    religious exultation of, 1, 40, 99,
        107–108
    "the white man's dog," 14
    as witness to suffering, 37–38
Stevenson, R. L., 124
Story of an African Farm, The
    (Schriener), 142, 156
Strange Fruit (Smith), 152
sublime, the, 113–132
    aesthetic modes, 124
    antisublime and, 122–123
    beauty of the land, 119–120, 122,
        123
    blackness/racial difference and,
        122
    colonial land question, 126–127
    definition of, 130
    emotion and, 118–119
    Kumalo's voice and, 128–129
    pain/peril and, 116
    utopian sublime, 127–128
subtitle, 43, 133
Sullivan, Richard, 136

Tabbi, Joseph
    Postmodern Sublime, 114

Tales from a Troubled Land (Paton), 4
thematic concerns, 45
Themba, Can, 147
Times Literary Supplement, 34, 95
time span, historicity and, 20–21
"To the Person Sitting in Darkness"
   (Twain), 7
Too Late the Phalarope (Paton), 4, 48,
   51, 162
Towards the Mountain (Alexander),
   62, 85, 123–124
town, life in, 11–12
townships, 88–89. *See also*
   Johannesburg
tragedy
   Greek tragedy, 36, 40, 137, 158
   of interracial love, 35
   literary mode of, 34–36
   mystery of injustice and, 36–37
   religious tragedy, 35
   white man and, 38–39
Transvaal Episode (Bloom), 69
tribal systems, 63, 70, 84. *See also*
   natives
   civilization and, 79–80
   destruction of, 34, 47, 53, 71, 79,
      89, 90, 91, 92, 104
   moral systems and, 39, 55
   union of South Africa and, 51
   white man and, 38–39
Trilling, Diana, 138
Trilling, Lionel, 54, 137
Trondheim, Norway, 135
Trotskyist Left, 143
Turbott Wolfe (Plomer), 109, 139,
   142–143
Tutu, Desmond, 1
Twain, Mark
   Huckleberry Finn, 135, 137
   "To the Person Sitting in
      Darkness," 7

Umzimkulu, 11, 52, 67, 120
"Uncle Tom" character, 44
union of South Africa, 51

United Party, 33, 60
United States, 63
Unity Movement, 143
Unskomaas, 11
urbanization, 39, 53, 67

van der Post, Laurens
   black identity and, 70
   The Hunter and the Whale, 69
   liberalism of, 77
   In a Province, 65–66
van der Vlies, Andrew, 133–165
Verwoerd, Hendrik Frensch, 33, 46,
   61, 103
Voegelin, Eric, 72

Walker, Eric, 9
Waste Land, The (Eliot), 98
Watson, Stephen, 33–48, 96, 101,
   102, 119, 158
Weill, Kurt, 4, 54, 157
white South Africans, 11, 14, 28, 45,
   55, 58
white supremacy, 53, 61, 62, 74, 123
White Writing (Coetzee), 113, 144
"Who is really to blame for the
   crime wave in South Africa"
   (Paton), 10, 87
Winfrey, Oprah, 135, 159
Wittenberg, Hermann, 113–132
Woods, Donald, 135
Wordsworth, William, 118, 124
Wright, Richard
   Native Son, 152
Wylie, Diana, 63

Yale Review, 63
"Yogi and the Commissar, The"
   (Koestler), 41
Young, Francis Brett, 140

Zulus, 28, 52, 57, 59, 125–126, 138,
   141–145, 143, 149
   language of, 154, 158
   "Mlung" Ungazikhohlisi, 146